How the Other Half Ate

CALIFORNIA STUDIES IN FOOD AND CULTURE

Darra Goldstein, Editor

How the Other Half Ate

A HISTORY OF WORKING-CLASS MEALS
AT THE TURN OF THE CENTURY

Katherine Leonard Turner

UNIVERSITY OF CALIFORNIA PRESS

BERKELEY LOS ANGELES LONDON

University of California Press, one of the most distinguished university presses in the United States, enriches lives around the world by advancing scholarship in the humanities, social sciences, and natural sciences. Its activities are supported by the UC Press Foundation and by philanthropic contributions from individuals and institutions. For more information, visit www.ucpress.edu.

University of California Press
Berkeley and Los Angeles, California

University of California Press, Ltd.
London, England

Library of Congress Cataloging-in-Publication Data

Turner, Katherine Leonard.
 How the other half ate : a history of working class meals at the turn of the century / Katherine Leonard Turner.
  p. cm.
 Includes bibliographical references and index.
 ISBN 978-0-520-27757-1 (cloth, alk. paper) — ISBN 978-0-520-27758-8 (pbk., alk. paper) — ISBN 978-0-520-95761-9 (electronic)
  1. Food habits—United States—History—19th century. 2. Food habits—United States—History—20th century. 3. Working class—United States—Social conditions. 4. Working class—United States—Social life and customs. 5. Working class—United States—Economic conditions. I. Title.

GT2853.U5T87 2014
394.1′2—dc23   2013029503

23 22 21 20 19 18 17 16 15 14
10 9 8 7 6 5 4 3 2 1

For Brian, Milo, and Felix

CONTENTS

ILLUSTRATIONS

ACKNOWLEDGMENTS

Sections of this book have been previously published as the article "Buying, Not Cooking: Ready-to-Eat Food in Working-Class Neighborhoods in American Cities, 1880–1930," *Food, Culture, and Society* 9, no. 1 (Spring 2006) and as a chapter entitled "Tools and Spaces: Food and Cooking in Working-Class Neighborhoods, 1880–1930," in *Food Chains: From Farmyard to Shopping Cart,* edited by Warren Belasco and Roger Horowitz (Hagley Perspectives on Business and Culture Series, University of Pennsylvania Press, 2008).

Since it first began as a dissertation at the University of Delaware, this book has been made possible by support from a wide array of institutions. First I must thank the University of Delaware and the Hagley Fellowship Program, which set me on the path to this research. I benefited from a great deal of help from the librarians at the University of Delaware and later at Philadelphia University, especially the Special Collections and Inter-Library Loan departments. Archivists at the following institutions helped me make the best of their collections: the Urban Archives at Temple University, the Archives of Industrial Society at the University of Pittsburgh, the University of Chicago Special Collections, the Chicago History Museum, the New York Public Library, the National Archives, the Library of Congress, the Historical Society of Pennsylvania, and the Hagley Museum and Library. I had the honor of grants from the Schlesinger Library of Harvard University, the Historical Society of Pennsylvania, and the Winterthur Museum and Library. At the University of California Press, Kate Marshall and Cindy Fulton provided support and encouragement to turn my manuscript into a book. Sharron Wood's copyediting saved me from many grammatical perils and vague comparisons. I thank Harvey Levenstein, whose clever chapter title in *Revolution at the Table* gave me the title for this book.

Special thanks to Susan Strasser, who advised my dissertation, and the members of my committee, Arwen Mohun, Anne Boylan, Warren Belasco, and Roger Horowitz, all of whom provided support and encouragement. The members of my writing group—John Davies, Tina Manko, Alan Meyer, and Christine Sears—provided daily encouragement, a never-ceasing cheering section, firm rebukes when needed, and really smart comments on my work, for which I am eternally grateful.

I must also thank the friends and family who have helped me along the long, lonely road to a book. The Leonard family has provided constant encouragement that I feel strongly, even over the distance that separates us. The Turner family has helped immeasurably with child care and other forms of household support. My husband, Brian, saw this project begin as a dissertation, and I could not have completed it without his love to sustain me. He is also a shining example of the kind of modern man who understands that food (and cooking, and cleaning up) is everyone's responsibility! I carried two sons while working on this book, and though they can't yet read it, they have been an important part of this journey. I thank them for helping me understand the difference between a household and a family, and the true meaning of a life of abundance.

ONE

The Problem of Food

IMAGINE SPENDING HALF OF YOUR income on food. If you were a member of the American working class in the late nineteenth or early twentieth century, food would have been the largest item in your budget, more expensive than rent or the mortgage, than heating fuel, than clothes or schoolbooks or anything else your family needed. About fifty cents of each dollar went toward food. Imagine how carefully you would buy and cook your food if you spent so much on it: looking for bargains on wilted vegetables and stale bread, walking an extra mile to buy meat at a lower price, fastidiously saving leftovers to make soup. Would you try growing your own vegetables or raising chickens, or would you use that time to work longer hours and earn more money? Would you spend the time to bake your own bread from cheap flour, or would you look for a good price on day-old bread? If eggs were only affordable for a few weeks in the summer, would you buy several dozen and try to preserve them for the winter, or would you just go without eggs for much of the year? How would you cook and eat if you could barely afford enough food for your family? Millions of poor and working-class Americans in the late nineteenth and early twentieth centuries faced this problem—the problem of food—every day.

Like us, they lived in a time of massive social and economic changes. Many were migrants or immigrants who had traveled hundreds or thousands of miles from their birthplace in search of work or to follow kin. The kind of work they did, their homes, their neighborhoods, and their household tools were all likely to be very different from those of their parents. The traditional ways of living, working, and supporting a family weren't always useful to them; they had to find new ways to live.

Amid all these transformations, they had to face the following important questions every day: What will I eat? What will my family eat? Working-class people often spent about 40 to 50 percent of their family's income on food.[1] The poorer the family, the larger percentage of their income they had to spend on food. The tools for cooking—stoves, pots, and pans—were also sometimes expensive, and the utilities that made cooking and housework easier, like running hot water and gas for cooking, were not common in poor neighborhoods. Men, women, and often children worked long hours to make enough money to survive, leaving little time to cook. And, perhaps most importantly, economic survival was uncertain. Everyday tasks like cooking were more difficult when family members worked different hours, some couldn't work at all because of illness or injury, and families might lack any income for long stretches when there was no work to be had.

Studying the food of working-class people is a challenge because, although they probably made up the majority of Americans at the time, they left few records, especially about commonplace tasks such as cooking. Working-class people did not frequently read or write magazine articles about how to keep house and cook. They rarely used cookbooks, nor did their recipes find their way into the published books. With a few notable exceptions, including the Lower East Side Tenement Museum in New York City, their homes have not been preserved as museums, and their possessions weren't preserved because they were used and handed down until they became worn out. And working-class people who wrote memoirs and autobiographies were more often concerned with the struggle for social justice or personal advancement than with the mundane matter of what they ate.

The largest body of evidence about the lives of working-class people of the time was generated by people of other classes, including journalists, nutritionists, doctors and nurses, philanthropists, social workers, and government researchers. These observers had a variety of reasons for investigating working-class lives, and were more or less critical, sympathetic, judgmental, or helpful. But they all considered food and cooking an important part of life that could be improved with study, and so they recorded reams of information about how working-class people cooked and ate. Government agencies studying the labor question gathered statistics on the price of food in relation to wages. Social reformers interested in nutrition estimated the caloric intake of working-class men, women, and children. Settlement-house workers and home visitors inspected kitchens, poked their noses into stewpots, and weighed the children of their immigrant neighbors. The information they gathered was shaped by social bias and political intent, and so it must be used with care, but it is invaluable in piecing together the food choices available to

America's working people. Their observations and advice shaped the public dialogue about food, and in fact their ideas continue to influence the way we think about food and poverty today. Ultimately, however, individuals solved the problem for themselves in a multitude of ways that shaped our country, and the foods we eat, forever.

WHAT DID THEY EAT—AND WHY?

As working people rose early, they ate breakfast in the warming kitchen at dawn or carried it to eat on the way to work.[2] Coffee or tea and a roll were considered sufficient by Jewish immigrants in New York. Mill hands in Massachusetts might have some beans and bread left over from the day before with coffee. Textile workers in the Piedmont had fried pork and wheat biscuits or cornbread with molasses. Single men in Detroit or Chicago might stop by the neighborhood saloon for a strengthening glass of ale before work.

After a long morning's work, those who had to pack their lunches ate quickly and simply: sandwiches, hard-boiled eggs, small cakes, pickles. Coal miners in southeastern Pennsylvania carried tin or aluminum lunch buckets down into the mines. The buckets of Slavic miners contained sandwiches of ham and homemade bread with pastries and fruit. Locally born "mountain folk" brought in their buckets fried or roasted rabbit or squirrel or simply bread and molasses. Meanwhile, Cornish and Finnish metal miners in Michigan and Minnesota carried pasties, turnovers of meat and vegetables wrapped in pastry. Working men in cities or industrial towns often turned into dark and noisy saloons, where the purchase of a nickel beer earned them access to the free lunch counter: bread, cheese, soup or stew, perhaps some cold ham or sliced corned beef, and vinegary vegetable salads and pickles. Schoolchildren bought cakes, candies, nuts, and fruit from peddlers outside their school gates. Those who could return home for lunch ate a home-cooked meal that was a preview of their evening meal.

At suppertime families who all worked the day shift converged back at home. In other homes, workers were constantly coming and going and there were no regular meal hours; a pot of beans or a pan of noodle kugel, some bread, and tea or coffee were left in the kitchen for people to help themselves. Many people still clung to the rural tradition of a big midday meal, so supper was simple: bread and milk, or leftovers from lunch. Some evening meals were cooked in a big hurry, as working women left work, stopped to buy the day's groceries, and cobbled together a quick meal. Other suppers were cooked by daughters while mother was away.

The substance of the meals was as varied as the workers' daily routines. Yeast bread was the staple of the northern working class. Whether homemade wheat or sourdough bread or puffy, white American bakery loaves, crusty Italian breads, rye, pumpernickel, or black bread from Eastern European bakeries, or bagels and bialys from Jewish shops, bread was the first food workers reached for. Spread with butter, jam, or sweetened condensed milk, bread was eaten with every meal and was sometimes a meal in itself served with milk or tea. In the South and parts of the West, corn was king in the form of cornbread or mush, often served with molasses. Also popular in the South and West, wheat-flour biscuits were considered a social notch up from cornbread. Other starchy foods filled up stomachs instead of or alongside bread. People of Eastern European ancestry made rich homemade egg noodles to eat alone or to enrich a soup; Jews baked their noodles into a kugel. Italians imported pasta from Italy or bought it from neighborhood pasta shops or regional pasta factories. The poorest families combined their bread with more starch: bread and potatoes, bread and cornmeal mush, bread and oatmeal. But for most, their daily bread was enriched and enlivened with meat, vegetables, dairy, and fats.

At the turn of the twentieth century, meat was a recently affordable luxury. European immigrants, accustomed to eating meat only a few times a year, were astounded that Americans of all classes ate it nearly every day. The most sought-after and highest-status meat was beefsteak, but working people also enjoyed pork chops, slow-cooked joints, bacon, and sausages. The steaks, chops, and bacon were fried quickly in a pan; other cuts of meat (especially large, inexpensive cuts like beef brisket) were simmered slowly and then stretched for several meals. Although fresh meat had become more widely available and cheaper than it had been in the past, preserved meat still had its place; Southerners ate salt pork or fatback nearly every day, using the grease for cooking and flavoring. Chicken was a treat for most, often reserved for Sundays and special meals. Jews particularly appreciated poultry, prizing the meat as well as innards such as chicken livers and using chicken or goose fat for cooking. Those who lived in coastal cities or along rivers ate fish, usually small ones like herring; people far from the water might get their protein from canned sardines. Men in rural industrial villages fished, hunted, or trapped to add trout, squirrel, or rabbit to the family table.

The workhorse vegetables were cabbage, onions, and potatoes. These appeared year-round on workers' tables, in soups and stews or cooked by themselves. From cities to small towns, workers with Eastern European roots shredded, salted, and preserved their own cabbage into sauerkraut every year. Other vegetables and fruits were eaten mostly in their seasons. Workers in cities could often buy fruit from pushcarts near their workplaces for a quick snack. Workers in more rural places bought bushels of fruit cheaply at the peak of the season and canned or preserve it themselves: after the 1870s, glass Mason jars made home canning affordable. Those who had gardens or lived in an area with a lot of vegetable farms could stretch their diets with a bounty of vegetable dishes. Italian immigrants, known for their passion for vegetables, established thousands of small commercial farms to supply their communities with the variety of greens, tomatoes, peppers, eggplant, broccoli, and other vegetables they demanded. Some working-class people foraged for produce, picking wild greens, berries, and mushrooms in the woods and fields around industrial villages, and even in the green spaces of industrial cities. In Pittsburgh, women and children picked dandelion greens from local parks to eat and sell. After 1900, working-class people could afford some canned vegetables and fruits, most commonly tomatoes, peas, and peaches, to add relish to bland food and a few vitamins and nutrients to monotonous midwinter diets. The favorite use for fruit was in pie, especially for native-born American workers; the American mania for pie was well known. Any fresh, canned, or dried fruit could be baked in a crust and serve as a dessert, a snack, or part of a meal. The poorest members of the working class ate hardly any vegetables and no fruit, clinging instead to a dreary but filling diet of oatmeal, bread, potatoes, and cheap stew meat, with perhaps some milk or butter.

Milk became a more common drink during this time. Before the late nineteenth century, milk produced in cities was commonly "swill milk" from urban cows fed inexpensively on food scraps or on the mash left over from brewing, which gave their milk a sour taste. In the 1880s and 1890s, newly established "milk trains" with refrigerated cars brought fresh country milk quickly into cities, making it less expensive than it once had been. (The milk was increasingly pasteurized after the 1890s, which reduced milk-borne disease but added to the cost.) Cheese and butter were also increasingly manufactured in factories rather than farmhouses; the new cheeses may have had less character, but they were also probably less expensive. Refrigeration also made cheese and butter available throughout more of the year. Butter was still relatively expensive; working-class people bought butter substitutes like margarine (made from animal and vegetable fats) when they were available, or they spread condensed milk or lard on their bread instead. Those from northern and Eastern Europe were most likely to drink milk and to eat other dairy products like sour cream, yogurt, fresh cheese, and buttermilk. The Irish had traditionally counted themselves lucky when they could have buttermilk with their potatoes; Russians scooped sour cream atop their beets and cucumbers. Italians bought small quantities of the expensive imported cheese they prized to season their dishes.

Alongside the traditional dishes, people often ate food that their parents, or their grandparents, had never eaten. Immigrants to the United States adopted new food habits to varying degrees. Italians clung resolutely to their traditional diet, provisioning their new American homes with produce from local Italian-owned farms, pasta factories, and olive oil importers. Others, especially those whose diets in the Old World had been particularly drab, adapted more freely, eating whatever was plentiful and cheap. One Polish woman, "asked if she had changed her diet in this country, replied, 'Naturally, at home everyone had soup for breakfast, and here everyone has coffee and bread.'" The "American diet" seemed to incorporate more cakes and other sweets, much more meat, and more coffee—in short, more of the food considered luxuries in the Old World. Those who migrated from country to city in this period changed their diet too. Southerners who migrated north learned to eat canned ham instead of country ham, sliced yeast bread instead of biscuits. And the forces of industrialization meant that everyone's diet changed over the generations, as canned food became cheaper, margarine substituted for butter or lard, and all-new foods like breakfast cereal and soft drinks were heavily advertised even to the working class.

Just as we do today, working-class Americans around the turn of the twentieth century combined desire with practicality in their daily menus. When we decide what to eat, we first think about the foods we like to eat, the favorite foods of people in our country or region or age group, or the foods our mothers made: our culture and our cuisine. Most of us also enjoy tasting foods from other cuisines and have incorporated some new dishes into our everyday menus. But our choice of food is not simply cultural. We are also constrained by material circumstances. We must also ask: What food can I afford? What food is sold in nearby stores? Can I grow any food myself? Must I buy raw materials and cook them, or is food sold ready-cooked? Is there someone else who will cook for me, and will I have to pay him or her to do so? What foods do I know how to cook? Do I have an oven, a refrigerator, a microwave, a plate, a fork? The answers to these questions often trump cultural considerations. No matter whether you crave a hamburger, a plate of gnocchi, or a green salad, you can't get any of these unless you have money and access to food and a kitchen, or access to restaurants. Material conditions are especially important for those in limited circumstances, who must choose carefully how to spend their money. Part of what defines poverty in any era is the inability to make free choices about necessities such as food. Poor people must eat what they have, or somehow manage to buy food with the money they can earn, and they must fit the time required to cook and eat into the grueling task of earning enough money to live.

Although I'm certainly interested in cuisine—that is, specific recipes and dishes—I'm more interested in how people got food when money was tight and life was uncertain. Food has so many cultural and social functions that we can forget its more basic importance. Food can mark celebrations of all kinds, religious holidays, and deaths and births in the family. Cooking can be fun and relaxing for people who enjoy it. It can be a competition between people showing off their skills, or it can be a tool of courtship. But in this book I've tried to uncover the repetitive and rather dull task of getting breakfast, lunch, and dinner on the table, day after day. This seemingly mundane task tells us about how people organized their lives, and how the massive changes of industrialization affected ordinary people

Food is always changing, but here I've focused on the period between 1870 and 1930. In the last quarter of the nineteenth century, America became fully industrialized. Millions of people left farms for cities and large towns and took up jobs in factories and mills. The growth of the railroad system (49,000 miles of track in 1870 became 163,000 miles by 1890) transformed the way food was grown, shipped, and sold, and entrepreneurs developed new technologies to process food.[3] In the late nineteenth century, American workers began a fight for political representation and better working conditions. Despite violence and setbacks, workers continued to organize and strike for justice until hard-won labor laws began to appear in the twentieth century. In the first thirty years of the twentieth century, the Progressive movement spurred thousands of social reform efforts, many aimed squarely at home cooking and the problems of poverty. Food processing continued to grow in sophistication, while prices for packaged foods dropped to within reach of working people. And for most of the sixty-year period, until immigration was limited beginning in the 1920s, European immigrants streamed into the country, affecting the American food scene even as they themselves adjusted to cooking and eating under the conditions of the New World. The working-class diet was changed because of all these events, but it was also during this time that the food of ordinary urban working-class people became part of the national culinary identity. American food after 1930 would never again be identified merely as the food of traditional, native-born, farming white Americans; it had been irrevocably marked by the street food, ethnic dishes, and "fast food" that began with the working classes.

America's working class was very large at this time and growing rapidly. Despite the size of the group, historical evidence about food habits is still elusive. The extant sources are unevenly distributed: we know more about urban people than rural people, more about northerners than southerners, more about easterners than westerners. The specific experiences of black Americans, though certainly shaped by pervasive racism and a unique culture, are not always delineated from those of white and immigrant Americans in the same areas. Unfortunately, the source limitations mean that this book cannot be comprehensive. My work focuses on the areas where efforts to "reform" members of the working class were strongest: the Northeast, Midwest, rural southeast, and, to a much lesser extent, the West. The food experience of people in other areas can be inferred to an extent; that is, working-class people in various industrial cities found similar opportunities and challenges, and people living in rural industrial areas faced some of the same conditions as coal miners and textile workers. I hope future scholars embrace the task of finding out more about what working-class people ate in those areas I have been unable to research in depth.

WHO WERE THE WORKING CLASS?

The working class might be defined in several ways: based upon income, occupation, standard of living, or a shared class consciousness. In the late nineteenth and early twentieth centuries, people may have been referred to as workers, workingmen, or laborers. They might have proudly called themselves "producers," people who made useful objects with their hands (implying that white-collar workers such as managers, lawyers, and clerks, who failed to produce any useful objects, were less than useful themselves). Some had the benefit of skill and training and therefore earned higher wages, while others were equipped only for grueling manual labor, but all worked with their hands, making things, extracting resources, or working in service industries.

Myriad small differences distinguished workers from one another. They would have been aware of distinct differences between races and ethnic groups, between skilled workers and unskilled workers, between immigrants and native-born Americans. In Chicago's meatpacking plants in the early twentieth century, for example, at least forty different ethnic groups worked in close proximity, speaking almost as many languages. Most were unskilled or "casual" laborers, hired by the day or hour; others were highly skilled butchers who zealously guarded their workplace status and privileges. Their wages differed based on their origin: American-born workers made 17.5 cents per hour, foreign-born ones 12.5 cents, women 10 cents.[4] Workers' ethnic or national background determined their language, their religion, their family life, and their cuisine. Their job status, as skilled or unskilled, determined their income, their standard of living, and their life chances. Any one of these factors might affect the food they ate: their traditional cuisine might not be available in a mixed-ethnicity industrial neighborhood, or a well-to-do skilled immigrant might be able to afford more meat than was customary in his traditional diet.

Although the working class is most often identified with cities, I have made a special effort to include in this book the rural working class, including people who worked in textile mills, lumber camps, and small coal-mining towns and others who did industrial work in a nearly rural setting. Many of America's industrial workers in this period, especially those engaged in extractive industries like lumber and coal, lived and worked far from large cities, and their living conditions were quite different from those of their urban counterparts. They did not generally lack living space, and they had plenty of space outdoors in which to raise vegetables and chickens. However, they lacked the amenities and opportunities that city dwellers enjoyed, including a variety of retail choices, the possibility of wage work for women, and particularly the freedom to seek another employer if conditions were bad. Some of these workers moved back and forth from industrial work to farming throughout their lives and preferred to live by farming if they could; they would have hesitated to lump themselves in with the full-time industrial workers of the cities.

In these ways and many others, the American working class was not cohesive; its members didn't always feel they had much in common with each other. These differences account for the often-mentioned fact that the American working class, though active in unions large and small and thousands of industrial actions, failed to form a politically strong worker's party, as those in several European countries did around the same time.[5] But all American workers, unified or not, had similar life experiences due to their class. And by their dress, bearing, ethnic background, and job status, they were clearly distinguishable from the middle class, which was growing in size, power, and assertiveness.

Although social mobility was possible, most people born in the working class stayed there. America was celebrated as the land of opportunity, where a Scottish immigrant could rise from a factory worker to a millionaire industrialist, as steel magnate Andrew Carnegie did. By the late nineteenth century, however, advancing through the ranks of industry was quite rare. The writings of Scott Nearing, a radical economist with a lifelong interest in social justice, provide detailed information about working-class lives from an economic point of view. In 1914 he calculated that workers in the railroad industry had a 1 in 300 chance of advancement, but a 1 in 20 chance of injury and a 1 in 120 chance of death in the course of employment with the railroad. As Nearing bluntly wrote, "The chance to rise considered over a lifetime was considerably less than the risk of death or serious injury."[6] Many working-class people hoped to improve their fortunes with a small business or through training in a skilled trade, and some succeeded. Those workers' lives could reach a level of comfort and stability near that of the middle classes, even if their employment status kept them firmly in the working class.

Workers might not achieve social mobility, but physical mobility was a part of life. Many members of the working class in the late nineteenth and early twentieth centuries traveled as part of two great movements of people: from rural areas in America to cities and towns, and from foreign countries to the United States. Domestic migrants streamed from America's farmland toward its industrial towns and cities. The industrialization of agriculture, along with an expansion of land under cultivation, meant that in each generation fewer farm workers fed more people. Young people from farming families moved to towns and cities to take up industrial work. Often entire families moved together from marginal agriculture to industrial work, like the southern families who moved from subsistence farming or sharecropping to work in cotton mills. White Americans moved from farms to small towns and from small towns to regional metropolises. After 1910 African Americans began moving as well, from sharecropping in the South to industrial jobs in the urban North. As blacks flocked to Detroit for work in auto and other manufacturing industries, their population grew from barely six thousand in 1910 to over forty thousand in 1920.[7] Vibrant black communities in New York, Chicago, and Cleveland owed their existence to the sudden concentration of migrants from the South, who were often crowded together in segregated housing.

Domestic migrants, however, were overshadowed by the huge numbers of immigrants from overseas. The late nineteenth and early twentieth centuries saw an influx of European immigrants, along with smaller numbers from Asia and Central America. The origins of the immigrants changed over time. From the 1850s, immigrants came in large numbers from Great Britain, especially from Ireland, and from northern European countries such as Germany. They were followed by increasing numbers of Italians. Finally, after 1900 a flood of immigrants came from central and eastern Europe, including Russia, Poland, and other Slavic countries. The number of immigrants in urban areas during this period can hardly be overstated. In 1880, 78 percent of San Franciscans were foreign-born or the children of foreign-born parents. The numbers were 80 percent in New York and Cleveland, 84 percent in Detroit, and 87 percent in Chicago.[8] In 1887 clergyman Samuel Lane Loomis observed, "Not every foreigner is a workingman, but in the cities, at least, it may almost be said that every workingman is a foreigner."[9]

Immigrants were both pushed and pulled into the United States. American manufacturers and business owners actively supported immigration because it ensured a constant supply of low-wage labor for factories, mills, and mines.[10] Many immigrants left their homes because, like the United States, their countries were converting to commercial agriculture and industrial production, leaving less room for farm laborers, small landowners, and skilled craftsmen. Others were lured by the promise of high wages, hoping to save up a nest egg and return home with money enough to buy land or a business. Immigration ebbed and flowed according to local conditions; for example, more Italian immigrants came during years when harvests at home were small, and fewer when harvests were good.[11] Some, especially the Jews, were drawn to the promise of a land where they wouldn't face the discrimination and persecution of their homelands. Almost all of them saw America as a land of abundant food, a place where they would not be stalked by hunger as in the old country.[12]

Immigrants and their food produced a constant challenge to American culture. Each successive wage of immigrants was more "foreign" to native-born Americans than the one before. The Irish were the first large group of Catholics in mostly Protestant America, and their ideas about drinking and sociability clashed with those of more sober, somber Americans, especially those who aspired to middle-class respectability. Their bare-bones cuisine of potatoes, based on English oppression in Ireland, drew contempt in the United States. But at least they spoke a dialect of British English; central and southern Europeans often did not speak English at all, and the customs of orthodox Jews and Eastern Orthodox Catholics seemed strange. Orthodox Jews maintained distinctive dietary and clothing traditions. Both Italians and Latin Americans ate food that native-born Americans considered too spicy and too strongly flavored, and Italians especially insisted on a huge variety of fresh vegetables, which were often eaten raw. These differences could create conflict. Popular pseudoscientific social theories suggested that northern Europeans had evolved into a people superior to other Europeans: taller, fairer, blonder, healthier, more intelligent, and with better moral character than central and southern Europeans, who were stereotyped as dark-haired, swarthy, unattractive, slow-witted, irrational, illiterate, and of dubious character. By the end of the 1930s, mainstream Americans had become more tolerant of difference and even exhibited a limited interest in "ethnic" foods and culture, but only after nativist activists had successfully called for immigration restriction laws that drastically cut the number of new immigrants after 1920.[13]

Immigrants and migrants faced the choice whether to retain their traditional foods as much as possible or to adopt mainstream "American" foodways. This will be discussed at length in the chapter on cities, since it was primarily in the cities that people faced this decision. Most immigrants tried to eat at least some of their traditional foods, and in the process they started thousands of small businesses to raise produce, import traditional foods, manufacture pasta, butcher kosher meat, and provide other ethnic or religious food necessities. Others found that, even when the raw materials were available, the new shape of their lives meant that traditional food-processing techniques had to be modified or abandoned. Faced with considerable pressure to "Americanize" by eating American food, some immigrants conceded—and their children generally ate American food with gusto.

The living conditions of the working class were as diverse as its people. Recent immigrants, along with migrants from rural areas and the native-born, crowded into industrial cities. Most manufacturing took place in cities and large towns, near the railroads and ports that brought raw materials and carried away finished products and where there was a large pool of labor available to ensure constant production when demand was high. The conditions of urban living depended a good deal on density. In the most crowded cities, like New York, people lived packed tightly together. Most working-class people rented small apartments in tenement buildings or in converted former private homes. Family members, relatives, and boarders piled into beds and slept on the floors in order to make the high rents. Large cities also had large populations of single men and women who lived in boarding and rooming houses and took their meals outside a family setting. (The question of where one ate was so central that it marked the distinction between boarding and lodging.) In less crowded cities such as Pittsburgh, working-class people were more likely to have a freestanding home, either owned or rented, to themselves. The homes were often in poor condition. A constant stream of new immigrants arriving meant that the demand for housing outstripped supply, which allowed landlords to charge exorbitant rents for low-quality rooms. Not all workers lived in cities, however; workers at mines and mills lived in company-built housing in small "company towns" across the nation, which were sometimes very isolated from other communities. In these towns working people were forced to live in the conditions created by their employers, and, without a larger community, they depended on their own families a great deal.

UNCERTAINTY

Life and work experiences differed by race, ethnicity, gender, age, and sex, but life for all was precarious and unpredictable. Many of the economic safety nets we take for granted today, like unemployment coverage, Social Security, and Medicare, as well as welfare and food stamps for the poor, did not exist. Workplaces were lightly regulated and often dangerous. In general, and over the long haul, industrialization meant higher wages and more food for everyone. But in the chaos of short-term reality, getting enough to eat was a balancing act. There was a fine line between a family with sufficient food and a family who was hungry, and it was very easy to slip back and forth across that line.

Native-born Americans and immigrants, in big cities and isolated company towns, tried to earn their daily bread in a climate of economic uncertainty. Either because employers couldn't hire, or because workers couldn't work, wage earners in America found it hard to count on a steady paycheck. In 1914 economist Scott Nearing identified five factors that "reduce or entirely eliminate income": overwork, sickness and accidents, labor-saving inventions, shut-downs of industrial plants, and industrial crises.[14] The

United States' economy fluctuated wildly, experiencing regular upswings and downturns. Years of investment and high employment were closely followed by years of massive unemployment. Many industries were still seasonal, hiring many men at one time of year and laying them off at another. Firms stopped producing when weather made work or transportation impossible, when there was no demand, or when workers went on strike. Many firms worked at batch production, meaning that many workers might be hired to fill a large order and laid off again when orders decreased. Nearing pointed out that in 1904, for example, three-fifths of all those employed in manufacturing worked less than a full year. Another third worked fewer than 270 days.[15] Wage earners might lose their jobs several times, or work reduced hours, or work only part of the year. Budgeting was difficult when income was uncertain.

Illness and injury, too, stalked the working class. Nearing estimated that in the early twentieth century there were half a million work-related injuries and deaths each year. In coal mining, for example, there was the constant threat of injury or death from accidents, such as exploding methane or tunnel collapse. But government investigators researching working conditions found that miners also often suffered from parasitic infections caused by working in damp environments without toilets, and miners contracted tuberculosis at ten times the national rate.[16] Most of those injured or made ill at work would receive little or no compensation or assistance, either from their employers or from the government.

Among the working class, who experienced poor living conditions and had little access to medical care, communicable diseases spread quickly. Infant mortality was also high. In 1900, about 110 white infants of every 1,000 live births died in infancy; for blacks, the number was 170. (The different rates for whites and blacks indicate the very real impact of racial inequality.)[17] And babies died more often in poor families. In some mill towns and other working-class areas, infant mortality was higher than 25 percent. In Johnstown, Pennsylvania, in 1913, children of the lowest-earning men were twice as likely to die as those in wealthier families.[18] Children and adults got sick from contaminated water, unclean milk, and filthy conditions in homes without running water and streets without sanitation. In 1909, 22 percent of Pittsburgh families in the poorest districts contracted typhoid each year through fecal-contaminated food or water.[19] In one Pittsburgh family, a sixteen-year-old daughter was out of work for thirty-two weeks after falling ill with typhoid; at the end of that period, she had developed tuberculosis.

Her family kept cows and sold milk to their neighbors, possibly transmitting the diseases further.[20]

Even small injuries such as cuts on the hand could become infected without proper treatment and become serious wounds or disabilities. In one cotton-mill family in Atlanta, Georgia, in 1911, most of the eleven children were covered in sores, probably pellagra, from poor nutrition. One of the boys was born with a disability that prevented him from working. The father had a bone felon on his thumb, an infected finger injury that eventually required amputation. He was reported to be "extremely emaciated" from the pain and stress of the injury.[21] Sick people couldn't bring in income, disrupting the family budget. Unlike today, sick people mostly stayed at home, which often required another family member to stay home to care for them. They needed expensive medicines and sometimes special foods as well, thus stressing the family budget even further.

Poor nutrition left people more susceptible to disease as well. Deficiency diseases such as pellagra and rickets were common. After about 1900 there was an epidemic of pellagra, a disease caused by vitamin deficiency that first causes diarrhea and a rash and lesions on the skin, then weakness, aggressiveness, and eventually dementia and death. Technological advances in flour milling had made white or "bolted" flour and cornmeal, with the bran removed, as cheap as the old-fashioned stone-ground whole grains that poor people had usually eaten. People greatly preferred white to whole-wheat flour once they could afford it. Poor Southerners who consumed most of their calories in cornmeal and ate few fresh vegetables, meat, fish, or eggs developed chronic cases of the illness, which grew worse in winter and hit women and children, who got a smaller share of the family's supply of meat, the hardest.[22] Poor children in northern industrial cities were more likely to develop rickets from a lack of vitamin D and calcium in their diets (and little exposure to the sun to generate vitamin D); their bones softened, causing bowlegs and other skeletal deformities. Communicable diseases like tuberculosis were also more prevalent among those with poor diets.

Because of the uncertainty caused by irregular work and illness, most working-class people depended on the participation of all members in the family economy. The "living wage," whereby one man's work could support his family so that his wife could keep house and his children could stay in school, appealed strongly to working-class men's sense of masculinity, but it was difficult for most to achieve.[23] Families needed each member's contribution to survive, and those families with the greatest number of workers (that is, with teenage or adult children who still lived at home) were the most stable and had the highest standard of living. Even women who didn't work for wages contributed materially to the family economy, either by performing labor that would otherwise have to be paid for (cooking, laundry, and growing and processing food at home, for example) or by "taking in" housework by doing other people's laundry, keeping boarders, or selling food. Almost all small businesses were family-run; wives and children all worked together. In rural areas, families often worked together in textile mills or in processing industries like oyster shelling. The middle-class ideal, in which the husband worked for a steady salary and the wife devoted all her time to household management, often did not fit working-class lives. Working-class women were often unable to be "just a housewife," even if they wanted to be.

Food is an important part of women's history, but food is not limited to women's history. Although cooking was certainly considered "women's work," food was a problem for the whole family. To be sure, the burden was not equally shared. Women bore the primary responsibility for finding, cooking, and serving food every day. Sometimes they had help from children or other family members, but often the dynamics of a patriarchal family meant that wives worked harder than anyone else in the family while receiving little comfort, security, or decision-making power in return.[24] Ultimately, however, both men and women had to make decisions about how best to earn money for, buy, store, and prepare food every day. Just as the realities of working-class life did not permit a separation between family life and the world of commerce, they also did not allow cooking to be relegated entirely to women. The living arrangements of many working-class people were not based on the traditional family unit. Young single men and women and single-parent families had to find nontraditional ways to solve the problem of feeding themselves.

WAGES AND THE COST OF LIVING

How much did working-class people earn, and was it enough to live on? The cost of living was a subject of constant public interest, as working people adjusted to the dislocations of the industrial economy, and workers, employers, and legislators wrestled over the definition of fair wages.

Wages were affected by industry slowdowns, by seasonal layoffs, by union activity, and by skill level. The process of deskilling lowered wages over time.

Employers sought to replace jobs performed by skilled, highly trained workers with jobs that could easily be filled by any unskilled worker. This trend lowered manufacturing costs but also eroded the privileges that skilled workers once held. For the sons of skilled tradesmen, learning their father's trade was no longer a guarantee that their standard of living would equal his, as employers were finding ways to make certain skills unnecessary. Many immigrants, though skilled in their home countries, could not find work in their skill areas due to language barriers or trade unions that controlled entry into lucrative trades, so they joined other immigrants in lower-paid unskilled work. Despite these dislocations, real wages slowly increased by 50 percent between 1860 and 1890.

The cost of living (including food, rent, fuel, and other basic requirements) during the same period also rose, but it did so more slowly, resulting in an overall increase in the standard of living.[25] Food prices fluctuated markedly in the late nineteenth and early twentieth centuries due to vast changes in farming, industry, and transportation. Americans paid less for food in the half century after the Civil War than before the war. The industrialization of agriculture was bad for the farmer, resulting in lower prices of the crops, but it was good for urban food buyers, as it resulted in lower food prices in the period leading up to 1900. Farm production had become so efficient by about 1900 that agricultural output increased faster than the population, and so food prices decreased and U.S. farmers were able to export its food surplus.[26] In general, people could buy enough food with their wages, but the margin of comfort was always slim. After food, rent was the second largest item in the working-class budget. Working-class people often paid a disproportionately high price for low-quality lodging because they had few options, because they were often discriminated against because of their race or ethnicity, and because they needed to live near their work.[27] But food was the most critical daily expense, and prices were unpredictable from day to day.

After around 1900, food prices for working-class people rose unevenly but steadily. With increasing mechanization, improved transport, and fewer new acres coming under cultivation than in previous decades, farm prices increased in the first quarter of the twentieth century before dropping abruptly at the end of World War I. Consumer food prices rose most sharply during the 1910s, especially after 1916, when international demand due to the war in Europe began to affect American food prices. Increased production meant employment, but also a skyrocketing cost of living. Government propaganda encouraging Americans to plant "liberty gardens" echoed existing working-class survival strategies. Housewives on the Lower East Side rioted in response to high food prices. Publishers put out books and pamphlets on economical cooking, and government officials and social workers took a renewed interest in family budgets.[28] Prices smoothed out in the 1920s, but hard times continued for many working people. In her study of family survival strategies in the early twentieth century, Susan Porter Benson writes, "In the comparatively prosperous 1920s, as well as in the depression 1930s, most working-class families had to wrestle with the consequences of insufficient or irregular income; the difference between the 1920s and the 1930s was one of degree rather than kind."[29] Food prices dropped again during the 1920s, as farmers were again distressed by overproduction and low crop prices, but decreasing wages meant continued hard times.

Almost everyone who wasn't wealthy was concerned with the cost of living during this time, but for the working class, the problem of food was one of life or death. Low wages or high food prices could mean starvation for working men, women, and children. Hungry men threatened the social order: without enough to eat, they might steal, strike, or riot. The problem of food and poverty was one of the central concerns of the Progressive movement of the late nineteenth and early twentieth centuries. The Progressives' interest in food not only provides us with valuable evidence of working-class foodways, but their ideas have also shaped the dialogue about food and poverty to this day.

PROBLEMS AND SOLUTIONS

The public discourse on food, including the food of the poorest Americans, was dominated by the Progressives. Although Progressives had many different and sometimes conflicting interests—poverty, public health, child rearing, sanitation, housing, Prohibition, prostitution, corporate power, the environment—they shared a belief that the ills of industrialization could be solved with its gifts. In other words, the modern industrial city, full of poverty, sickness, immorality, and despair, could be improved by the application of modern social thought, rationality, and state power. When considering the labor question and other issues surrounding working people, Progressives positioned themselves as disinterested third parties. Neither working people nor capitalist business owners, they could mediate disputes so that industrial capitalism could be saved and the threat of Marxist or Socialist workers' movements defused.

Progressives were very interested in food. The Progressive movement was largely powered by women, especially women of the middle and upper classes who had received college educations but were informally barred from most professions. With too much energy to confine themselves to the traditional charity work performed by elite women, they created and utilized social sciences in an attempt to eliminate poverty rather than simply ameliorate its symptoms.[30] These journalists, activists, and settlement-house workers felt uniquely qualified to help with "women's problems," including the feeding of families. Cooking was almost inseparably associated with women and motherhood. Women traditionally fed their families, from breast-feeding to preparing dinner to packing school and work lunches. Cooking reform was a way for female settlement-house and charity workers to enter the public realm via the private sphere, and to use their natural authority as women to set in motion changes that would benefit all of society.

Food was a private matter with public implications. Unclean food and food businesses could cause disease. Poorly fed children would become poorly educated delinquents. Poorly fed men were prone to drink. Women who were trapped at the stove had no free time to educate themselves. "Environmentalist" theories suggested that people could be changed by their surroundings: bad food made bad people, but good cooking could make better citizens. Legislation was considered the key to establishing safety and accessibility, education the key to banishing irrational prejudices. Food and cooking were steeped in tradition and superstition, but now rational inquiry could determine the "best way" to select, cook, and serve food. Perhaps most importantly, food could no longer remain a personal matter between a man and his appetite, or a woman and her children. Traditionally, food and cooking were part of the "domestic sphere" of women, a realm that was supposedly distinct from the men's world of business, politics, and science. But, as Progressives showed, food was closely entwined with business when it came to food prices and concerns about adulteration and sanitary processing. Food became political when working people asserted that their wages were insufficient to buy bread for their families. And science, in the form of the new field of nutrition, seemed to offer hard, verifiable facts about food, including exactly how much people needed and which foods were "best." In short, Progressives were very modern, with concerns similar to ours today about food quantity, quality, and safety and what we would now call food justice.

Their interest in food carried Progressives into the homes of millions of Americans on a search for detailed information about what Americans ate.

Without the budget studies, photographs, price lists, recipes, anecdotes, and legislation they produced, our understanding of working-class diets would be much poorer. Throughout this book I have used images from a sociologist and reformer named Lewis Hine. In the early twentieth century Hine used photography to document living and working conditions among working-class people and to fight for change, most notably with the National Child Labor Commission. Hine's photographs showed children at work in tenements, fields, and canneries in order to draw public attention to their plight. His photographs also incidentally recorded details of working-class life that are hard to find elsewhere. Other Progressive sources are documentary, like the 1918 Department of Labor budget study. From 1917 to 1919, investigators for this massive study interviewed thousands of working-class families around the country to determine what they spent their money on, and whether their wages were sufficient to get by. The study recorded food purchases in dozens of categories, providing unusually detailed information about what foods working-class people bought and ate, as well as the kitchen utilities (running water, gas, etc.) they had available and whether they gardened or raised chickens for extra food and money.

The spur for all this documentation was a deep interest in food as a social problem. In the late nineteenth century, charity workers had begun to perceive a paradox about food. Despite advances in farming, distribution, and food processing that promised better and more abundant food for all, it was clear that working-class and poor people in America were very often hungry. In fact, it often seemed that industrialization had made the food situation worse, not better, for city dwellers. In large, dirty industrial cities, meat and milk were tainted with filth. Unscrupulous food processors adulterated food with valueless nonfood substances at best, or dangerous poisons at worst. Cheap "junk food" like pies and candy tempted workers away from plain, wholesome food. The long hours of grueling work required of wage-earning families made it impossible for mothers to devote much time to cooking. And the inhuman conditions of industrial workplaces distorted natural appetites, driving men to drink when they were simply hungry for nourishing food. The food problem was not limited to poor Americans. The "socialism of the microbe" meant that all urban Americans were at risk if unsafe cooking practices and dirty, adulterated food were produced and consumed anywhere in the city.[31]

With their interest in food, charity and settlement workers merged with the domestic science or home economics movement. Since the mid-nineteenth century ambitious, intelligent women had been pushing for a more systematic approach to the myriad tasks that comprised housework. As early as the 1840s, Catharine Beecher had argued for a more thorough study of "domestic economy" in order to improve housewives' working conditions and their status. Later in the nineteenth century, women such as Ellen Richards (Vassar, 1870 and MIT, 1873) and Isabel Bevier (University of Wooster, 1885 and Case Western Reserve, 1889) earned degrees in chemistry and other branches of the natural sciences. But when they wanted to go on to graduate work or careers in science, they did so under the aegis of "household science." Richards became an instructor in "sanitary chemistry" at the Lawrence Experiment Station, applied chemical and scientific principles to household work and organization, published books on home science, and was the first president of the American Home Economics Association.[32] Bevier was advised while in school that "the place for women in chemistry was in food chemistry," and thus went on to found an important home economics department at the University of Illinois that covered every branch of household science.[33] Home economics was a field in which women could assume professional scientific identities within the university without threatening the definition of "women's work." As home economists saw it, making housework more scientific would help women by making their work lighter, more systematic, and more intellectually challenging. Society would benefit as well, as cleaner and better-organized houses and more nutritious food would produce better citizens. And home economists certainly shared the Progressive belief that food should be a public matter, the subject of study, education, and legislation.[34]

The emerging field of home economics found useful partners in medical science and nutrition, reinforcing the idea that the home kitchen had an important effect on public health. Bacteria, microbes, and flies replaced "bad air" as the accepted source of disease transmission, justifying a more intensive scrutiny of household cleanliness and sanitation methods.[35] Home economists and settlement workers thus entered workers' homes, chiding them to open windows, clean up dirt, and sanitize kitchen and baby equipment in order to control germs that caused disease. For example, the Connecticut Daughters of the American Revolution published Yiddish-language guides for new Jewish immigrants. The 1913 edition urged recent immigrants to keep milk covered, to wash hands frequently, to wash meat and produce before eating it, and to obey the Board of Health. Readers were *not* to spit, beat rugs out of windows, throw garbage on the street, or keep chickens. The guide exhorted its readers to keep a watchful eye on public cleanliness: "Select a milk man who has *clean* hands, *clean* clothes, *clean* wagon, *clean* cans, *clean* bottles. Tuberculosis kills 5,000,000 people annually. It may be carried through infected milk. Do not forget that *dirty milk may kill the baby*."[36] Every household had a private duty to its members and a public duty to the community to maintain standards of cleanliness and prevent diseases like tuberculosis. Home economists and settlement workers embraced this responsibility, arguing that a well-ordered home was cleaner, safer, and better for the community than a dirty, disordered home.

The most important scientific research for food reformers was in the new field of nutrition. In the 1880s and 1890s, early nutritionists like William O. Atwater at Wesleyan University theorized that the human body was a machine that required precise caloric inputs. Calories could be supplied by carbohydrates, fats, or proteins interchangeably. To early nutrition researchers, the precise foods that supplied these nutrients did not seem to matter very much.[37] As Atwater wrote in 1899, "A quart of milk, three-quarters of a pound of sirloin steak, and five ounces of wheat flour contain about the same amounts of nutritive material, whereas the prices are very different. . . . This is a fact which very few people realize."[38] The cheapest source of nutrients was surely the best for poor folks.

Cookbook writers and other food reformers eagerly adopted this new perspective, arguing for rationality over preference in food choice. In cooking instructor Mary Hinman Abel's 1890 cookbook, *Practical Sanitary and Economic Cooking Adapted to Persons of Moderate and Small Means,* she encouraged her readers to substitute the cheapest possible source of nutrients for expensive ones, "for example, the proteid [protein] of beef instead of that of chicken, fat of meat instead of butter."[39] To experts of the time, lard was nutritionally equivalent to butter and therefore absolutely comparable; people on a small budget must buy only the cheaper substitute. Foods were to be selected only on the basis of their constituent nutrients. Abel wrote, for example, "Eggs at their cheapest, as in April when they often sell at 15 cents a dozen . . . [are] still much dearer than the cheaper parts, flank, neck and brisket, at 8 cents. So that even at this low price, they are somewhat of a luxury to the man who must get his proteid and fat in their cheapest form."[40] Since eggs were usually even more expensive than they were in April, there was no nutritionally defensible reason for buying eggs instead of cheap cuts of meat. Taste and preference were irrational distractions from the true purpose of food. The fact that one might prefer butter and eggs to lard and beef was irrelevant to Abel.

This mechanistic view of human nutrition could have some outrageous results, as nutritionists (and candy manufacturers) insisted that candy was a tremendously nutritious food because of its hefty servings of calories and fat. In a public lecture in 1910, Professor Jon C. Olsen of the Brooklyn Polytechnic displayed jars of chocolate creams and salted peanuts and declared, "Candy is a nourishing and sustaining food. . . . Any vigorous adult could make a good breakfast on those chocolate creams and peanuts."[41] Olsen pointed out that, at almost three thousand calories for thirty cents worth of candy, it was cheaper per calorie than oysters and many other wholesome foods.

Simplistic views of nutrition were tempered by the "newer nutrition" of the twentieth century. Vitamins were discovered in the 1910s, when researchers realized that not only could certain nutrients, such as those found in milk, butter, fruits, and vegetables, cure diseases like rickets and pellagra, but that their absence could actually cause them.[42] The discovery of vitamins elevated the importance of fruits and vegetables over that of candy (and, incidentally, served to legitimate the dietary choices of certain immigrants, such as those of Italians, who had always insisted on plenty of produce when nutritionists were pushing cornmeal and boiled beef). Nutritional science still backed home economists' claims that there were more important, more scientific criteria by which to judge food choices than the old-fashioned and irrational criteria of taste and appetite.[43]

BUDGET STUDIES AND THE PROBLEM
OF MANAGEMENT

Armed with this new scientific knowledge, charity and settlement workers, sociologists, and nutritionists converged on working-class neighborhoods in order to make quantitative studies of working-class food habits. Home visits, surveys, and budget studies were the tools that Progressive reformers used to study the problem of food.

Budget studies, in which investigators recorded an individual or family's income and expenditures for food, rent, and other necessities, had been performed occasionally by statisticians and economists since the seventeenth century.[44] The first large-scale American budget study, featuring interviews with 397 working-class families, was published in 1875 by Commissioner of Labor Carroll D. Wright in the *Massachusetts Labor Report*. Wright had hoped to find that working-class families could earn a decent living on one income, but instead he found that most families fell far short. Wives earned little (in terms of cash income), and children provided between one-quarter and one-third of household income.[45] Wright became head of the United States Bureau of Labor in 1888 and went on to organize ever-larger studies of working families' diets.[46] In 1890, his bureau gathered budgets from 2,490 families of coal, iron, and steel workers, and in 1891, the bureau studied the families of textile and glass workers. In an attempt to create a statistical basis, the investigators generally studied only families defined as "normal": "having husband at work, wife, not over 5 children, none over 14, with no dependent boarder, lodger, or servant."[47] Yet even these families, selected for their completeness and stability, had trouble making ends meet. Life was even more difficult for the many families defined as "abnormal" because of a single parent or more than five children.

Meanwhile, from the 1890s onward, other investigators were making smaller-scale budget studies in cities and towns across America. Budget studies and nutrition studies relied on quantitative analysis of data gathered by paid or volunteer workers and meticulous record keeping, and they incorporated as much of the evolving field of nutrition as possible. Researchers recorded everything the family bought and its price in order to carefully compare the amount of money spent with the actual number of calories consumed. In addition to his lab work in chemistry and nutrition, Atwater performed dietary studies on working families in several cities in the 1890s.[48] Robert Coit Chapin's study of New York City families, published in 1909, was funded by the Russell Sage Foundation. Louise Bolard More did another study of some two hundred families on New York's West Side, which was published in 1907. Numerous other settlement-house workers, social scientists, and government bodies continued to perform budget studies throughout the 1920s, including a massive study conducted by the Bureau of Labor Statistics in 1918.[49]

Historian Daniel Horowitz points out two major problems with the information gathered by these studies. First was the problem of communication. Budget studies relied on personal interviews conducted by an American-born, college-educated investigator or government employee with a (usually) foreign-born worker's family, and a great deal may have been lost in translation. As Horowitz writes, "In 1875, for a worker's family to have a representative of the state, of a different social and ethnic background, ask about personal details must have elicited an immensely complicated series of interchanges, especially from poverty-stricken immigrant families."[50]

The second problem was related to the categories chosen by the investigators. Interviewers of the late nineteenth century focused on market exchanges like wages, purchases, or sales in cash. The investigators did not ask about or consider the many nonmarket transactions that filled working-class lives: barter, shared work, household production, garden produce, gifts, and loans. Some excluded the many families who kept boarders, thereby ignoring a major strategy for making ends meet. Also, cooking at home is a form of home production, with costs and benefits, the same as keeping chickens or sewing clothes, but it was not seen or recorded that way by most budget investigators. Later budget studies partially remedied this fact, and by the 1920s those who planned budget studies examined sources of income and expenditure more comprehensively. In the 1918 Bureau of Labor Statistics survey, for example, investigators asked about seven categories of family income: earnings; board and lodging; the net yield from gardens, chickens, and similar pursuits; gifts of money, food, or clothing; net income from rents and interest; fuel picked up; and "other."[51]

As researchers investigated family budgets using nutrition studies as their guide, they saw a baffling tendency for the poor to spend too much on food and still be hungry and malnourished. In 1899 home economist Ellen Richards asserted, "The $200 which a Lowell factory operative spends on food, out of his $360 total income, is largely spent on costly meat, sugar, butter, and fine flour, instead of on well-chosen cuts of meat, peas, beans, and corn meal. He could have secured better nutrition for $100."[52] In other words, his income was perfectly adequate to secure "good nutrition" via legumes, corn meal, and cheap cuts of meat, regardless of whether that's what he wanted to eat. Armed with new studies of human nutrition, the social scientists found what charity workers had long suspected. The same amount of money could be used for radically different amounts of calories and nutrition. It *was* possible, these researchers felt, to live better—that is, to acquire more calories and nutrients—for less money.

The budget studies were attempts to solve the problem of wages, a problem that had serious political and social implications. Were workers being paid enough? Exactly how much money was required to support an individual or a family? This inquiry was central to the "labor question," the controversy over the rights and duties of workers and employers under industrial capitalism. Workers organized to demand better wages and safer working conditions and, indeed, to protect their very right to organize. As Lawrence Glickman and other labor historians have shown, the idea of a "living wage"—a wage on which a male breadwinner could support his wife and children—was an important goal, both emotionally and politically, for generations of American workers.[53] To those of the employers' class, workers' seemingly capricious and selfish demands, strikes, and riots threatened the social order and might soon topple the system of industrial capitalism that had brought so much wealth and material comfort to the upper classes. Budget studies offered a seemingly rational and unassailably disinterested solution to the central question of wages. If workers were ragged and malnourished, did the fault lie with their low wages or with their intemperate habits? Facts and figures—in budget studies, cost-of-living analyses, and retail price series—would answer the question once and for all. Either the prevailing wages could buy adequate nutrition at market cost, or they could not.

Progressives, like those who investigated poor and working-class food budgets, saw themselves as impartial mediators in the war between the rich and the poor. As historian Michael McGerr has argued, they held up their own middle-class lifestyles as an example for all: frugal but not penurious, comfortable but not extravagant.[54] Ultimately, many of their writings are tinged with a moral disapproval of the working class for being insufficiently middle-class in their behaviors and priorities. To be sure, many investigators and reformers sympathized with the poor and wrote with compassion about their difficulties. Margaret Byington, for example, in her 1910 study of steel-workers outside Pittsburgh, clearly identified low wages as a reason for poor living conditions. "In spite of the reputed high wages among steel workers," she wrote, "the problem Homestead housewives face in trying to provide food and a good home on the man's earnings is no easy one."[55] The middle-class Progressives who headed the budget studies cast the problem of food as one of individual skills and self-discipline—a problem of management.[56] If workers could simply put aside their irrational appetites and cook cheap, nutritious foods rather than buy expensive luxuries like butter and steak, they would have plenty to live on.

Those who gave poor people advice on what to eat struggled with the tension between individual and public responsibility, a tension that was complicated by the heavily gendered nature of cooking. Although they recognized that food was everyone's problem, they did not veer from the conviction that the solution rested on women's shoulders. Often the solutions they proposed hinged on individual women's hard work, skill, and discipline. Although these are all noble qualities, the reformers who suggested these solutions tended to turn a blind eye to the structural inequalities that conditioned food choices. Hard work could mitigate, but not eliminate, the fundamental problem of feeding a family on insufficient wages. Working-class people and those who offered advice about food viewed each other across a class divide that influenced both the way the problem of food was perceived and recorded, and the solutions that were offered. This inability to see past class differences, despite good intentions and a wealth of data, continues to inform the way we perceive the problem of food today.

Although the Progressive food reformers were sometimes judgmental and critical, they still left a priceless legacy of information about the food habits of working-class Americans in the late nineteenth and early twentieth centuries. We can combine these reports with other kinds of information to understand the actual conditions under which food was purchased and eaten, the limitations and opportunities faced by poorer people, and the structural changes that affect the entire food system. In order to understand people's food choices, we first have to uncover how people got their food, and how they cooked and ate it.

_____

TWO

Factories, Railroads, and Rotary Eggbeaters

FROM FARM TO TABLE

INDUSTRIALIZED AGRICULTURE AND THE TRIUMPH OVER SEASONALITY

The American foodscape was transformed in the late nineteenth and early twentieth centuries. The industrialization of agriculture changed the size and nature of American farms, which were becoming larger, more efficient "factory farms" that required enormous inputs in the form of machinery and chemical fertilizers. Improvements in transportation changed the way food was bought and sold and lowered its price. Perhaps most importantly, the combined effects of industrialization and transportation worked together to reduce seasonality.

These structural changes profoundly affected working-class diets by lowering food prices and making the purchase of out-of-season foods at least possible. These changes allowed everyone, including working-class people, to eat more like wealthy people of the past, with more access to high-status foods like meat and white sugar and access to a larger variety of produce throughout the year. In fact, twentieth-century advertisers and promoters seized on this idea, crowing that industrialization made it possible for a poor man to eat like a king. However, these changes to the food system occurred at the same time that America's "second industrial revolution" concentrated new immigrants and American rural migrants into crowded industrial cities. Despite the long-term movement toward lower food prices, frequent industrial depressions and job insecurity meant that working-class city dwellers frequently had trouble stretching their food dollars to feed the family. Eating like a king was still a dream rather than a reality for most.

The triumph over seasonality was probably the biggest revolution in food of the time. For the whole of human history, the food supply had been limited by the annual cycle: plants will grow only during certain times of the year, and animals follow a seasonal reproduction cycle. To be eaten out of season, food had to be preserved; for example, pigs slaughtered in the fall were salted and apples gathered at the same time were dried so that they could be eaten, in altered form, throughout the year. Food could be grown in controlled environments, such as greenhouses, or transported to areas where it was not in season, but until the twentieth century, these options were both impractical and expensive. Prior to the twentieth century, people ate fresh foods only in season, and they ate preserved food or did without during the rest of the year. Although foodies today advocate a more seasonal way of eating (both for better taste and better sustainability), for those without a choice, seasonality seemed like a curse. It meant long stretches of dull food and poor nutrition through the winter and early spring. The decrease in seasonality would eventually transform the American diet entirely from its nineteenth-century format.[1] Like other technological changes, the increased availability of fresh food regardless of season carried moral and social implications as well. Working-class people, like other Americans, would have to decide whether the novelty and variety offered by out-of-season food was worth the extra cost.

In the 1870s foods were already becoming available outside their traditional times of year through improved transportation and new technologies in farming and food processing. Faster transportation effectively shortened distances, so that ripe fruit could be brought from southern or western states or even from other countries and sold before it rotted.[2] Refrigerated train cars meant that animals could be slaughtered and their meat shipped at any time of year, not just in the cold months, as before. New farming technologies could also reduce seasonality. For example, chickens normally lay fewer eggs in winter, meaning higher prices for eggs in the cold months. If they are exposed to a source of artificial light, however, hens can produce more eggs year-round. Improvements in food processing, such as canning, also made preserved food seem fresher. Canned food was much closer in taste and texture to fresh foods than dried or salted foods were, so the improved availability of canned foods represented an impressive reduction of seasonality.

The industrialization of agriculture also helped smooth out seasonal variations and pressures on the prices of staples and grains. Industrialized agriculture was more like factory production than traditional farming, with increased use of mechanization, increased dependence on capital and credit, economies of scale, and market specialization. America had more land available for plowing: in the thirty years after 1870, farmers began to flood into the Great Plains, which were previously considered a useless desert.[3] More land under cultivation meant a larger supply of food on the market and lower prices, especially for grains and meat. Farmers changed their tools as well. Innovations such as mechanical planters, reapers, and binders (tools that still used horses as the motive power rather than steam or gasoline) increased the amount of crop farmers could produce with less labor. Wheat production increased 250 percent in the last quarter of the century.[4] Farmers needed significant capital to farm in the West in order to pay for the now-critical inputs of mechanized tools and fertilizer, leading to increased dependence on banks. Larger farms resulted in lower commodity prices, which in turn made it even harder for small farmers to compete.[5] These changes in American farming combined to bring a greater variety of food into American markets and, at least for a while, lowered prices for food as well. The urban working class, who bought all of their food and needed to count their pennies, benefited from these changes, destructive as they were to the traditional American small farm.

Railroad transportation and related technological changes altered the nature of food as a commodity. First, railroad transportation decreased food prices. As historian William Cronon argues, Chicago's growth as an entrepôt of grain sales and the use of grain elevators combined to encourage standardized grain grading systems. Instead of being hauled into the city by farmers in their wagons and sold as bags of grain from a single source, grain was increasingly brought in by railroad and classified by grade, such as number two spring wheat. Graded grain could be bought and sold in any quantity or traded as futures. The commodification of grain increased its supply and lowered its price by streamlining its transport and sale.[6] Secondly, the railroads transformed food by increasing the supply radius. Food could be transported quite cheaply over long distances, which both lowered prices and increased the variety of food available. By the 1880s, the use of refrigerated railroad cars was beginning to transform agriculture, as fruits, vegetables, meat, and other perishable goods could be shipped long distances. In some instances, the railroad system transformed entire industries.

The development of the refrigerated railroad car made it possible to develop a centralized meat-processing center in Chicago. In the 1850s, cattle from Texas were herded through Kansas and into Chicago by rail. From

Chicago the cattle would be shipped, still "on the hoof," to slaughterhouses throughout the East. In the 1870s, Gustavus Swift built a more efficient system, shipping chilled butchered meat rather the entire living cow. His plan required refrigerated cars that would chill the meat without damaging it; icehouses along the way to refresh the car refrigeration; and butchers who would consent to sell "chilled beef" instead of beef that they had butchered themselves. Once Swift was able to perfect this system, other packers followed suit. As this "western beef" flooded the market in the last quarter of the nineteenth century, prices for beef dropped considerably, as much as 30 percent between 1882 and 1893.[7] Meat, traditionally a scarce item in working-class diets, became vastly cheaper. Americans could now eat fresh meat instead of preserved meat, and replace salt pork with fresh beef. The changes in the meat industry affected individual neighborhoods as well: local slaughterhouses disappeared, and retailers concentrated on selling the most desirable cuts rather than having to dispose of all the parts of a locally slaughtered animal.[8]

In tandem with the increasing availability of fresh packed beef and pork, wild game and shellfish declined in numbers due to overhunting. By 1900, for example, Americans living in New York, Philadelphia, and Baltimore could easily buy inexpensive beef butchered and packed in Chicago, but the ducks, oysters, and crabs that were once plentiful in the Chesapeake Bay were becoming scarce.[9] The decline in seasonality went hand in hand with a more centralized food system in which more food poured out of fewer processing locations.

The milk supply was also drastically altered by the railroads. Until the 1870s, city dwellers drank milk from cows kept right in the city in locations derided as "swill dairies," where the cows ate discarded distillery and brewery mash and were penned in small, filthy stalls. The milk traveled only a short distance to customers, but it tasted sour and was often dirty. In the late nineteenth century, "milk trains" carried milk from large rural dairies into the city. As "country fresh" milk became more widely available, demand increased; city dwellers drank more fresh milk and fed it to their babies instead of breast-feeding them. However, railroads increased the distance and time that milk could travel between cow and consumer, and bacterial contamination plagued urban milk supplies until pasteurization became widespread in the 1910s.[10]

The railroads had possibly their greatest effect on produce. Seasonal fruits and vegetables were being shipped from the warm South into colder northern cities even before the Civil War, but by the 1870s this had increased considerably. Southern states like Florida, Georgia, and South Carolina, with their longer growing seasons, specialized in fruits and vegetables that were shipped to New York and other northern cities. The use of refrigerated railroad cars made it easier to ship perishable produce. Historian Richard Hooker notes that after 1878, "cities near sea or rail transportation . . . had, even in winter, fresh tomatoes, radishes, cucumbers, spinach, cauliflowers, eggplants, Valencia onions, and salad greens, all but spinach from the Deep South."[11] Fresh produce was shipped not only from the South to the Northeast and Midwest, but all the way from California to the cities of the East. The first carload of fresh fruit reached the East Coast from California in 1869, and the California agricultural economy boomed in the last quarter of the nineteenth century, as refrigerated cars could ship produce almost anywhere in the country without significant damage—especially after sturdy varieties like iceberg lettuce were specially developed for long transport.[12]

This meant that city dwellers, even in cold northern states, could enjoy locally out-of-season fruits and vegetables. Americans in much of the country were able to benefit from the long southern and western growing seasons instead of being limited to what was locally available. Cooking teacher and home economist Maria Parloa, in an 1880 cookbook, wrote about the temptations of supplementing Northeast produce with southern items, warning of their higher cost: "The railroads and steamers connect the climes so closely that one hardly knows whether he is eating fruits or vegetables in or out of season. The provider, however, realizes that it takes a long purse to buy fresh produce at the North while the ground is yet frozen."[13]

Cold-storage warehouses attached to the railroad network also extended foods' seasonal range. Home freezers were not common until the 1950s, but cold-storage warehouses, cooled by mechanical refrigeration, were common at the turn of the twentieth century. Refrigerated food could be sold as fresh, helping to eliminate seasonality long before the mass retailing of frozen food. In 1891 *Harper's Weekly* reported that large cold-storage warehouses in New York and Chicago were keeping eggs, meats, and other items fresh for weeks or months out of their seasons. The buying public was often suspicious of cold-storage foods: the food seemed unnaturally fresh though months old, and the cold could conceal spoilage.[14] For *Harper's,* however, cold storage promised a "peaceful revolution" in which eggs would sell for the same low price year-round, spring lamb would be available any time, and "people of very small incomes will be able to enjoy a bill of fare such as the richest man was unable to procure within the memory of the reader."[15] The changes in food distribution promised a sort of "democracy of goods" in which even poor people would be able to buy plenty of fresh, luxurious food. Whether or not this promise was achieved, most Americans did benefit from the wider seasonal availability of food. Anthropomorphic measurements (height and weight) indicate that until the widespread adoption of refrigeration, many groups of Americans were perennially underfed. The better nutrition from refrigerated meat and dairy allowed everyone to grow a little taller and heavier.[16]

After the turn of the twentieth century, working-class people in cities could afford a bit more variety in produce than previously, able to purchase produce perhaps a few weeks earlier or later than it would be available locally. In 1893 William T. Elsing, an activist minister on New York's Lower East Side, thought that even the poor in New York could afford early or late-season produce "raised in hot-houses, or sent from Southern markets" at "reasonable prices."[17] The rural population, who lived far from railroad terminals or shipping ports, did not benefit from this new transportation technology, of course; they were still largely limited to produce that grew locally or could survive longer, slower hauls. Out-of-season produce was mostly an urban phenomenon.

INDUSTRIAL FOOD PROCESSING

Beginning in the late nineteenth century, food-processing industries worked along with transportation to change Americans' experience of food. There were two major sets of changes to American food processing. First, traditional processes such as cheese making, brewing, bread baking, and meat curing were accelerated and converted from small-batch, artisan production to continuous factory production. Second, new processes such as canning and breakfast cereal manufacture created new processed foods that had the potential to radically change American eating habits. These changes came to fruition during the 1920s. Working-class people incorporated processed foods into their diets very slowly during this period, but the growth in processed food changed the American diet more generally.

Traditional food-processing techniques changed slowly but steadily throughout the nineteenth century. To use cheese as an example: by the 1870s, most cheese was produced in large cheese factories rather than small farmhouses. Newly available laboratory-produced rennet (the enzymes that separate milk into curds and whey) was more reliable than that extracted on farms from calves' stomachs. In the early twentieth century, food science researchers at land-grant colleges and state experimental stations attempted to "rationalize" cheese making, instituting the use of pure milk with a precise butterfat content and replacing naturally occurring bacteria with precise inoculations of the correct cultures. Processed cheese, which did away with troublesome natural variations, was being sold by 1916.[18] By the 1930s, the cheese that Americans ate was likely to be prepared in large batches under sterile, standardized conditions. This was true of bread, beer, ham, pasta, and other traditional foods as well.[19]

Canned food was the processed food most commonly eaten by working-class people in this period. Food had been canned since the early 1800s, but for most of the nineteenth century canned food was an expensive luxury, often sold to travelers and those who wanted to enjoy out-of-season or rare delicacies. In the 1850s, a small can of oysters, salmon, lobsters, tomatoes, corn, or peas might cost fifty cents in an Eastern grocery store.[20] (At that time a skilled mason working on the Erie Canal earned about $1.50 each week.)[21] After the Civil War, canned food was often sold to miners and others on the far western frontier. In "boom" areas where few vegetables were yet cultivated for sale, canned fruits and vegetables were sometimes the only ones available at any price. Newly rich miners in California lavished money on canned delicacies, paying exorbitant prices for exotic "prepared" foods like turtle soup and lobster salad in cans.[22] In the late nineteenth century, the industry expanded and canned food's retail price dropped as manufacturers found ways to eliminate costly human labor: that of the skilled tinsmiths who made and soldered the cans, as well as that of the unskilled, low-paid women and children who prepared the food to be canned.[23]

Canned food finally became affordable for the middle classes in the 1880s, and for most people around 1900. Technological advances and the elimination of high labor costs lowered the prices of common canned foods, especially tomatoes, corn, and peas, to within the reach of the working class. By 1900 middle-class cooks were already accustomed to using canned fruits and vegetables when fresh ones were seasonally unavailable.[24] In Fannie Farmer's 1905 cookbook, aimed at the urban middle class, a recipe for "Green Peas" began, "Open one can of peas."[25] Even poor working-class families used a small amount of canned food. At about the same time as Fannie Farmer's cookbook was published, working-class New York City families

FIGURE 1. Sociologist and photographer Lewis Hine devoted his career to exposing and eliminating child labor in the United States with the National Child Labor Committee. This photograph, taken in July 1909 near Baltimore, Maryland, shows women and small children stringing beans before they are canned. Photograph by Lewis Hine for the National Child Labor Committee, July 1909. Library of Congress, Prints and Photographs Division, National Child Labor Committee Collection, LOT 7475, v. 1, no. 0855. Reproduction Number: LC-DIG-nclc-00031.

that spent only $10 per week for food regularly spent 10 cents for a can of tomatoes.[26] Americans' consumption of canned foods increased steadily through the 1910s and 1920s, as the foods available now included convenient prepared dishes such as canned soup and spaghetti. By 1930 Americans consumed twice as many canned vegetables and four times as much canned fruit as they had in 1910.[27] Canned food joined abundant meat and out-of-season produce as former luxuries that were now everyday foods available to the working class.

There was, however, some continuing resistance to canned food. Some recent immigrants, especially those from less industrialized parts of Europe, refused to use canned foods. Italians in particular made a point of seeking out and, if necessary, creating local sources of fresh vegetables.[28] Even native-born Americans believed that canned food was a necessary evil. In a 1926 Department of Commerce study, the consumers polled overwhelmingly preferred fresh food to canned in terms of flavor, and more than half believed that fresh food was more nutritious.[29] The reality of canned food hadn't lived up to the canners' extravagant promises of a bounty of flavor.

The path food took from farm to kitchen had changed almost beyond recognition. Farms were larger, food traveled faster and farther to market, and some food was transformed along the way into a growing selection of packaged and processed foods. The kitchens where this food was processed for the last time before it was eaten had changed too. In working-class kitchens the economic and political food system met the private world of individual decisions, preferences, and cooking ability. The types of tools and utilities available to working-class people, and the shape and character of their kitchens, dictated how food was cooked.

WORKING-CLASS KITCHENS: THE WORKPLACE AT THE HEART OF THE HOME

In the late nineteenth century, working-class and middle-class people thought about kitchens in very different ways and used them for different purposes. Among the middle class, the kitchen was a separate, clearly defined room that reflected the family's orderly social life. Well-designed homes had kitchens whose activities would not be seen, heard, or smelled by anyone else in the house, especially guests. At a time when most middle-class people could afford to hire one or two servants, the kitchen was a place for cooks and maids to work unobtrusively. Ideally, the heat, noises, and smells of cooking would be completely blocked from the semipublic social areas of the home, such as the parlor or sitting room.

After the turn of the twentieth century, architects and "domestic feminists" (reformers who wanted to redesign the home to improve women's work in it) planned kitchens that used new technologies to lighten household work. By the early twentieth century, it had become more socially acceptable for middle-class women to "do their own work" with few or no servants, partly because their kitchens were now clean, light, and well designed.[30] Even in these modern kitchens, middle-class women preferred to screen off the dirt, smells, and labor of the kitchen from the rest of their family's life.

In contrast, working-class kitchens were not isolated, specialized spaces. The kitchen was the center of the home, busy with activities such as eating, bathing, socializing, and working. The kitchen might be a small or large room, or it might simply be one area of a large room where the stove, sink, and table were located. Anecdotal and photographic evidence shows stoves, sinks, and kitchen tables in the midst of family activities. On dark evenings and during cold winters, families huddled around the stove, a source of heat and light. In summer, people tried to use the stove as little as possible or used small tabletop gasoline or oil stoves to save fuel and reduce heat in their living and working area.[31] For present-day observers, the most striking feature of working-class kitchens as shown in many photographs is the presence of a bed or other seemingly out-of-place furniture or objects, as well as the lack of a formal dining space. People slept in the kitchen if that was the most comfortable room, or if there was no other space. They ate wherever it was convenient and comfortable: near the stove in winter, near the open door or windows in summer.

This lack of specialized functions and formal spaces was the primary characteristic that differentiated a working-class home from a middle-class one. The difference, however, was only partly due to a lack of space and resources; it was equally the result of a choice that working people made about their living spaces. Historian Lizabeth Cohen explains that there were both material and cultural reasons that working people simply were not interested in clearly differentiated home spaces. Working-class homes, whether apartments or houses, were generally small and full of people, with little in the way of built-in storage or single-function rooms. Practically speaking, working-class people could not afford to light and heat several rooms of the home at once, so it made sense to huddle together around the source of heat and light, or to work on piecework in the same room where the children played and slept.

Working-class people were accustomed to sharing their living and working spaces closely with others. While middle-class women believed their homes should be a refuge from the economic world, working-class women constantly performed wage-earning work there, keeping boarders, doing piecework, or working in the adjoining family business. The kitchen space was functional and social, not symbolically separated, as it was in middle-class homes. Working-class families would no doubt have appreciated larger functional spaces, and the ability to separate messy tasks like laundry and food processing from the family's living space. (Whenever the weather and access permitted it, they took messy tasks outside.) But they didn't seem to want to wall off the kitchen from the rest of the home, even if it was possible. The material culture evidence shows that although working-class people were

FIGURE 2. This Hine photograph from the National Child Labor Committee shows a nine-year-old girl named Jennie Rizzandi performing piecework sewing with her parents rather than attending school—but it also offers a glimpse of the interior decoration of a working-class tenement apartment in New York City in 1913. Photograph by Lewis Hine for the National Child Labor Committee, January 1913. Library of Congress, Prints and Photographs Division, National Child Labor Committee Collection, LOT 7481, no. 3256. Reproduction Number: LC-DIG-nclc-04306.

constrained by cramped living spaces and a lack of storage, they still sought to arrange and adorn their living spaces according to their own preferences, and they often refused to rearrange their lives according to middle-class ideas of propriety.

Even when working-class families had more room, they retained the practice of eating, living, and working in the same room. If there was a separate dining room in the home (a rarity), it was kept for "company" or for other purposes, not for family dining.[32] Margaret Byington, who studied steelworkers' families in Homestead (a mill town just outside Pittsburgh) as part of the Pittsburgh Survey, reported, "Though a full set of dining room furniture, sideboard, table, and dining chair, are usually in evidence, they are rarely used at meals. The family sewing is done there . . . but rarely is the room used for breakfast, dinner, or supper."[33]

Although their homes were small and crowded, working-class people worked hard to decorate their homes. Nearly every photograph of a working-class home shows embellishment of some kind. Families that had a steady income or a sudden windfall bought the largest, grandest furniture they could afford (often purchased on installments), and they were particularly fond of luxurious-looking items like plush furniture, drapes, lace curtains, and mirrors.[34] Kitchens and dining rooms were festooned with extensive lace or paper lambrequins (decorative short, stiff drapes) on every shelf, with deep ruffles of fabric around sinks and stoves.[35] The ruffles decorated, but did not attempt to hide, the utilitarian appliances. Sideboards and cupboards displayed stacks of ceramics and rows of glassware. Walls were adorned with colorful chromolithographs, advertisements, religious images, and calendars. Working people in cities clearly intended to live in and enjoy their kitchens rather than isolate the space from their family and social life or hide its productive capacity.

UTILITIES

Despite the curtains, mirrors, and lambrequins, kitchens were also workplaces. The utilities and tools in working-class kitchens were usually older and less efficient than those in middle-class kitchens, which made the women's work demonstrably more difficult. As historian Susan Strasser writes, "Well into the twentieth century, indoor plumbing remained a matter of class: the rich had it, the poor did not."[36] In the late nineteenth century, most working-class people had to haul water, either from a single sink in their apartment building or from a pump in the backyard or on the corner. In Homestead, Pennsylvania, in 1907, only about half of families of mill workers lived in buildings with running water, even including those few who owned their homes.[37] Plumbing was expensive to install, and landlords who rented to working-class people avoided installing it until required by law. For instance, a 1902 Chicago city ordinance required that every new tenement have one sink with running water on each floor of the building. Older buildings were required to have a sink with running water in a location easily accessible to each apartment, which usually meant the hallway.[38] Hallway sinks were common in city apartment buildings well into the twentieth century; in some cities, a sink with running water in each dwelling was still not required as late as 1920.[39] The authors of *Middletown* estimated that one out of four residents of Muncie, Indiana, lacked running water in 1924.[40]

By the 1930s almost all working-class housing, even the most dilapidated, had running water. This water, however, might still have to be carried to the stove to be heated. Throughout this period utilities that had been installed grudgingly to satisfy the letter of the city law were not always kept in good working order. Tenants repeatedly suffered from backed-up toilets and drains, which landlords ignored. In the hallway sinks of some New York tenements in 1911, the *Daily People* reported, "the pressure is insufficient, and it is necessary for tenants on each floor to pump the water after turning on the spigot."[41]

In some places the lack of utilities was a function of the physical location of working-class neighborhoods and their lack of municipal clout. In Pittsburgh, the mills on the river flats used so much water that those living in the surrounding hills had no water pressure. As Susan J. Kleinberg writes, "During the summer, many neighborhoods in the largest industrial section of the city (the South Side) had no water from seven in the morning until six at night when the mills operated."[42] Women had to carefully plan their working days around the mills' schedules, scheduling the heavy work of laundry and cleaning for the very early morning or evening hours. Kleinberg argues that this directly affected the efficiency of working-class women's work: "Her washing and cleaning chores, made difficult by Pittsburgh's heavy particle pollution and the grime and sweat on her family's clothes, were made more arduous by the city decision to provide decent [municipal] services only to those who could pay for them."[43] In this instance, the labor of working-class women was less efficient because of their living conditions.[44] The South Side did not have access to municipal water supplies until 1914.[45] Any working-class neighborhood near a large water user such as a factory or mill might have had this problem. And as Kleinberg points out, other effects of proximity to factories, such as pollution, affected housework for the worse.

Even such simple amenities as sinks and fixed tubs were not always present. Built-in washtubs, replacing old moveable wooden or metal washtubs, became commonplace in working-class housing by World War I.[46] In Betty Smith's semiautobiographical novel *A Tree Grows in Brooklyn,* around 1910 Francie Nolan's family lives in a tenement apartment in Williamsburg with a pair of built-in soapstone washtubs with a wooden lid. The tubs were designed for laundry and other chores, not for bathing. As Smith wrote, "It didn't make a very good bath tub. Sometimes when Francie sat in it, the cover banged down on her head. The bottom was rubbly and she came out of what should have been a refreshing bath, all sore from sitting on that wet roughness."[47] The family had previously lived in a nicer apartment in another part of Brooklyn with a real bathtub, "an oblong wooden box lined with zinc."[48] As the family's fortunes fell, they found themselves using poorer-quality plumbing fixtures. The tubs in Francie's Williamsburg tenement at least had faucets attached; older tubs simply had drains, requiring the user to pour buckets of water into the tubs to use them.

Women adjusted their patterns of work around the fact that every drop of water used for cooking, cleaning, and bathing had to be carried in and heated on the stove (and sometimes carried back out again). In 1899 the New England Kitchen was established in Boston by dietary reformers who wanted to offer nutritious cooked food and promote plain, healthy recipes. The kitchen's organizers began offering hot water to neighborhood people who could not (or would not) carry and heat water in their own kitchens, especially in hot weather. "The people started it by first asking for what we should never have thought to offer, and now the whole neighborhood draws on our supply of hot water, and this means a great deal for health and cleanliness, especially in the summer months."[49] The kitchen, fitted up with restaurant-style cooking capacity, most likely had running water that was piped directly into the stove to heat, or the building might have had a water heater for hot running water. The large cookstoves of middle-class houses had hot-water reservoirs—large covered metal basins attached to the stove, with a faucet for access—that could produce a constant supply of hot water as long as the stove was kept lit and the reservoir refilled as the water was used. But someone in those houses still had to carry water and the coal to heat it with.

Imagine the logistics of a home kitchen in which producing hot water was so arduous that people would rather walk down the street, or even several blocks, to carry hot water back with them. The people who took advantage of the New England Kitchen's hot water may not have had a reservoir on their stove, may not have wanted to heat the stove in the summer, or may have been boarders or lodgers with no cooking facilities at all. In these kitchens, working-class women avoided cleaning tasks in the summer, and their families bathed less frequently. And if they avoided heating the stove for hot water, they must have avoided cooking on it as well.

It was simply harder to keep one's home clean and to perform other household tasks like cooking in a poor or working-class neighborhood. The Progressive settlement-house workers and home visitors who tried to understand the problems of working people were often taken aback by the difficulty of life under these conditions. One visiting housekeeper wrote in 1917, "With modern equipment, steam heat, electric utensils, and new and sanitary apartments, it is not a difficult task to keep [a home] fresh and clean, but in rickety, shadowy apartment buildings or houses where the floors are worn and rough, with no hot-water service, and too often without even gas for lighting, we can at once recognize the trials and handicaps which confront the housewife in the poorer districts."[50]

Gas was another kitchen utility that was distributed unequally. The wealthiest Americans had experimented with gas fixtures in the 1870s, and by the late nineteenth century many factories, schools, and city streets were lit with utilitarian gaslights. By the early twentieth century working-class homes commonly had gas lighting fixtures, sometimes installed at the renters' own expense.[51] Some urban tenements had coin-operated gas meters to power appliances. In his memoirs of growing up in East Harlem around 1900, writer and educator Leonard Covello recalled that his family had a meter in their apartment that operated the gaslights and the stove. When the money ran out, "in the middle of a meal or at night while I was reading, the gas would lower under a boiling pot of spaghetti or the light would dim" until more coins were inserted. Covello remembered, "My father said it was like having an extra mouth in the family."[52]

Like other fixtures in cheaply built, poorly maintained tenement housing, gas fixtures were often improperly installed. Two women working at the College Settlement in New York City rented a tenement apartment for themselves in the working-class neighborhood surrounding the settlement house. They found that, although new, the house was very poorly built. They reported, "The gas fixtures were poor and ill fitted, so that we had a constant leakage which was both expensive and far from healthful."[53] Some buildings lacked even poorly installed gas or other amenities. On a working-class street in Boston in 1895, all the tenement houses had water and sewage connections, but "not one of them has gas, a hot-water heater, a bath-room, or—trifling but portentous detail—a fly-screen. One badly kept water-closet, located in the cellar, has to answer for all the families of a house."[54] Again, although a landlord might eventually be prevailed upon to improve the toilet facilities or install window screens or (less likely) a water heater, residents might have to count on the city to run gas lines into the neighborhood.

Although kitchen utilities in working-class homes routinely lagged behind those in middle-class homes, American kitchens could still seem very luxurious to European immigrants. A woman who emigrated from Bulgaria in 1929 explained how her new home in America seemed lavish because there was gas: "I drew a picture of the house and sent it to my people and said, 'I'm so lucky to be here. I bet you King Boris doesn't live the way I live.' Because there was no gas in Bulgaria, so I knew King Boris couldn't have no gas."[55]

TOOLS

Utilities were a part of the house, the building, or the neighborhood, but kitchen tools were owned by each individual family. The most important tool in the kitchen, the stove remained essentially unchanged from the Civil War until the widespread adoption of gas stoves around 1900. The only major innovation in stoves during that time was the change in fuel, from wood to coal. Most stoves could burn wood or coal interchangeably, so cooks could switch back and forth depending on what was cheaper. In the late nineteenth century, more working-class people probably burned wood, even though coal burned hotter and longer and was less bulky to store. Hard (anthracite) coal was more expensive but burned cleaner and hotter than the cheaper soft coal. The only real advantage to wood over coal was that, in some rural and semirural areas, it was still possible to forage for wood. A woman who emigrated from Austro-Hungary in 1909 at the age of eight recalled that, in her parent's home near Pittsburgh, they used a wood stove since they could not afford coal: "Of course you could have bought coal if you had the money, but if you didn't have the money you had to substitute the wood."[56] Urban dwellers could sometimes pick up coal in the streets that had been dropped by coal haulers or scavenge wood from construction sites and packing boxes.[57] In the early twentieth century, working-class people with coal stoves lagged behind those in the middle class who were acquiring new gas ranges.[58] Cooking on a coal stove of 1900 was more or less the same experience it had been on a wood stove of 1850. Though perhaps slightly more efficient and more convenient to use, the stove still required hauling fuel, tending the fire constantly, and standing uncomfortably close to the source of heat in order to cook. The experience of cooking began to change only with different types of fuels and stoves that could be turned on and off more easily, and that did not emit so much radiant heat.

A stove and fuel of some kind was necessary for any kind of cooking and was therefore an unavoidable expense. When working-class families moved into rental housing, a stove was sometimes provided as part of the furnishings. In other circumstances families had to bring their own stoves. As late as the 1920s, Russian immigrants living in cheap tenements in New York had to bring their own small coal stove.[59] In 1897, the cheapest kitchen stove from the Sears, Roebuck catalog cost $7.20; in that year the average weekly wages of a man working in industry were about $8.48.[60] Used stoves could be purchased for less. In 1911, Mabel Hyde Kittredge, who wrote a book advising tenement dwellers how to furnish their apartment, gave the price of a stove as $9 (for a tenement apartment with five people).[61] Those who wanted a fancy stove "with much nickeling" (shiny metal ornamentation) might pay $20 or more.[62]

Guides for housekeepers regularly acknowledged that cooking stoves were difficult and time-consuming to operate and maintain and warned that they required constant supervision and care to work properly. A wood or coal stove required maintenance every day. If the ashes were not removed each day, the fire would not light; and if the stove were not cleaned regularly, it would not "draw" properly, smoking up the room. Any stove would rust into uselessness if not "blacked" with stove polish as often as every few days. Inexpensive stoves were more or less simple boxes whose heat was hard to control; a complicated system of dampers controlled the heat in more expensive models, requiring time and attention to learn. Wood and coal stoves did not have temperature gauges. To test the heat, cooks used traditional methods that were essentially unchanged from the days of brick hearth ovens, such as holding one's hand near the heat and counting the seconds until it was unbearable.[63] They were dangerous appliances to have in the home. Stoves—even coal-burning ones—could emit noxious gas if used improperly. They could topple over, and hot-water reservoirs might spill and scald.[64]

Finally, stoves had to be fueled constantly in order to maintain the heat while cooking. Susan Strasser makes an important point about these stoves: "Wood and coal stoves were never 'turned on'; they were used only when economical in time, in labor, and in fuel. This made them less flexible than modern gas and electric stoves, which cooks can use one burner at a time."[65] In other words, stoves were either entirely off or on for hours. Wood and coal stoves were very impractical for cooking for one. They were more suited to the full-time housekeeper whose other tasks kept her in the house and who could maintain the fire and cook a variety of dishes at different temperatures as the fire waxed and waned than they were to the wage worker who returned home only to eat. They were also most practical when used for slow-cooking dishes like stews, or when used for several dishes at once to get the most use from the fuel. In this way they were still like the old-fashioned hearth.

Stoves using different kinds of fuel were patented beginning in the 1860s. These new stoves used coal oil, kerosene, or gasoline. They were inexpensive and relatively easy to use, but the burning oil smelled bad and there was great risk of fire and explosion.[66] The 1897 Sears, Roebuck catalogue offered one-burner oil stoves for as little as 85 cents and gasoline stoves for $2.63, adding, "There is positively no danger in using the Acme Gasoline Stove. It cannot explode"—suggesting that consumers were aware of gasoline stoves that *did* explode.[67] Small cooking appliances allowed people to juggle a few different types of fuel to keep costs down. Social reformer and home economist Helen Campbell wrote of the struggles of two formerly genteel women who were reduced to sewing to make a meager living. Campbell was surprised that they only used twelve cents' worth of coal per week, and asked, "How could twelve cents' worth of coal do a week's cooking?" One of the women responded, "It couldn't. It didn't. I've a little oil stove that just boils the kettle, and tea and bread and butter are what we have mostly. A gallon of oil goes a long way, and I can cook small things over it, too."[68] Small families who depended on an oil stove might find themselves limited to cooking "small things" as well: baking bread or cooking a large, economical joint of meat would be more difficult.

Working-class families who had gas lines into their homes and could afford fuel had a variety of appliances from which to choose. Many homes pictured in the photographs taken by journalist and child-labor reformer Lewis Hine had small one- or two-burner gas stoves that connected to the wall or ceiling fixture with hoses. Placed on top of their old coal stoves, the gas stoves were presumably for use in the summertime. These could be used for heating a pot but not for more time-consuming baking. In 1902, a two-hole portable gas stove cost $1.50, or less if secondhand.[69] Early gas stoves could be dangerous as well. Newspapers carried constant mentions of exploding stoves, as in November 1905, when "Gussie Paulkovin, 25 years old, of 244 First Avenue, was preparing Sunday dinner on a gas stove yesterday morning, when the gas blew out violently and enveloped her in a sheet of flame."[70]

Well into the twentieth century manufacturers produced hybrid stove models that could burn coal and wood on one side and gas or oil on the other at the same time.[71] A woman who grew up in Pittsburgh recalled that when her family moved into a new house around 1922, they "had big pot belly stoves. When we moved in that house, my dad bought a combination stove, a great big one with four burners of gas and four coal. We used to burn coal."[72] By the 1920s gas was becoming commonplace in working-class homes. In the 1920s about two-thirds of the families in Muncie, Indiana, cooked with gas; most of the remainder used gasoline and coal, and a few cooked with electricity.[73]

FIGURE 3. This family, including all the children, worked together crocheting caps on the Upper East Side of New York City in 1912. On top of their coal stove is a gas hot plate, which could be used without heating the apartment as much as the coal stove would. Photograph by Lewis Hine for the National Child Labor Committee, November 1912. Library of Congress, Prints and Photographs Division, National Child Labor Committee Collection, LOT 7481, no. 3123. Reproduction Number: LC-DIG-nclc-04273.

Gas burners allowed for much more flexibility in cooking. They could be turned on and off, and so they could reasonably be used for both quick heating and for longer-term cooking. Families who paid for gas by the nickel, like Leonard Covello's, might hesitate to feed the gas meter long enough for a long-simmered sauce, but they could boil the spaghetti quickly and then turn it off when done. Gas burners (sometimes in the form of "hot plates") also made it practical to cook a meal for one and made possible bachelor apartments with kitchenettes where a single person could live alone and prepare his or her own meals.

But what utensils did working-class Americans have in their kitchens? In the late nineteenth century cookware on the American market was made from new, lightweight, and inexpensive materials. Pots, pans, kettles, buckets, and other vessels, previously made of heavy and relatively expensive cast iron, were now made using lighter metals such as aluminum, which appeared after the 1880s. Enameled goods (the lightweight white or blue-speckled pans called enamelware, agateware, or graniteware) were made by a process developed in Germany in the eighteenth century. They were manufactured in large quantities in the United States after the 1870s.[74] Enamel pots and pans sold in the Sears, Roebuck catalog for between fifteen cents and a dollar in 1897.[75] (Sears prices were cheaper than retail but more expensive than those for similar used items.) Formerly expensive items like ceramic dishes and pressed glassware were now mass-produced, and thus sold more cheaply.

There was a general late nineteenth-century enthusiasm for specialized kitchen implements and serving ware. In an era when factory work was increasingly rationalized and mechanized, inventors and manufacturers created kitchen tools for very specialized tasks. Patented gadgets like rotary eggbeaters and apple corers became more common. From the mid-nineteenth century, domestic advisors like Catharine Beecher advocated having the right tool, utensil, or dish for the job. This was related to the ideal of having clearly defined, separate rooms for different household activities; it was simply considered more appropriate to use the correct item. Beecher, writing for a middle-class audience, advised a full complement of at least 144 items for the service of an ordinary middle-class dinner party, counting only cutlery, plates, and bowls.[76] Other items for table service included sauceboats, soup tureens, vegetable and pudding dishes, platters for meat, and specialized dishes for desserts, fruit, and other courses. Wealthy Victorians delighted in even more specialized items, such as cake baskets, caster sets, ice-water pitchers, doilies, asparagus forks, grape scissors, and so on.[77]

Families at all levels of society, though they may not have felt the same need for grape scissors, aspired to a similar profusion of objects. This is one way in which working-class kitchens might have lived up to middle-class ideals. Mabel Hyde Kittredge listed required household goods in her 1911 guide to keeping house in a tenement apartment. Her requirements for the kitchen (including cleaning supplies but not the stove or laundry tools) totaled $22.66. The list included some highly specialized items probably lacking in most working-class kitchens, including a potato masher, an apple corer, a lemon squeezer, and popover cups. Her list is otherwise reasonable and includes dishpans, bread pans (although it seems unlikely that working-class families would also have separate pie tins, layer pans, cake pans, and gem pans), knives, two frying pans, and two saucepans. She noted, "This is a full list, and in case of a very limited income one *can* do without many things."[78] Dishes (including individual butter, sauce, and dessert dishes) totaled $5.74. By the 1920s the list of kitchen items necessary or desirable for working-class families had been pared down somewhat, but it still included a dozen place settings, four sizes of frying pans, three granite (enameled) pans, a boiler, a dishpan, a grater, a bread box, water pitchers, and more.[79]

Though working people might not have had quite as many dishes and utensils as their middle-class counterparts, visual evidence suggests that most seem to have had plenty for ordinary use and for display. The Lewis Hine photographs, taken to demonstrate child labor conditions in the home, show extensive collections of glassware and dishes in some apartments. The working-class families who resorted to low-paying piecework to survive could still afford lots of kitchen goods. One Hine photograph shows Mrs. Palontona and her daughter, Michaeline, making pillow lace in their tenement on East 111th Street in New York in 1911. Although Hine noted that the Palontona's kitchen was "dirty" and both mother and daughter were "very illiterate," the photograph shows several pieces of kitchenware carefully hung on the walls. There were seven different pots and pans, a colander, a funnel, a spatterware coffeepot, four pot lids, a ladle and measuring spoons, a pie plate, and a salt holder.[80] Another 1911 photo was meant to illustrate that in Italian families, the father was often idle while the mother and children worked hard at piecework. In this New York family, in which the father's income was uncertain ("Sometime I make $9.00, sometime $10.00 a week on the railroad; sometime nottin'") and the piecework brought in only $4.00 a week, stacks of dishes are visible on the decorated shelves. A pitcher, large bowl, coffee pot, sugar dish, and at least a dozen each of dinner plates, smaller plates, bowls, cups, and saucers can be seen.[81]

Of course, a household could be operated with a bare minimum of equipment. A woman from Czechoslovakia, who emigrated in 1937 remembered that when she arrived in McKeesport, Pennsylvania, and met her husband, who had emigrated ahead of her, he bought kitchen tools for them: "He went to the store and he buy three cups, three spoons, three forks, three dishes, coffeepot and that—and he buy coffee—then I can make a pot."[82]

By the end of the 1920s, America's food system had irrevocably changed from the form it took in the 1870s. The majority of Americans who lived in cities were buying brand-new food products, as well as more processed versions of familiar foods. Trucks were beginning to surpass railroads as the means to get foods from farm to market (or to factory), and cars were replacing delivery wagons as customers carried home their own groceries. Workers cooked the food in their small kitchens, which were crammed with whatever tools they could afford and surrounded by all the other tasks of living.

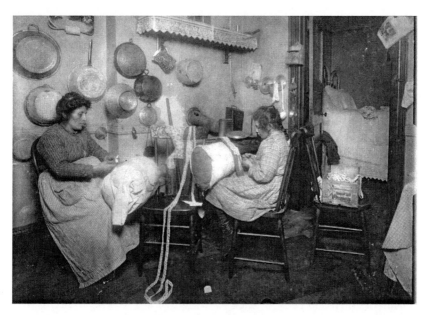

FIGURE 4. Mrs. Palontona and her daughter, Michaeline, making pillow lace in their tenement apartment, New York City, 1911. Notice the wide variety of pots, pans, and tools hung from the walls (probably for convenience and for display), the shelf lambrequin, and the lace trim on the neatly made bed in the second room. Photograph by Lewis Hine for the National Child Labor Committee, December 1911. Library of Congress, Prints and Photographs Division, National Child Labor Committee Collection, LOT 7481, no. 2711. Reproduction Number: LC-DIG-nclc-04111.

Despite the enormous changes, however, food remained at the heart of working-class family life.

Today we have transcended seasonality far beyond the dreams of the people of 1900. In our supermarkets we can easily buy blueberries in November, tomatoes in January, and apples in April. The produce might be grown in hothouses, raised year-round in the Southwest, imported thousands of miles from South America, or just held in cold storage for months after harvest. Critics of the modern food system argue that the industrialization of agriculture has gone too far. They point out that seasonal, local produce tastes better and is more environmentally sustainable. And industrialized foods such as processed American cheese are seen as bland, dishonest, or simply less tasty than "real" cheese. But for Americans of the late nineteenth century, the beginnings of these changes looked like progress. The greater availability of fruits and vegetables rescued consumers from their monotonous diet and the nutritional deficiencies that had been common during the cold months. Processed cheese, although perhaps less tasty than natural cheese, was at least much more consistent, the same every time you bought it. Even relatively simple innovations, like the artificial lighting in henhouses that made eggs more affordable in winter, improved nutrition for everyone. The trade-offs and disadvantages of industrialized agriculture and food processing are undeniable and have become much clearer to us over time, but it's important to remember that in the late nineteenth and early twentieth centuries Americans believed that these changes were making food better for everyone: more widely available, more nutritious, and more reliable.

As they embraced the industrialization of food that brought cheaper meat and produce, working-class Americans were ahead of their time in making the kitchen the heart of the home. Modern American homes—even large, expensive homes designed for the upper classes—are built to showcase the kitchen, with the expectation that families will do most of their living and socializing there. Since 1974, the size of the average American kitchen has grown from 150 to 300 square feet.[83] But in the late nineteenth and early twentieth centuries, the middle class considered the kitchen a hot, odorous, slightly disreputable place where servants or harried housewives did unpleasant work; it was not thought fit for company or public display. In contrast, working-class people truly lived in their kitchens. In part this was because they had no choice: in small, cramped houses and apartments, there were no specialized rooms or much privacy. But the centrality of the kitchen in working-class homes also suggests that the work done there was not limited to women but consisted of a set of tasks that involved the entire family. The work done there might be hot, unpleasant, and monotonous, but the kitchen was where daily life happened.

THREE

Food and Cooking in the City

IMAGINE A WORKING SINGLE MOTHER who finds herself without much time for cooking, or even for shopping. She delegates the tasks to her older children, who buy mostly salty, processed "heat and eat" food along with plenty of sweets. A social worker studying the family is sympathetic to the difficulty of juggling family and job but points out that this food is really more expensive than home cooking. Part of the difficulty is that this family lives in a neighborhood where fresh food can be expensive and inconvenient to get.

Although this tale sounds familiar to us today, it is from 1907. The "social worker" was Louise Bolard More, who was studying the wages and expenses of working people living in Greenwich Village in New York City. The family she studied got most of their "processed food" from the delicatessen: "The most striking feature of this budget is the large amount of delicatessen food which was bought—cooked ham, pickles, sardines, pickled fish and canned fish, potted tongue, etc. This was because the mother was not at home to do the marketing or cooking. . . . Cake and pies and coffee and condensed milk were also largely used."[1] This family paid a high price for food that required no cooking or other preparation. Neither the mother nor her children even needed to heat up the food they bought except for the coffee. The great difference from today, however, is that their food was prepared right in the neighborhood, probably by the family's close neighbors, not manufactured in a distant plant and shipped long distances. In fact, this German-American family bought their food from a German-style delicatessen, where the dishes as well as the language were familiar. In her report, More stated with some surprise that the family seemed healthy enough, but she noted that their food "was probably more expensive than necessary if it had been more intelligently selected and prepared."[2] At that time, however, Greenwich Village was a working-class immigrant neighborhood, and buying fresh groceries required a tiring trek to a chaotic marketplace and perhaps a complicated interaction with someone who spoke a different language. For a single mother, the slightly higher price was a welcome trade-off for familiarity and less work.

Most working people lived in cities or large towns, near the workshops, mills, or factories where they worked. Getting food was difficult in cities, and the task was disorientingly different from the rural areas in Europe and America from which these workers had come. Shopping required an exhausting battle of wits in a hectic market. Apartments were too small and crowded to store more than a day or two's worth of food. But cities also offered a new advantage: entrepreneurs—on the street, in small restaurants, and in saloons—were selling rye bread, apple pie, smoked fish salad, and a hundred other foods that were already cooked and ready to eat. Many working-class people in cities eased their cooking tasks by buying some of their food already prepared. Other people—sometimes the same people—turned their tiny apartments into factories, making pasta or wine or preserving vegetables or fish to sell to their neighbors or local shops. The consumption of what we might consider "fast food" coexisted with labor-intensive home food production. The nature of urban working-class communities heavily shaped the possibilities for food, offering both challenges and opportunities.

SHOPPING FOR FOOD IN URBAN NEIGHBORHOODS

At the turn of the twentieth century food shopping was a difficult, time-consuming task.[3] Shopping required knowledge and skill: where and when to get the best-quality food for the lowest prices, how to judge the quality of food, and how to avoid adulterated products. Working-class women were also mindful of the limited storage space available to them at home and how long things could be stored, because food bought in bulk was no bargain if it could not be saved.

As farming, processing, and transportation transformed food, the way that most people bought food changed too. In rapidly growing industrial cities and towns, a dizzying and ever-changing array of retailers sold fresh food and groceries. Working-class people had to learn to navigate these changes to find decent-quality food at low prices.

At the beginning of the nineteenth century, groceries had represented a very small proportion of the food that Americans ate. Dried, preserved, or long-keeping foods such as flour, cornmeal, and dried fruits were sold by grocers in cities and general stores in the country. Groceries were imported or luxury items, such as coffee, tea, spices, liquors, and preserved foods, as well as staples like salt. Families who lived far from cities or had very little money might buy almost no groceries at all except for grains, some sugar, coffee or tea, or whatever food they could not grow or trade for locally. People who could afford to buy staple foods in bulk (and had the storage space to keep them) usually did so, buying perhaps several barrels of flour and sugar and boxes of dried apples per year. People in cities who lived a hand-to-mouth existence or who lacked storage space might buy small quantities of staple foods—for instance, two cents' worth of sugar, enough for a few days—several times a week. During the nineteenth century groceries gradually became a more important part of daily food shopping. The category of dry groceries expanded as more foods were packaged and branded, that is, sold with a brand name instead of in bulk. After the 1880s, canned foods, packaged crackers, breakfast cereal, and other processed foods filled grocers' shelves.[4]

Groceries were small local businesses that offered flexible credit and other services to meet their customers' needs. They were usually full-service operations, meaning that they offered credit and home delivery. Both wealthy and poor households availed themselves of credit to buy food. In wealthy households, servants could be sent food shopping without being entrusted with money; in poor ones, credit kept food on the table during periodic unemployment. Local stores charged relatively high prices to cover their overhead. Retail grocery and food stores were businesses that were easy to enter but hard to succeed in. A relatively small amount of capital was needed to start a store, but it was a very competitive field, and the expenses of making deliveries and extending credit put many retailers out of business.[5]

During the first decades of the twentieth century, different types of retail stores began to emerge as a result of changes in manufacturing, distribution, and marketing. First, "combination stores" combined groceries with fruits and vegetables, or with meat. For example, in Chicago around 1914, about 10 percent of meat markets carried groceries as well.[6] Then, in the 1910s, chain stores began to edge out small neighborhood grocers. The best-known examples of these were the new "economy"-style A&P stores. These stores operated on a cash-only basis, offering low prices but no credit and no delivery.[7] Cash-and-carry chain stores could be operated much more cheaply than traditional groceries, allowing for a larger store with less staff. High stock turnover and more efficient accounting ensured profits.[8] These new stores attracted mostly native-born Americans, while recent immigrants still shopped at smaller, more traditional grocery stores and still patronized separate butchers, bakers, and greengrocers. With the increased use of the automobile by middle-class and working-class families, in the 1920s and 1930s chain stores began relocating to larger lots of cheap land in the new suburbs just outside the urban core. Chain store owners built large stores with parking lots, called "supermarkets," and encouraged shoppers to drive there and buy a week's worth of groceries instead of walking to traditional corner stores and carrying groceries home every few days.[9] Although older styles of food shopping still existed in the 1920s, the shift toward the modern supermarket had begun.[10]

For most of the late nineteenth and early twentieth centuries, city dwellers could choose between different places and ways to buy food as the types of retailing evolved. Most still bought fresh food—meats, dairy, and produce— every few days or every day. The most important decision to make was where to buy: from small, specialized retailers, such as butcher shops, dairy stores, bakeries, or greengrocers, from stands at outdoor or partly covered public markets, or from peddlers on the street.

Public markets offered flexible pricing: customers could shop early in the day, for the best quality, or late in the day, for the lowest prices, and vendors could change their prices quickly based on inventory, supply, and demand. Public markets and street peddlers also generally sold food more cheaply than brick-and-mortar stores because sellers needed to pay only a small stall rent or license fee and thus had lower overhead costs than those who owned or rented store space.[11] At some markets consumers could buy directly from producers who hauled their fruits, vegetables, meats, or dairy products into the city. Public markets offered low prices and sometimes fewer middlemen, but they could also be crowded and unsanitary. Around 1900 there was a burst of public interest in more efficient, sanitary markets. Many city governments replaced the traditional sprawling outdoor markets with clean and orderly "closed" markets in large public buildings. Despite reforms of this nature, public markets became less important after the 1920s. As trucking replaced trains for shipping goods, markets were no longer limited to central railway terminals. Both public markets and the small groceries would eventually be crowded out by the large chain "combination" stores and, later, supermarkets.[12]

Public markets offered intrepid housewives the chance to get wholesale prices and restaurant-quality goods if they were clever and quick. The markets opened early—at about 4 A.M. in New York City. Restaurant workers,

FIGURE 5. Baltimore's Centre Vegetable Market, between 1890 and 1910. Wittemann collection, U.S. GEOG FILE—Maryland—Baltimore. Library of Congress Prints and Photographs Division, Washington, D.C. Reproduction Number: LC-DIG-ppmsca-12326.

caterers from fashionable hotels, and the housekeepers of the wealthy came first and paid the highest prices for the freshest, best-quality food. After they had made their selections, housewives and boardinghouse keepers arrived around 6 or 7 to look for bargains. As the day went on the food became cheaper and cheaper, as the produce wilted and the fish began to stink.[13] Public markets offered a variety of price and quality levels, with a long list of factors influencing prices. Peter Shergold has tracked the inconsistent prices that resulted from this complex system of supply, demand, and barter in Pittsburgh public markets. "Fresh herrings, for example, which cost 2¢ each on Friday, were reduced to six for 8¢ by Saturday morning and by the evening of that day could be bought at eight for 4¢." This meant that shoppers paid a wide variety of prices. "Veal, for example, varied by as much as 16¢ a pound in one day!"[14]

Shopping at this type of market required considerable skill and aplomb. A buyer had to know just what he or she wanted and how much could be stored, had to judge the quality of what was offered and determine how long it would keep in the storage facilities available, and had to evaluate the seller's need to unload his produce and his willingness to bargain. Indeed, despite the bargains available, many buyers shied away from the hectic markets and this battle of wits.

If they would not come to the market, the market would come to them. Working-class people in cities bought food from peddlers and hucksters who sold from pushcarts, wagons, or baskets. Pushcart peddlers sold fresh fruits and vegetables, meat and fish, bread and bakery products, groceries, and all manner of prepared snacks, in addition to clothing, shoes, fabric, notions, household goods, books, and other items. Peddlers and hucksters took the advantages of the public market—that is, price and variety—and added mobility: they traveled about the city, enabling consumers to buy right outside their doors or on nearby streets. New York and other large cities had the largest populations of pushcarts.[15] In some New York neighborhoods, pushcarts were the main retailing outlet for the poor and working class. New York's densely populated immigrant neighborhoods made it worthwhile for pushcart peddlers to stop wandering and instead establish themselves in a semipermanent market. These markets were established on certain streets, such as Hester Street on the Lower East Side, as early as the 1880s.[16] The great competition among peddlers resulted in the lowest possible food prices for immigrants in the neighborhood.[17] Especially in crowded working-class neighborhoods, pushcarts offered convenience: they were right outside the door. Housewives could buy while carrying out other household tasks and caring for children. In *Out of This Furnace,* a 1941 semiautobiographical novel about Pittsburgh steelworkers, the protagonists in 1903 lived on a street in Pittsburgh "so narrow that Mary could buy from hucksters' wagons without moving off her own doorstep."[18] Pushcart sellers often catered to an ethnic population, since knowledge of English was not required to set up a pushcart or to buy from it. Olsa Elsen, born in Ankara, Turkey, moved to the Lower East Side in 1913 at age ten. She lived on Orchard Street, a busy gathering place for pushcart sellers, and remembered that buying from pushcart vendors was easy for a recent immigrant: "My mother couldn't speak English. At the beginning, she didn't know anything, so she would point."[19]

The flexibility and lack of middlemen that pushcart vendors enjoyed meant that their produce could sometimes be both cheaper and of much better quality than what brick-and-mortar stores offered. Pushcart sellers could buy wholesale in small quantities: for example, if a fruit jobber or wholesaler was unable to sell a large, ripening shipment of fruit to regular retailers, he could sell it in small lots to pushcart vendors. The pushcart vendors could dispose of overripe fruit quickly without much waste, because they were willing to offer discounts on less-than-perfect fruit.[20] A 1924 travelogue of New York called *Around the World in New York* described the "beauty and variety of the vegetables and fruit sold there in what is supposed to be one of the poorest quarters [i.e., the Italian district]." The author described fresh, tempting, and unique produce: "peaches with blooms on, and the softest and the most luscious plums, the largest apples and most beautiful pears, the cleanest salads . . . lying near and between each other so as to form a color-scheme."[21] By the same token, the food could also be overripe or rotten, but that was where the bargaining skills of the buyer came into play. Pushcart vendors could also sell in quantities to suit their buyers. Peddlers in New York's Jewish community could find buyers for damaged eggs "for a song," for a single white or yolk from a broken egg, or for a single chicken wing or an ounce of butter among residents of tenement houses who had little storage space and bought food every day.[22]

Street peddlers were being legislated off the streets, especially in congested cities, by about 1910. In later years motorcar traffic completed their decline except in isolated areas and in some strongholds in New York City. After World War II, remaining peddlers were more likely to use trucks.[23]

Not every neighborhood had pushcarts or access to public markets, but all had a few small local grocers. Common to all American cities and industrial towns, these family-run businesses were often financially shaky. Opening a small grocery was possible with only a small capital investment, although the odds for success were not good.[24] Local grocery stores could be miniscule and quite casual; one street in Boston in the 1890s featured within its tenements "one corner and two basement groceries, with bread, bundled kindling-wood, milk, and salt pickles for staple articles of traffic."[25] Prices were higher in small groceries. Poles living in Chicago's Packingtown neighborhood in 1909 spent more than 51 percent of their income on food. This was a function not only of their small incomes, but also the high cost of food in poor neighborhoods.[26] Working-class residents were often effectively limited to these and other small stores, since lower prices in other stores were not justified by the difficulty and expense of traveling long distances to shop.

Local groceries were closely tied to the ethnic identity of a neighborhood. One Italian neighborhood in Chicago boasted several greengrocers selling a huge variety of the vegetables and greens (including Swiss chard, mustard, dandelion leaves, endive, squash blossoms, and escarole) that Italians held dear. In a Lithuanian neighborhood in Chicago around the same time, the only grocery stores were small combined meat markets and food stores that sold cheap meat, canned food, baker's bread, and no produce. If families in that neighborhood wanted produce, they had to buy from a wagon or push-cart.[27] The sometimes poor selection was offset by the advantages of trading with a countryman: there was no language barrier, familiar foods were available, and shoppers were more likely to be offered credit.[28] These same advantages made small groceries uncomfortable or even hostile toward people of a different ethnicity. The insular nature of local groceries explains why African Americans often embraced packaged food and the new chain stores: they hoped standardization would mean less discrimination in pricing and hiring.[29]

The limited amount of storage space in urban working-class homes dictated shopping decisions. Built-in storage was rare in working people's small, crowded homes. There simply wasn't much room to store household goods, much less food bought in bulk. The difficulty of storage in urban tenements can be gauged by the amount of advice offered on this subject by household advice writers. Home economist Mabel Hyde Kittredge, in her *Housekeeping Notes: How to Furnish and Keep House in a Tenement Flat* (1911), recommended building a covered window shelf for cool food storage to replace or supplement space in the icebox.[30] A high school textbook for consumers in 1913 recommended creating one's own storage: "Dry groceries can be put away in small spaces, stowed in plain packing boxes, set one above another, high toward the ceiling, to be reached from a chair, their lids opening sidewise *[sic]*, like the cupboard door."[31]

The lack of household storage naturally made cooking more difficult, but its most critical effect was on shopping. Urban people bought food—even staples like butter, flour, and sugar—daily in small quantities. In 1893, housing reformer Marcus T. Reynolds explained that low-income families bought in small quantities for lack of both money and storage space. Working people "cannot buy a barrel or even a bag of flour, for if they did they would be without other provisions. They do not want a pound of butter or a leg of meat, for they have no ice to keep it on."[32] Journalist Abraham Cahan agreed. In 1902 he wrote of the Jewish housewife of the Lower East Side of New York, "There is absolutely no provision in her tenement for storing table supplies, and she spends a good part of her time each day running back and forth between her home and the various shops."[33] These housewives generally lacked iceboxes, and so if they bought ice, it was "used principally to cool off the drinking water and not as a means to keep perishable supplies. The latter she purchases only as they can be used."[34]

Though certainly inconvenient, this system had one advantage: it put the burden of storing perishable food on the retailer. When refrigeration became more common in the early twentieth century, butchers invested in large refrigerators and display cases to keep meat fresh. One writer advocated "living on a little" by investing in a large cut of meat, like a quarter of a lamb, and keeping it cold at the butcher's until pieces were wanted: no home refrigeration was needed.[35] Shopping every day allowed one to get the freshest items, but buying in small quantities also resulted in the highest prices, as Reynolds acknowledged. "Butter, bought by the quarter of a pound at a time, brings from 32 to 40 cents a pound; elsewhere it may be obtained for from 25 to 30 cents a pound, or for very much less if bought by the tub."[36] Tracey Deutsch has demonstrated that women of the early twentieth century considered food shopping to be difficult and tiring work; they might well have welcomed the chance to shop a little less often for the necessities of daily life.[37]

The local conditions of stores and markets, combined with the added difficulties caused by lack of home storage and high prices, made food shopping a difficult task for urban working people. People in cities, however, did have one important advantage: they were surrounded by opportunities to buy prepared food that they did not have to cook themselves. And sometimes they did just that.

RESTAURANTS: BUYING, NOT COOKING

By the late nineteenth and early twentieth centuries, some working-class families were slowly but surely moving away from home cooking. Although some home food production remained, working-class urban Americans were at the vanguard of a trend toward the labor of cooking being transferred outside the home, leaving (in the extreme case) only reheating to do. Historians have tended to locate this change within the middle class; to pinpoint the critical time of change as the 1920s through 1960s; and to emphasize the role of industrial food-processing technologies and advertising.[38] However, evidence from photographs and food reformers shows that important changes in home cooking took place much earlier among the urban working classes, beginning around the 1880s or even earlier. Urban working-class people began to replace home cooking in part, not with the products of nationally advertised firms, but with local sources of ready-to-eat food.

These local sources were usually not "restaurants" as we think of them, with tablecloths, menus, and attentive service. That sort of restaurant dining has been the province primarily of the middle class in the twentieth century, and of the wealthy in the centuries before that. However, working-class people still bought food they did not have to cook in many other sorts of places. In the years from 1875 to 1930, workers in large towns and cities could buy ready-to-eat food at bakeries, saloons, lunchrooms, delicatessens, pushcarts, and tiny restaurants. These options add up to a significant range of possibilities to supplement or replace home-cooked food. Working-class families bought cooked food selectively to relieve themselves from the labor, expense, and inconvenience of cooking at home.

Ready-cooked food for working-class people can be divided into two general categories. First, workers could buy food to eat at home that replaced or simplified home-cooking tasks. Bakery food (both plain bread and pastries) and delicatessen food could be brought home and either eaten with little additional work or used to simplify the preparation of a more complex meal: for example, one could buy cold cuts instead of cooking and slicing meat at home. Workers also bought and ate food that was ready to eat outside the home at saloons and small restaurants, or from pushcarts and stands. This category of food required the least amount of work, as even the eating utensils and dining spaces (such as they were) were provided and maintained by the seller. Both categories replaced home cooking, but the latter moved the production and eating of meals out of the home entirely. These two categories could be considered the forerunners of "convenience food" (processed food purchased to simplify home preparation of meals) and "fast food" (inexpensive prepared food, bought outside the home and eaten in a casual setting).

BAKERIES

Bakery items were the most common choice for a worker who wanted cheap ready-to-eat food, such as the family's daily bread or pies and cakes for a quick snack or lunch. Most urban workers, in fact, depended on baker's bread as the staple of their diet, a pattern that dates to the earliest years of the Industrial Revolution in England. Commercial bakeries had, of course, existed in Europe before the Industrial Revolution, but wage workers in the new factories worked long hours away from home and therefore ate more baker's bread than homemade bread. Sidney Mintz has argued that white baker's bread, along with jam, tea, and sugar, was the fuel that largely sustained the urban British working class from the eighteenth century onward. Mintz evoked the critical place of bread in nineteenth-century British working-class diets in his description of jute workers in the Scottish city of Dundee: "When the mother is at work there is not time to prepare porridge or broth. . . . Usually breakfast and dinner become bread and butter meals [and] the children have to unlock the house and get 'pieces' for themselves."[39] Buying bread freed women from the work, time, and fuel expenditure of baking it themselves or preparing other traditional foods, such as porridge or broth (both of which required time, attention, and fuel to simmer). Bread and butter was also easier to serve; unlike porridge or broth, children could serve themselves bread without having to heat it. Bread could not be spilled like porridge, and it required no bowl or spoon. Mintz argued that bread became a more important staple food as more working-class women traded housework for wage work. The availability of baker's bread was therefore a crucial factor in British women's decisions to work outside the home. They could not have done so without a replacement for their work at home producing and serving food.

Urban working-class Americans of varying ethnic backgrounds similarly depended on baker's bread as a basic food in the late nineteenth century. Although Americans in rural areas continued to bake their own bread well into the twentieth century, in towns and cities families depended on daily bread from the baker and often enjoyed pies, cakes, and other bakery treats as well. Like the workingwomen of Scotland, American women found that buying bread from the baker relieved them of a significant amount of food preparation and serving work. Home bread baking was also particularly difficult in cramped urban kitchens. Home-baked bread was considered a luxury as baker's bread became the norm for busy working-class women and their families.

As Americans moved into towns and cities, they had more opportunities to walk to a neighborhood baker and buy bread rather than baking it themselves. The American baking industry expanded along with American industrial cities. In 1879 there were 6,396 bakeries in the United States, roughly one for every 7,800 Americans. In 1899 there was one for every 5,100 Americans. By 1909 there were 23,926 bakeries in the United States, or one for every 3,800 people.[40] In other words, there were twice as many bakeries per capita in 1910 as there had been in 1880. Population density per square mile nearly doubled in the same years, meaning that more people lived in cities and towns, close to bakeries.[41]

Home baking was gradually superseded in towns and cities by commercially baked bread. By one estimate, in 1901 bakers made a third of all the bread eaten in cities, and by 1918 they made two-thirds.[42] In the Lynds' study of Muncie, Indiana, a local baker estimated that only 25 percent of the bread eaten in the city in 1890 had been commercially baked. By the 1920s, 55 to 70 percent of bread was commercially baked.[43] As truck transportation expanded the delivery areas for large bakeries, loaves of baked bread appeared in groceries even in smaller towns. In 1930 more than 60 percent of all bread consumed in the United States—in both urban and rural areas—was baker's bread.[44]

Most of the growth was in relatively small local bakeries. In 1899, 78 percent of bakeries had four or fewer employees. Small bakeries with no hired employees —"one-man" or family operations—served their own neighborhoods and small towns.[45] Some neighborhood bakeries were almost microscopic. In Boston in the 1890s, a tiny bakery, "about six feet by six, opening out of Mrs. Flanagan's kitchen," served the occupants of one working-class street.[46] Larger bakeries that mass-produced bread that was advertised and sold regionally appeared in the 1920s.

Bread was consistently cheap. The baking industry benefited as the flour and sugar industries grew and the prices of these staples dropped by more than half between 1872 and 1898.[47] Bakers were able to pass these lower prices on to consumers, keeping the retail price of bread low. In Pittsburgh in 1894, Isabel Bevier recorded the price of the cheapest kind of bread as two and a half cents per pound.[48] The cheapest bread was sold at the same price in New York City a year later.[49] In 1902, Abraham Cahan reported that Jewish housewives on the Lower East Side bought white bread for four or five cents a loaf, and "black" or dark wheat bread for two cents a pound.[50] In 1909, Robert Chapin's budgetary studies among New York City workers (who, he wrote, "universally buy bread") revealed a range of prices paid for bread: from two and half cents a loaf for stale bread, to an average of five cents a loaf for "regular" bread, and up to eight cents per loaf. Cakes cost ten cents; rolls cost ten cents per dozen. Pittsburgh workers studied by Margaret Byington around the same time bought bread for five cents a loaf. Pie cost ten or twelve cents.[51] And according to Department of Labor budget studies, in 1918 families in New York, Pittsburgh, and Chicago paid between five and ten cents per pound for bread.[52]

The five-cent loaf of bread was consistent between about 1890 and 1920; its price equates to about two or three dollars today.[53] It is hard to know whether a five-cent loaf in New York was equivalent to a five-cent loaf in Chicago or Pittsburgh or anywhere else, either in size or in quality. Some states, including Pennsylvania, required bread to be sold by weight so that bakers could not cheat the customer with large, puffy loaves.[54] It seems likely that each locale or ethnic community had an accepted standard for the price of a "regular" loaf of bread; individual bakers, of course, may have provided higher or lower quality at that price. In 1899 a writer at *American Kitchen* magazine thought that the price of five cents per one-pound loaf was standard in New England; in fact, she said that consumers would assume that lower-priced bread must be of lower quality.[55] Stale or day-old bread was usually available at a reduced price, and "dark" bread was cheaper than light.[56]

With prices fairly low and stable, urban working-class families in northern cities depended on bread as their daily staple and bought several loaves a week. Dietary and budget studies revealed the frequency and quantity of bread purchased by almost all the families studied. For example, the families Chapin studied averaged between seven and twenty-one loaves of bread per week, spending between 15 percent and 35 percent of their food expenditure on bread alone.[57] Inexpensive loaves of baker's bread, bought daily, formed the basis of their diet; meat, pastries, and fresh vegetables and fruits were added (in that order of priority) when there was extra money. According to W. O. Atwater and Charles D. Woods's "Dietary Studies in New York City in 1895 and 1896," only a few of the dozens of families studied baked their own bread. The other families purchased bread daily at the bakers.[58] All nineteen of the families in Louise Bolard More's 1907 study of New York City families bought baker's bread.

Earlier budget studies sometimes emphasized the poorest of urban families, but the 1918 Department of Labor budget studies encompassed a wider cross-section of the working class. The study, carried out in cooperation with the War Labor Board, was intended to determine whether wages had kept up with rising prices.[59] Many skilled workers and members of the "labor aristocracy" were included in this study. And in 1918, even many of the wealthier working-class families of northern cities bought baker's bread. In Pittsburgh, 78 percent of families purchased more baker's bread (by weight) than flour, indicating that they probably bought bread more often than they baked it themselves. In Chicago, fewer families relied on baker's bread: only 59 percent bought more bread than flour. But 48 percent of Chicago families bought more than a pound a week of other baked goods; thirty-three of those families bought more than two pounds a week. And in New York City, the vast majority of families—95 percent– bought more bread than flour, and 62 percent of families bought a pound or more of other bakery products each week.[60]

In addition to daily bread, bakeries also sold sweet rolls, pies, cakes, cookies, and doughnuts to working-class people for snacks and light meals. The budget studies recorded a huge variety of sweet bakery treats bought by almost everyone. Atwater's 1896 budget study in New York City mentioned six different kinds of cake, three kinds of sweet buns, doughnuts and crullers, and three kinds of pie bought by the urban working-class subjects.[61]

Sweet bakery foods were popular because they were readily available, inexpensive, and tasty. And, as Mintz argues about earlier industrial workers in Britain, sweet baked goods such as bread with cheap jam delivered a lot of calories quickly in a tasty, satisfying form. Exhausted workers often had little appetite but could tempt themselves with a sweet cake. Pies and cakes were particularly popular as quick meals for young, single workers, who particularly needed the convenience of ready-to-eat food. Single people living in the city, if they did not get board with their room, survived with meals cooked in makeshift kitchens in their rooms (made much more feasible after the spread of gas and electric hot plates in the 1910s and 1920s). Or they ate in public dining rooms (some, aimed at boarders, offered weekly rates), or in lunchrooms. Or they made hasty meals from ready-to-eat food picked up from the delicatessen or bakery. Louise Bosworth reported that factory girls in Boston, left to their own devices for feeding themselves, would eat bakery food almost exclusively, to the detriment of their health: "'We tried boarding ourselves,' said three Jamaica Plain shoe factory girls, 'but we bought so much stuff from the baker's windows because it was easy to get and we were tired, that we all got sick, had doctors' bills to pay, and went in debt.'"[62] The girls eventually began waitressing after work to get enough to eat. Exactly how they got "sick" is not described. Bosworth's account moves on quickly from this anecdote, as if it were not necessary to explain sickness brought on from eating nothing but bakery treats. Nutritional science around 1911, when Bosworth wrote, was vague on the necessity of fruits and vegetables, but it did endorse the need for protein and dairy products in addition to carbohydrates and fats. No one pretended that a diet of cake and pie was healthful, but it was seen as a common vice among young and heedless workers, especially women.

Food reformers and nutritionists like Bosworth considered bakery food extravagant and unhealthy, and their response to families who bought it ranged from pity to scorn. Margaret Byington juxtaposed a Homestead housewife who was a "good manager" with one who was "poor and unintelligent." The first baked her own bread and bought no prepared food; the more slovenly housewife bought bread as well as fig cakes, rolls, pudding, doughnuts, and pie.[63] Atwater and Woods's 1895 study of New York City mentioned the folly of a family who bought "buns at 5 cents a pound when wheat flour was worth 2 cents a pound."[64] They also highlighted a very poor family of eleven, whose mother kept three boarders as well as took in sewing. The family bought bread as well as expensive cakes, buns, and crackers, which, among other facts, caused the authors to characterize the mother's shopping as "not judiciously done" and the housekeeping as "hopeless."[65]

Wasting money on sweet treats was the worst sin, but reformers also disapproved of baker's bread more generally. They believed it was more thrifty, as well as more healthful and more virtuous, to bake bread at home. In the reformers' understanding of food and women's home labor, the home production of food was economically sound. If one didn't count effort and time, bread baking seemed to require only the cost of flour, and flour was cheaper than bread.[66] Florence Faxon, writing in *American Kitchen* magazine in 1899, calculated that bread cost two and a half cents per loaf to make at home (not counting labor and fuel), as opposed to five cents per loaf from the bakery.[67] However, even apart from economics, food reformers believed that home cooking was conducive to good morals and family stability.

The reformers sometimes did not sufficiently understand the material conditions of urban working-class homes that encouraged workers to buy baker's bread rather than make their own. Bread was difficult to prepare and bake in cramped urban working-class homes. Bread making also required time: yeast bread took three to five hours to rise and bake, plus time was needed for the mixing and kneading. It required an oven and fuel, either wood or coal—or, later, gas—to bake for between thirty minutes and an hour. Baking also required raw materials—flour and perhaps milk, yeast, and eggs, depending on the recipe—as well as tools, including a stove, bowls, and pans. Less tangibly, bread baking required knowledge and skill: knowledge about what flour was the best and how to buy a good quality at a good price; skill in mixing, kneading, and shaping the bread and in regulating the heat of temperamental coal or wood stoves.

Ovens heated for baking put out a tremendous amount of heat, making small homes very uncomfortable in summer. Marcus T. Reynolds, in his 1893 book on *The Housing of the Poor in American Cities,* described the intolerable conditions of tenement kitchens: "Ask any of the summer physicians of our sanitary boards, and he will bear witness to the terrible sufferings of the poor in summer from the stove, whose heat reaches to every side of the small rooms."[68] Even Florence Faxon, who calculated the lower price of home-made bread, conceded that many more people bought bakery bread in summer to avoid the heat.[69]

Time was the most important factor in home bread baking. Women who worked for wages six or seven days a week simply could not allot hours in any given day to making bread when bread could be bought ready to eat at the bakery. As Mintz argues, eighteenth-century British factory operatives had already realized that factory work, especially women's factory work, cut into the time traditionally devoted to baking bread for the family. Although married women in American cities at the end of the nineteenth century did not usually work outside the home, many did piecework at home. The more densely populated the city, the more likely women were to work for wages. In cities, where married women rarely did wage work, many women worked as boardinghouse keepers instead, adding one or more paying strangers to the household. Women who kept boarders were generally exhausted by the demands of cooking, cleaning, and washing laundry for boarders in addition to their own husbands and children. They needed to provide food at the lowest cost and effort in order to turn a profit while retaining their health.[70] Although some did bake bread, most of those with access to bakeries quite understandably chose to lighten their workload by buying instead of baking. And, of course, most of the single men who emigrated to the United States came from traditions in which men did not cook; they would have bought bread rather than attempting to bake their own.

A final obstacle to baking bread at home was that urban working-class families had difficulty buying groceries in bulk, lacking both the money to invest and the space to store them. As a result, families had trouble buying flour in the large quantities necessary to provide a family with bread. Isabel Bevier found that even if Pittsburgh working-class families wanted to buy flour to make their own bread, they often could not afford to do so advantageously. Of the family of a consumptive blacksmith working in the steel mills who had four small children, she wrote, "When they could get together enough money to buy a sack of flour they baked their own bread; otherwise they bought baker's stale bread in small quantities."[71] A woman in New York City whose budget was recorded by Atwater and Woods in 1896–97 baked bread at home and estimated she saved $4 a month by doing so. "It was the ambition of the mother to be able some day to buy a whole barrel of flour."[72] The budget shows that even this family bought at least some baker's bread, perhaps to supplement the home-baked variety or as a special treat. Home bread baking required an investment of money in a bag or barrel of flour rather than a small, frequent expenditure. And the cost of bread also included the cost of the fuel and equipment used to bake it, as well as the money the housewife might otherwise have earned in wages.

Being able to bake bread at home required significant resources. In fact, increasingly in the late nineteenth and early twentieth centuries, home bread baking was a privilege reserved for well-off workers and the middle class. As Mintz suggests, baker's bread had long been identified with working-class people. In *Middletown,* a baker reminiscing about the 1890s recalled that baker's bread was considered "poor-folksy": "It was the working class who bought baker's bread. It was in the factory districts that groceries first began about 1890 to keep baker's bread for the accommodation of their customers."[73] A Pittsburgh study of the 1890s that compared six dietary studies (deliberately taken from different income levels: families of a professional man, a skilled artisan, a skilled laborer, an average day laborer, and unskilled mill workmen) found that bread baking correlated to higher income and social status. Only in the household of the professional (a lawyer) was bread regularly baked at home (and there was most likely at least one maid or cook to help). The lawyer's family used sixty-four pounds of flour over the thirty days of the study. The other families all used baker's bread and cake; each family also bought crackers, pies, and other bakery goods.[74]

Yet for industrial workers of the turn of the century, eating baker's bread might have been a long tradition rather than an embarrassing makeshift option. Urban Europeans had bought baker's bread at least since the Middle Ages. Food historian Ken Albala notes that in European cities from the Middle Ages onward, "Baking was only generally done by those who could afford an oven and the fuel to heat it"—a category that left out much of the urban laboring poor.[75] Immigrants entering the United States from Europe likely had no personal or ethnic traditions of baking their own bread. Or they may have baked bread in a more communal way, mixing the dough at home and paying a small fee to bake it in a baker's ovens. Although urban colonial Americans had often used community ovens, this practice seems to have faded during the nineteenth century.[76] Atwater and Woods mention one New York family who made the dough at home and took it to a baker to be baked for one cent per loaf during the warmest weather.[77] And Robert Chapin mentions that "among the Italian families the custom prevails of mixing the bread at home and taking it to a bakery to be baked at a charge of 10 cents a week."[78] But these are among the few American references to what seemed to have been a common practice in Europe.[79] European immigrants who had been accustomed to using public bake ovens may simply have started buying bread if they were unable to find a baker who would bake their dough. For example, in southern Italy around the turn of the century, people baked bread once or twice a week in communal ovens. No one was expected to have the space for a large oven or the fuel to heat it to bake bread for just one family. Southern Italians who migrated to Chicago were therefore unlikely to attempt home bread baking in their cramped new industrial homes and bought high-status white baker's bread instead.[80] Centralized or community kitchens were proposed but never executed. The communal kitchens espoused by Marcus Reynolds, and by better-known experts such as Charlotte Perkins Gilman, existed mainly in the minds of their creators and as short-lived, failed enterprises.[81]

The large number of European bakers who set up shop in American cities seems to attest to the willingness of immigrants to pay for baker's bread. Many European immigrants were from urban areas in their home countries, where they expected to buy bread along with other foods rather than make it at home. A short story written by journalist Abraham Cahan in 1902 described a German immigrant who hit on a means for sure business success in New York:

> One day he overheard a conversation between two men who were singing the praises of a certain kind of bread they used to eat at home in a German-speaking town in Bohemia. . . . He discovered a whole block where most of the tenants were from the Bohemian province in which the bread in question was baked. "If I could get a good baker from that place and the two of us opened a bake shop in this neighborhood we might be kept busy." . . . So thrilled were the housewives of the neighborhood when they tasted the new bread.[82]

These German immigrants had come with the tradition of baker-made bread, which they could not or did not replicate in their home ovens once they arrived in the United States. According to the story, the bakery was a huge success, and "people came all the way from Brooklyn" for the bread. In the mostly Jewish Lowest East Side of New York, there were seventy bakeries around 1900 and nearly five hundred by the 1930s.[83]

Americans who migrated from rural areas into cities and towns didn't always bake bread at home either. They made traditional yeast-free "quick breads" such as biscuits and cornbread. Appalachian women at the turn of the twentieth century made beaten biscuits for special occasions and corn bread for everyday use, and they were generally uninterested in the yeast-risen breads that Progressive community leaders taught them to make.[84] Like urban women, rural women had material reasons for their bread preferences. Historian Elizabeth S. D. Engelhardt notes that beaten biscuits were made only for special occasions and by well-off families because they "work[ed] better with marble rolling boards, rolling pins, biscuit cutters, mallets or cleavers, and ovens with consistent and steady temperatures. Corn bread needs only a bowl, a spoon (although fingers will do), a skillet of some kind, and a heat source."[85] Women who migrated to the cities from the country were more likely to continue making simple quick breads at home or to begin buying baker's yeast bread; they were unlikely to begin baking yeast-risen bread at home. The prevalence of European immigrants and American rural migrants in turn-of-the-century cities meant that an American "tradition" of home bread baking was not as widespread as middle-class reformers liked to believe. Certainly the reformers had forgotten that bakeries were common in colonial American cities, and that even Ben Franklin bought baker's bread.[86]

Baker's bread was associated with the working class because it represented having little or no space or time at home for preparing bread; it represented a mother who worked for wages, inside or outside the home; and it represented the inability to buy basic raw materials at an advantageous price. Quick, easy, and requiring no fuel or materials, baker's bread was the choice of many urban working-class families. To some, this choice was a desecration of the wife's traditional role and a scandalous extravagance; to others, it was a blessing. Social worker Mary Simkhovitch, in her study *The City Worker's World,* noted, "When one considers the limited space there is for all the functions of housekeeping it seems a mercy that much that formerly took place in the home is now done outside."[87] After surveying the quality and cost of baker's bread and the effort required to make bread at home (which might, as she pointed out, be very poorly made), Florence Faxon conceded, "Bread is one of the articles the production of which can best be eliminated from the household."[88]

Even if baker's bread was "a mercy," it is difficult to say whether working people regarded it as a less appealing but practical alternative to homemade, or whether they particularly enjoyed the taste and variety of baker's products. Present-day Americans tend to romanticize homemade bread as more health-ful, delicious, aromatic, and spiritually rewarding than purchased goods, and there has been a resurgence in recreational home bread baking and "artisan-style" commercial breads since the 1960s. But working-class Americans of the time may well have appreciated maintaining a cool apartment, having quick, easy access to a meal staple, and the taste of certain treats from the bakery just as much. On the other hand, people who lived on little but bread and tea, or bread and potatoes, or cornbread with fatback might well have wished for greater variety, and the reformers were correct in pointing out the nutritional inadequacy of this diet.

Bread baking was a particularly time-consuming task. But what about everyday meals? Urban Americans, it turns out, bought their other food items ready to eat almost as often as they did their bread.

WORKING-CLASS RESTAURANTS

American cities had a thriving tradition of restaurants since colonial times, but the number of restaurants exploded in the late nineteenth century. Workers and immigrants played an active role in the development of restau-rants, maintaining them at times when genteel people preferred to eat in private homes. In the late nineteenth and early twentieth centuries, urban working-class people ate at a wide range of restaurants, from chain cafeterias to tiny restaurants operated out of private homes, surprisingly often. In 1908, budget investigator Robert Chapin calculated that 42 percent of the 318 families studied took some meals away from home.[89] The 1918 Department of Labor study recorded a fair number of working-class families that ate some meals away from home. One-third of workers in Pittsburgh ate some meals away from home, half of Chicago workers ate out at least occasionally, and more than two-thirds of New York families ate some meals out. Families that ate out did so regularly, eating an average of about 250 meals out per year. That was more than four meals a week—it could well have been a lunch nearly every day.

Even many of those who didn't eat entire meals out supplemented their home-cooked food with purchases. The Department of Labor interviewers frequently made notes about the nature of the meals eaten out. On many budgets (in which the average price for meals out was only five or ten cents), there were notes such as "Buys sandwich every day beside lunch from home."[90] A purchased cup of coffee or soup could enliven a lunch of leftovers, and purchased bread, cheese, salami, cake, or pie made a quick lunch to be carried to work.

The restaurants, saloons, pushcarts, and other venues at which working-class Americans bought lunches had evolved during the urbanization and subsequent immigrant rush of the late nineteenth century. From the colonial period through the mid-nineteenth century, public dining was mostly limited to taverns and inns that served travelers or local businessmen. Street vendors sold food such as oysters, roasted corn, fruit, and sweets at low prices to all classes. These hucksters, such as Philadelphia's vendors of "hot corn" and "pepper pot soup" (a spicy tripe soup), remained traditional in many cities until the twentieth century.[91] Oysters in particular were a cheap and popular street food, eaten from small stands and in basement "oyster saloons" by the millions until their prices rose around 1910 due to overfishing and pollution.[92] Elites considered dining in any public place inferior to dining in a well-appointed private home; middle- and lower-class people probably depended upon street snacks and on meals eaten in taverns and oyster houses and prepared at cook shops more heavily than did the upper classes.[93]

Over the course of the nineteenth century restaurants began to proliferate in American cities. European-style fine dining began to develop in eastern cities in the century's second half.[94] From the 1840s well into the twentieth century, Delmonico's restaurant in New York City (actually a series of restaurants in different locations around New York, owned by a Swiss family) symbolized fashionable, lavish European cuisine served in a luxurious atmosphere. Other restaurants such as Sherry's, Rector's, and the dining rooms at the Waldorf-Astoria followed in the same vein. Toward the end of the nineteenth century, middle-class Americans began to imitate social elites, eating out more often than before at more modest, but still genteel, establishments. Originally available only to businessmen and the wealthy, the practice of fine dining gradually lost some of its masculine and extravagant connotations and became more open to unaccompanied upper-class and middle-class women, as well as to families.[95]

After the turn of the twentieth century, increasing numbers of white-collar workers commuted to work from outlying suburbs and found it inconvenient to return home for lunch. Restaurants sprang up to serve quick lunches to these city workers. Some were in the traditions of taverns or chophouses, serving heavy, substantial food to businessmen in a clubby atmosphere. Other new restaurants were more in the "lunchroom" style, serving quickly prepared, simple, and relatively light meals of sandwiches, soups, egg dishes, or a few slices of meat with side dishes in environments dominated by clean, sanitary white tile. By the second or third decade of the twentieth century, American cities and towns boasted a range of inexpensive places to eat out: diners, doughnut shops, hot dog stands, Automats, fast-food restaurants. Urban white-collar workers and suburban families flocked to these new, inexpensive eateries after the 1930s. Urban blue-collar workers, however, had been eating at a large range of eating places, from pushcarts to chain restaurants, since the late nineteenth century. These restaurants were an important part of immigrant entrepreneurship and neighborhood social life.

Increased immigration in the second half of the nineteenth century caused a major change to the restaurant scene in large cities, both in the types of restaurants and in the clientele who patronized them. The earliest and best-known "ethnic" restaurants were the *Biergartens* opened and patronized by German immigrants beginning in the 1860s. *Biergartens* offered a festive environment with live music, plentiful food, and lager beer (which took America by storm when it was first introduced in large quantities in the 1870s).[96] Other immigrants opened restaurants in ethnic enclaves in order to sell familiar foods to the single male countrymen who emigrated in large numbers. For the most part, these restaurants were unknown outside the ethnic enclaves. They were small (in fact, they were sometimes operated out of an apartment kitchen and known only to the neighbors) and went mostly unnoticed by those outside the community. Nevertheless, numerous examples can be glimpsed in city directories, photographs, and anecdotal accounts.

Food businesses were easy and popular first businesses for new immigrants. Recent immigrants were often helped into businesses by their countrymen and so tended to go into the same line of business. Greeks, for example, were known for opening candy shops and small cafes, which sold both Greek and "American-style" food. The author of 1913's *Greeks in America* noted that Greeks operated many "chop houses," but "these do not include the Greek restaurant proper, where the Greeks themselves go and eat Greek food. These are found in every good-sized Greek colony."[97] Greeks found success serving both middle-class Americans and ethnic Greeks at separate types of establishments.

Jewish immigrants also found the food business accessible and lucrative, as well as an important community service. Jews who wanted to keep the laws of kashruth needed kosher butchers, bakers, and other food sellers. As historian Hasia Diner puts it, "Jews lived primarily where they could buy Jewish food."[98] The Jewish community was most closely identified with the Lower East Side of New York, but many other cities harbored significant immigrant Jewish populations, and in those enclaves Jewish-owned food businesses sprang up. In the early twentieth century immigrants who settled in Pittsburgh's largely Jewish Hill District, for example, recalled numerous food businesses, including Black's Grocery, Diner's Confectionery, Abramovitz's Butcher Shop, Frank's Bakery, and "the delicatessen at Logan and Epiphany."[99] Herman Gordon, born in 1912 in the Hill District, recalled the mix of food businesses in his childhood: "[There] were butcher shops, bakeries, restaurants which specialized in ethnic food, kosher restaurants. . . . They had many little restaurants, confectionary stores, in the back room of which they had pool tables."[100] Many immigrants went straight to work in those businesses on arrival. For example, Louis Arenson, born in 1894 in Kolno, Poland, moved to Pittsburgh in the early twentieth century and went to work in Kaplan's bakery. He remembered, "A *landsman* [a countryman] took me in, he was a baker . . . [and so] I became a baker."[101] In Chicago, Jews created a number of food businesses to serve the community, whose workers formed strong and enduring unions. The Jewish Waiters' Union and Jewish Bakers' Union were active throughout the 1910s and '20s, enforcing high wages and fair work hours.[102] In Chicago's Jewish community, women often ran the businesses, which included fruit and fish stands, candy stores, bakeries, and butcher shops, by themselves.[103] Finally, Jews in America, following a European tradition of work in the alcohol business, often opened lucrative saloons where food might be sold as well.[104]

African American migrants from the South formed their own enclaves in northern cities after the migrations of the early twentieth century. A 1928 study found that black entrepreneurs were concentrated in the restaurant and grocery businesses.[105] Like other minority groups, African Americans found food businesses relatively easy to start up and could count on steady customers from the neighborhood. Advertisements for black-owned restaurants in Chicago emphasized their southern roots and specialties with names like Florida Eat Shop, Georgia Food and Fish Hut, Hanson's Chitterlings Shack, and Arletta's Creole Food.[106] In the midst of Jim Crow restrictions on black consumers, the Chicago *Defender,* the country's foremost African American newspaper, carried advertisements for restaurants in major cities where blacks could get good service, such as Tabb's Quick Lunch in New York ("A clean, up-to-date place to dine. Our specialty: Southern cooking") as well Chicago's own J. A. Bell's Lunch Rooms ("Open Day and Night").[107] Blacks in Harlem enjoyed the food that would become known as "soul food"—pork, cornbread, greens, fish—and also mingled with other working-class residents of New York as they learned to eat Italian sausage sandwiches, Jewish snacks of chickpeas and knishes, and Puerto Rican meat patties.[108]

The tightly knit Italian community also offered advancement through food business jobs to its members. Italians, even those from small villages, were accustomed to food businesses: restaurants, cafés, and street stands sold food to even the poorest Italians. They naturally created similar businesses in the United States.[109] Every city with an Italian enclave supported businessmen (and women) who imported olive oil and cheese from Italy, or who made pasta in tiny storefronts. The existence of numerous small pasta manufacturers is revealed by negative articles in both American and Italian newspapers denouncing the lack of cleanliness in storefront "macaroni factories."[110] Italian fruit and grocery stores, saloons, and restaurants were extremely common. In Chicago in 1880, there were 22 fruit stores, 30 restaurants, and 33 saloons owned by Italians. By the mid-1920s, Italians in Chicago owned 60 bakeries, 30 cafes, 27 ice-cream parlors, 257 restaurants, 12 sausage manufactories, and 15 macaroni factories.[111]

Historian Tracy Poe points out that large numbers of Italian men came to the United States alone, creating a market for resident Italian women to run boardinghouses and otherwise enter the food trade. She argues that women participated significantly in businesses nominally owned and operated by men: "Many women cooked in their husbands' saloons [or] ran small food shops right out of their homes or storefronts, even though these businesses were technically owned by their husbands."[112] One Italian woman, whose mother had owned a bakeshop in Potenza where she baked other people's bread for a small price, migrated to America with her husband around 1890 and operated a grocery store for thirty years. Three of her sons worked in the fruit business, using their own children for labor. Two of her daughters, who married men that operated a tavern and a grocery store respectively, worked in the businesses alongside their husbands. The remainder of her ten children stayed with her to work in the grocery store. Thus four generations of this family worked in some kind of food business, with their spouses, siblings, and children as partners.[113] Other single men learned to cook for themselves,

FIGURE 6. This small restaurant was photographed on the Chicago docks in 1906 for the *Chicago Daily News*. The sign reads, "Lunches put up at quick notice." DN-0003793, Chicago Daily News negatives collection, Chicago History Museum.

and men in families took on food-production tasks such as making wine, pasta, or dried fish.[114]

Immigrants so commonly ate at ethnic restaurants that the practice contributed to their cultural isolation. J.W. Howell, in the reform journal *Charities Review,* wrote, "As soon as an Italian lands in America he hastens to the Italian quarter and there he is likely to stay. He finds men and women who speak his language. He lodges in an Italian house and eats in an Italian restaurant."[115] A 1920s study of Russian immigrants in Brownsville, Brooklyn, found that immigrant men ate exclusively at Russian, Polish, or Jewish-operated restaurants. The authors reported, "The result is that patronizing a restaurant does not ordinarily bring Russians into contact with Americans."[116]

Recent immigrants and native-born Americans alike operated a variety of small urban food businesses to meet the needs of their working-class clientele. Many eateries clustered around workplaces. Almost all factories, mills, and other workplaces were surrounded by small restaurants and street vendors who sold quick, cheap meals. Along New York's wharves, very small restaurants and street vendors sold coffee, doughnuts, hash, codfish balls, macaroni, and pie.[117]

Other small, casual restaurants operated out of apartments and basements to feed people near their homes. A basement on West Houston Street in New York around 1904 sheltered a restaurant catering to the many Italians from Milan in the neighborhood. An American journalist and his wife who were researching a book on the lives of Italian immigrants described the patrons, the food, and the atmosphere:

> Around the uncovered tables of varying sizes were Italians to the number of a score or more. More than half of them were in rough working clothes. Some had beer, some had wine before them and some were eating the stringing macaroni from large dishes heaped with it. . . . It was evidently a restaurant and used as a sort of club house by a company of the convivial and congenial. There was not the slightest indication on the street front that the place was anything but an ordinary tenement basement.[118]

The restaurant featured a communal table and was patronized almost entirely by local Milanese immigrants who knew each other. The Americans who ventured into the restaurant felt conspicuous and out of place there: "Looks of suspicion passed, and though [the patrons] greeted us in a constrained sort of way as we took places at the foot of the table, I could see that we represented a note of discord."[119] Small restaurants such as this one probably did not advertise, hire cooks or waitstaff, or particularly try to bring in new customers. They existed merely to feed the people of the neighborhood (and friends of the proprietor) at low prices.

Other small restaurants evolved in districts with many boardinghouses in order to feed the single men (and some single women) who were "roomers," or paying for room without board. For instance, a 1912 survey found ninety-three restaurants and sixty-two bakeries in an area of Chicago one mile square that was known as a rooming-house district.[120] Some rooming houses expressly forbade cooking in the rooms, either for safety reasons or simply to save the landlady the annoyance and mess. Louise Marion Bosworth's study of working women in Boston in 1917 found that there were several options for single women to eat: "girls" could eat at one of the larger boardinghouses or separate dining rooms for three dollars a week ("$3.50 for gents") or buy single meals for fifteen or twenty-five cents.[121] There were also cheap restaurants,

FIGURE 7. This undated photograph was taken in Chicago around 1895. It shows what was probably either a boardinghouse restaurant or an inexpensive restaurant for workingmen, who can be identified by their clothes. Chicago neighborhoods glass negative collection, ca. 1895. G1981:0293. Subject: "Restaurants," print 156. Chicago History Museum.

delicatessens, and grocery stores to choose from. Young, single workers had to choose among these different options, weighing their budgets, their tastes, and the convenience of these eating places to their homes and work. Bosworth found most of these options fairly dismal: the home dining rooms were unhomelike, with rude staff, and the food was served in scanty portions or was badly cooked. Ruth Katz, who emigrated to Chicago from Poland in 1913, found her food options cheap and satisfying: "I didn't cook. . . . You could get for twenty cents a good dinner in a restaurant." She ate out three times a week and snacked on smoked fish and cream cheese for other meals.[122] Small food businesses remained in operation by feeding the city's army of young, single workers.

Cheap restaurants that were not linked to a specific ethnicity or workplace were an important part of the urban male subculture in the last quarter of the nineteenth century. Encompassing a broad spectrum, from dirty places for semihomeless men to efficient cafeteria-style spots for businessmen's lunches, the cheap restaurants provided a wealth of local color for journalists such as George Ade of Chicago.[123] These restaurants maintained their low prices with a basic, unvarying bill of fare and by offering smaller portions when wholesale prices rose.[124] Several reports suggested that cheap restaurants economized in another way: by reusing leftovers from customers' plates. In a Socialist account of the injustices of the restaurant world, journalist Pasquale Russo revealed that the dishwashers were ordered to save food from dirty plates: "Bits of lettuce, celery, meat, bread, cakes, potatoes, wafers, butter, cream, fruits and vegetables are all carefully put aside for future use in one way or another."[125]

The cheap restaurant's primary clientele was men eating alone. It is difficult to determine whether women and families ate at these restaurants. It seems that although restaurants did not formally bar women, those who considered themselves respectable did not generally eat in restaurants, preferring boardinghouses, dining rooms, and other options. Most working-class women probably experienced restaurants as workplaces rather than as places to relax and enjoy a meal. The cheap restaurants that working-class men enjoyed, and which provided a modest income for the immigrant families that ran them, were built on the labor of women and children. A man who emigrated from Naples around the turn of the century opened a restaurant in Greenwich Village. Rather than hire workers, "he brought from Italy his parents, two brothers and a sister. This he did in the interest of himself for his relatives could be relied upon as trustworthy and industrious helpers." His daughter Josephine was kept out of school in order to wait tables and wash dishes, and she led a difficult life. "When caught on the street or daydreaming while washing dirty dishes, Josephine was frequently whipped by her father."[126]

A QUICK LUNCH: SALOONS, CAFETERIAS, DELICATESSENS, AND PUSHCARTS

After bakeries and small restaurants, the next common source of ready-to-eat food for urban working-class Americans was probably the saloon. Between 1880 and the First World War many saloons offered "free lunches" with the purchase of a beer. A peculiar combination of circumstances during those years meant that the free lunch was often a substantial addition to the working-class diet, especially that of men. Like baker's bread, it came with a certain social stigma, but it also offered convenience and replaced some home production of food.

Saloons began offering free lunches in the last quarter of the nineteenth century. As more Americans moved to cities to work in factories and mills, more and more saloons sprung up to compete for their business. The number of saloons in the United States tripled between 1870 and 1900.[127] In 1901, there were 6,217 saloons in Chicago, or about one for every 273 people.[128] In 1910, New York City had over 1,000 saloons on the Lower East Side alone.[129] Most of these were "tied-house" saloons, which sold beer from only one brewery in exchange for fixtures, furniture, and other start-up costs provided by that brewery.[130] In order to compete in the crowded urban market, breweries and beer distributors began providing food or funds to the saloons in order to put out a free lunch spread. The lunch was free with the price of a beer, which was usually a nickel.[131]

The free lunch began in the Midwest and West because of the greater number of single men in those regions and greater number of competing saloons. Free lunches were notably more plentiful in the West than the East not only because of the greater competition but also because wholesale food supplies were generally cheaper in the West.[132] Free lunches in Chicago tended to take the form of generous spreads of hot and cold dishes, which were supplemented with ethnic or daily specials. In *The Jungle,* Upton Sinclair wrote that on the street of saloons called Whiskey Row, "One might walk among these and take his choice: 'Hot pea soup and boiled cabbage today.' 'Sauerkraut and hot frankfurters. Walk in.' 'Bean soup and stewed lamb. Welcome.'"[133]

Since the liquor licensing laws were more stringent in the East, there were not as many saloons competing with each other there. The free lunch spread in New York saloons typically consisted of either a "hot lunch" of soup, or a cold lunch consisting of bread, cheeses, meats, and salads. Some New York saloons offered only the most miserly of free lunches—moldy cheese and crackers, or an assortment of pickles and cheap bread—but a decent if not extravagant selection was usual. In 1904 a *New York Times* writer described the summer free lunch in East Side saloons: "sliced onions and cucumbers, smothered with vinegar; sliced tomatoes, treated ditto; pickled beets, sauerkraut, potato salad, cold baked beans, leberwurst, bologna sausage, and smoked fish," as well as bread and cheese.[134] Most of the food offered was highly spiced, salted, or pickled, both because those foods kept better at room temperature and because they provoked thirst. A journalist for the

New York Socialist newspaper *Daily People* suggested that saloon cooks were under direct pressure to add more salt: "Sometimes the 'chef' gets a hint from the manager or proprietor that the demand for beer is not what it should be. He accordingly puts a little more salt in the soups, a little more pepper in the chowder, and an extra shake of curry in the goulash. Then the patrons are dissatisfied and complain, and the poor 'chef' is at his wit's end; for he must not drive away his customers, yet he must make them thirsty."[135]

Workingmen often got their midday meal at saloons. Raymond Calkins, author of the detailed, thoughtful, and sympathetic temperance work *Substitutes for the Saloon,* wrote, "The number of men that go straight from their work to a saloon for luncheon . . . will outnumber, ten to one, those that enter any eating-house in the vicinity."[136] For this very reason, temperance advocates found it difficult to come up with acceptable substitutes for the saloon. Calkins admitted that the saloons were "the base of the food supply of thousands of men of all classes in our cities."[137] Sociologist Royal L. Melendy studied the saloons and restaurants available in the working-class districts in Chicago. Along four miles of Madison Avenue in Chicago there were eight "workers' restaurants," most of them very cheap and unpleasant, which served meals for five or ten cents. (These were probably similar to the "cheap restaurants" described above.) Melendy described these five-cent restaurants as "unfit for even a dog" and "indescribably dirty," and he noted, "The air of poverty about these places is intolerable."[138] The ten-cent lunch places were somewhat better, offering a meal equivalent to that of the saloon free lunch—but for twice the price, and without the beer. Along the same four-mile stretch there were 115 saloons that served plentiful free lunches with the purchase of a five-cent beer in relatively clean, pleasant surroundings. (Other restaurants, offering lunches for twenty-five to thirty-five cents, catered to middle-class office workers.)[139]

Melendy argued that not only were the saloons a good value, but they were much more congenial than either nonsaloon restaurants or the workers' own homes. Sinclair made this point as well: in addition to a plentiful and (usually) delicious meal for only five cents, the saloon offered warmth, light, companionship, and entertainment. In the saloons described in *The Jungle,* "there was always a warm stove, and a chair near it, and some friends to laugh and talk with. There was only one condition attached—you must drink. . . . But all of the men understood the convention and drank; they believed that by it they were getting something for nothing—for they did not need to take more than one drink, and upon the strength of it they might fill themselves up with a good hot dinner."[140] The social functions of the saloon and its cheap, tasty meals were the reasons that temperance leaders found it so hard to replace.

Although the main purpose of the free lunch was, of course, to increase saloon patronage and sell more beer, it provided another major, if unintended, service: it eliminated the need for a packed or carried lunch. Men who ate lunch at the saloon would not need to carry a lunch pail to work, and their wives or boardinghouse keepers would not need to fill and clean the lunch pails each day.

Some women may have enjoyed the free lunch themselves. Saloons did, after all, have "ladies' entrances" or "family entrances," often on the side, so that women could enter the bar discreetly. In *The Long Day,* Dorothy Richardson's semifictional account of life as a New York City working girl, the narrator one day goes to lunch in a saloon while working in a steam laundry. Usually the younger girls ate cold sandwiches, pickles, and cakes brought from home for lunch, but one day they go with the older Irish women to Devlin's Saloon for beer and hot soup. The women go in the ladies' entrance of the bar, but all the men immediately leave the room, either out of chivalry or discomfort.[141] The women then enjoy a filling and companionable meal of soup and beer.

For the most part, however, working-class women who considered themselves respectable did not go into saloons. No doubt this was partly because saloons were often workplaces for prostitutes and partly because drunken men were likely to insult, proposition, or otherwise mistreat women.[142] Women avoided saloons even when the free lunch might have meant a significant economic advantage. In 1913 a young woman on strike from her job in the garment industry explained her financial problems to a *New York Times* reporter. She had to spend $2.75 of her $4.50 weekly wage (more than 60 percent) on food. There were cheaper ways to get food, but they were not open to her. "'You see,' she said, 'the boys can go to the saloons and get free luncheons with a nickel beer, but we have to buy from a pushcart.'"[143] She did not specify why she could not go into saloons—she seemed to think that the reason would be obvious—even though she could have saved significantly on her food costs.

Saloons were becoming scarce even before Prohibition. In the late 1910s, due to a revitalized temperance movement, some counties and municipalities used their "local option" to outlaw liquor. In 1917 the Chicago City Council, along with many other municipalities, prohibited the free lunch completely, hoping to reduce saloon drinking during the war.[144] Starting in 1920, the

saloon, of course, disappeared. Some former saloons were converted to restaurants, but a new type of restaurant was elbowing aside older forms of
cheap eateries: the lunchroom, which became increasing popular in the 1910s
and '20s. Although they served primarily white-collar, lower-middle-class
city workers, their doors were open to the working class as well.

There were endless variations on the lunchroom idea. A 1916 book on
lunchroom management recommended that proprietors stick to simple
food: "The most successful lunch rooms are those that are confined practically to breads, pastries, cereals, a few sandwiches, boiled eggs, and quickly
made side dishes, or entrees, as they are called on the restaurant cards."[145]
Cafeterias further simplified the lunchroom idea by almost completely
removing the waitstaff; patrons in these "grab joints" would select their
food from a counter or buffet, pay for each item, carry their tray to a table,
and bus their own dishes when finished. Historian Perry Duis asserts that
the idea of a self-service cafeteria originated in Chicago in the early twentieth century, as a women's dining club decided to eliminate waitresses and
serve themselves to reduce their overhead charges. (Duis also claims that the
drugstore lunch counter originated in Chicago as well, in a Walgreens in
1908.)[146]

The number of lunchrooms skyrocketed in the years after the First World
War. The elimination of saloons after 1920 (as well as their gradual decline in
the previous years as numerous states and counties established local prohibition) contributed to the growing popularity of lunchrooms.[147] The saloons
had always been the cheapest source of meals, but they were usually limited
to men. Unlike saloons, cafeterias and lunchrooms served no alcohol and
were therefore always appropriate for women. Lunchrooms and cafeterias
were a large contributor to the restaurant boom of the 1920s, a decade during
which the number of restaurants and lunchrooms increased by 88 percent.[148]
In major cities, lunchrooms and cafeterias often developed into chains in the
1910s and 1920s, such as Childs' in New York.

Lunchrooms were most often found in business districts. The new armies
of young white-collar secretaries and clerks in American cities after World
War I provided a major market for lunchrooms. As historian Harvey
Levenstein put it, "Short lunch hours and expanding cities made going home
for lunch impossible. Hot lunches were regarded as a necessity and lunch
pails were too working-class."[149] Lunchrooms could also be located near large
workplaces like factories or mills. These might offer quick lunches or takea-
way food, such as a box lunch packed with a sandwich, a piece of fruit, and a

cookie or an éclair, sold for ten cents.[150] At one point in her varied life, in 1892 anarchist Emma Goldman, along with two associates, opened a lunchroom and ice-cream parlor in Worcester, New York, as a moneymaking venture. The lunchroom served coffee, sandwiches, pancakes, and ice cream to a working-class clientele.[151]

Lunchrooms and cafeterias always featured a number of small items, such as coffee, pastries, or a bowl of oatmeal, that could be purchased for five cents or less. It seems likely that at least some non-white-collar workers found their way into these common and inexpensive restaurants, where they could get a light meal for ten cents or less.

When workers wanted a quick meal or snack, they could turn to local delicatessens or to pushcarts on the street. New York in particular was known for its Jewish and German delicatessens. Jewish "appetizing" stores sold smoked fish and dairy products, while delicatessens sold meats and sausages. Non-Jewish German delis offered sausages, fish salads, sauerkraut, wursts, and smoked ham.[152] Over time the different types of delis began to mingle, as some Russian and other Eastern European Jews began to eat German-style deli meats like pastrami as part of a homogenization of "Jewish-style" food in America.[153] Much of this food could be eaten cold: salads, pickles, smoked fish, bread, cheeses, ham, sausages, desserts. Like bakeries, delis offered ready-to-eat food that was appetizing and not too expensive that could be part of a complex meal served at home, or simply eaten alone.

A women's use of delicatessen food was often seen as a mark of laziness by reformers. Social worker Louise Bolard More, who wrote about the single mother whose children bought lots of deli food, was relatively restrained in her criticism. She recognized that without the mother's labor to shop and cook, the children needed to purchase mostly ready-to-eat foods. Other reformers saw delicatessens, like bakeries, as the refuge of the indolent house-wife. A cooking-school teacher advocated the importance of teaching girls to cook in the public schools by asking rhetorically, "Is it not better to train a girl to be interested in home cooking rather than have her go about talking to her neighbors, when she is a married woman, then rushing off to a delica-tessen shop just before her husband comes home and paying for ready-made dishes?"[154] Even the Socialist press agreed that only the most shiftless kind of married woman, "the girl who wants to loaf around in a kimono all day," depended on delicatessen and bakery food for daily meals: "All she has to do is to make a cup of coffee, serve baker's rolls in the morning to her husband, make a bed or two and visit the delicatessen shop just before he comes home at night. The rest of the day she can hang out of the window gossiping with her neighbors."[155] The cooking teacher and the Socialist journalist may have exaggerated to make their points, but it seems likely that delicatessen food at least theoretically made it possible for married women to dispense with cooking altogether. Critics were ready to attribute the desire to eliminate cooking as laziness on the wife's part. With all the obstacles that working-class women faced in their kitchens and neighborhoods, however, it is rather surprising that more women did not abandon cooking for deli takeout.

Pushcarts were another source of ready-to-eat food for urban working-class people. New York was the city best known for its pushcarts, but they could be found in working-class districts around the nation. In addition to selling groceries and dry goods, many pushcarts specialized in snacks, such as fruits, nuts, candy, and cakes. Pushcart snacks were usually cheap in every sense of the word. According to the reformers who developed school lunch programs beginning in the 1890s, many children relied on unsanitary and unhealthy food from pushcarts and candy stands for their lunches while in school.[156] In 1902 one Hessel Broidy, seventy-two years old, was brought before the New York Board of Health and charged with selling dirty candy to children. According to the newspaper account, Broidy "covered pieces of apple with syrup, run [sic] a stick through them, and sold them to the children of the east side. The sweets were described as being filthy and exposed to the dust and dirt of the streets."[157] Broidy's sentence was suspended when he promised to stop selling the candy. Pushcarts could be found in any place where inexpensive snacks could be sold to those with little money: for example, pushcart vendors stationed themselves at Ellis Island to sell snacks to the immigrants as they waited to be admitted. Around 1900 a writer observed the pushcarts selling overpriced apples and, for ten cents a slice (the cost of two beers in a saloon), "a thick yellow cake that was the worst mess of coloring-matter, adulterated flour, and soda, I have ever set my teeth into. It was as heavy as a stone and equally gritty."[158]

Some pushcarts, however, operated more like lunch wagons, serving more substantial meals. Royal Melendy, who reported on the saloons and their free lunches in Chicago, noted that workers could also get food from lunch wagons which (despite the name) were only open at night, perhaps serving men when other restaurants were closed. The wagons sold chicken, pork chops, eggs, coffee, hamburger steak, pie, and other such dishes for between five and fifteen cents.[159] The food was eaten while standing on the sidewalk or street. But, Melendy pointed out, the lunch wagons could not compete with the saloons in offering comfortable, warm, dry surroundings in which to eat, and they could not compete in price with the free lunches. Around 1900, journalist George Ade reported that some Chicago vendors changed the products they sold throughout the day. They began by selling hot waffles or egg sandwiches in the morning "to rooming-house residents who needed a quick breakfast" (and lacked the facilities to fix one for themselves). Later in the day they would move to work sites and factories, selling sausages, sandwiches, watermelon, and corn on the cob to workers on breaks.[160] Like the saloon and the cafeteria, lunch wagons provided a hot lunch to workers who could not return home; unlike the lunch pail, these options required no work on the part of wife or mother, nor did they require shopping, purchasing fuel, or owning any kitchen tools.

Working-class people in turn-of-the-century American cities had innumerable opportunities for buying ready-to-eat food, and they often did so. The majority of food most working-class people ate was probably cooked at home. Cooking at home was still the cheapest option, at least when only the cost of materials is considered. But, mindful of the true cost of household labor, working people bought at least some of their food, whether baker's bread and pies, salads and pickles from the deli, or a quick lunch from a saloon or lunchroom. These local sources replaced some of the home production of food, because they were often cheaper in time, effort, skills, or equipment. Ready-to-eat food was a solution to the material difficulties of the working-class home. It also offered companionship, status, convenience, or tastier food than was available at home. Hasia Diner points out that, especially for Italian and Jewish immigrants, restaurants and food businesses symbolized America's abundance and novelty and offered a way to solidify and share cultural identity.[161] Working people had a variety of reasons for choosing to eliminate some or all home cooking, and it is clear that there were many ways for them to do so.

URBAN HOME FOOD PRODUCTION: COOKING AND PRESERVING IN THE CITY

Buying cooked food was one part of the working-class household food economy. Home food production was another. Despite the difficulties inherent in buying food and cooking in small kitchens without running water, efficient stoves, or storage space, many working-class women and their families not only cooked but produced vast quantities of food at home, either for their own use or for sale. Entrepreneurs selling bread, pasta, pickled vegetables, and pushcart snacks usually produced their wares at home or in a small shop. Mass-produced and advertised foods also made gradual inroads on working-class diets during this time, especially in the form of small treats like Coca-Cola or candy bars.[162] For the most part, however, the food that working-class people bought in the city was produced right there, in the same neighborhood, and often by people of the same ethnic background.

Several examples from Pittsburgh allow a glimpse into home food production. Pittsburgh experienced an influx of immigrants from Italy and central Europe around 1900. Some of those immigrant women, as well as their daughters and their granddaughters, were interviewed in the 1970s as part of an oral history project. Their reminiscences often featured the food that they and their families had produced each year. One woman, whose mother who had been born in Czechoslovakia in 1898, was born in Pittsburgh in 1930. She remembered the food-processing work done in their ethnic neighborhood in Pittsburgh: "A few of the neighbors around where we lived, they had an outdoor oven. They used to bake bread out there. They had a pig which they would slaughter themselves. My father made smokehouses, to smoke the hams and everything."[163]

Another woman, who was born in 1901 in Yugoslavia and emigrated in 1905, recalled that every fall her mother bought sacks and sacks of cabbage and other vegetables. She "would make her own sauerkraut, make her own wine and butcher a 300–400 pound hog. Then she would have that smoked and some meat, it would be fresh. She would salt it down and garlic it and everything."[164] An Italian woman, who was born in 1891 and emigrated in 1920, remembered canning tomatoes, peppers, pears, apples, prunes, and green beans and making her own egg noodles and bread every week.[165] Some immigrants foraged for food in the urban wilderness; Italians were particularly adept at this.[166] Several Italian women remembered picking dandelions in the parks to sell:

> And we'd go for dandelion, my mother and all of us—5 o'clock—because the police would come then and chase you. They didn't want you to pick dandelion there. And I don't know why, because it's better if you pick them out of the ground. . . . We would take them home, wash them, sell some, and eat them in soup or cook them with oil and garlic. We sold them to Kramer's restaurant downtown—and that was a real classy restaurant those days.[167]

The mother, who emigrated from Naples with her young daughter in 1901, foraged for wood at building sites and gathered dandelions. "We had no warm water, we had no gas, and she used to wash these dandelions out in a tub in the back yard." The daughter recalled, "Well, we couldn't eat the best of everything but we always had a lot of bread. My mother baked her own bread. She had an outside oven and she used to bake great big loaves of bread. Sometimes you could hit them up against the wall [and] it would come back to you. But we used to soak it and eat it anyhow."[168] And a woman who emigrated in 1899 from Naples remembered how her grandfather made wine while living in Pennsylvania: "His was supposedly one of the best recipes and I don't know how to get these recipes. But it was so good that all the other members in his particular community who were all Italian, would come for bottles of his wine."[169]

Immigrants to Chicago during the same period expected to produce their own food as well. In yards and cellars working-class Chicagoans made wine, cheese, and pasta, raised chickens, butchered pigs, and smoked meat. Slovak and Polish immigrants to Chicago kept chickens and smoked meat on Chicago back lots—activities considered public nuisances—as late as 1929.[170] Italians in Chicago who couldn't manage their own home production bought from their neighbors who did. Some neighborhood storekeepers would charge to can or dry their customer's homegrown produce. Eventually, these community food-production tasks evolved into private businesses, which also reduced the price through economies of scale. When it was done for reasons of nostalgia or taste rather than thrift, home food production could actually be more expensive than buying from a local store.[171]

Other immigrants and working-class families kept home gardens or raised livestock on any available scrap of land. Workers who lived in areas that were less densely populated took advantage of the open space around them. In Johnstown, Pennsylvania, immigrants who worked in the coal mines or iron and steel industries lived in "foreign colonies" surrounded by livestock and gardens of beets, cabbage, turnips, potatoes, parsley, and dill.[172] An 1890s survey indicated that around 30 percent of iron and steel workers in the state of Illinois had productive gardens or cows, pigs, or poultry. Between 15 and 50 percent of workers in New York State had gardens or livestock, and up to 93 percent of Pennsylvanians did.[173] In 1918 a United States Bureau of Labor Statistics study found that in Chicago, 95 of the 348 families surveyed (27 percent) had income from gardens, poultry, or similar pursuits. Many more families must have had yards that provided food for the family but no profits. Most of the families who had garden income (63) had total family incomes of $1,200 to $1,800 annually, which put them about in the middle of the working classes: they were not destitute, but nor were they able to depend on a single income as more well-to-do working-class families did. In Pittsburgh, only 16 percent of the families surveyed (41 of 254) had income from their gardens.

In New York City, a scant 3 percent of families (17 of 518) had income from gardens, poultry, or other agricultural pursuits.[174] Yet those who did were tremendously productive. Italian housewives in New York bought and "put up" peppers in salt water or vinegar for out-of-season use, rendered their own lard, and made bread daily.[175] A long tradition of keeping pigs and poultry in city dwellings began to end in the later nineteenth century, with great reluctance on the part of the urban keepers. In New York City Irish immigrants who kept pigs through the 1860s were replaced by Jewish immigrants who kept chickens, turkeys, ducks, and geese in the basements of tenement buildings.[176] The sanitary police force had eliminated most poultry operations by 1900, but new immigrants had to be warned. A *Guide to the United States for the Jewish Immigrant,* published in 1913, warned, "It is a crime to keep a live chicken within the built-up sections of New York without a permit from the Board of Health, or to kill such chicken within the city limits."[177]

Why did working-class people tackle such large productive tasks, as well as numerous day-to-day cooking tasks, when their kitchen facilities were inadequate? Culture played a large role. People from some ethnic groups were more likely to participate in home food production than others. Many Italians, like those mentioned above in Pittsburgh and Chicago, produced food at home. They had a strong cultural attachment to fresh vegetables and either grew their own or established extensive retail produce networks in their new cities.[178] An American-born man remembered that in his Brooklyn neighborhood in the early twentieth century, the Italians stood out from the Jewish, Polish, Russian, and German immigrant families because of their vegetable garden and milk goat:

> On that street, studded with apartment houses, there was to be found a strange little world, shut off from the rest of the block, as though separated by a vast ocean, rather than by a mere picket fence. . . . Flanking the house on the left was a field of corn and on the right, vegetables grew abundantly. Tethered to a tree was a goat. In this house, lived a very large family, we whispered, of "Italians." . . . They were different from other people as proven by the existence of vegetation, the goat and their segregation.[179]

FIGURE 8. This Hine photograph of a backyard in Central Falls, Rhode Island, in November 1912 demonstrates the unsanitary conditions that resulted when privies and garbage dumps coexisted in cluttered backyards. However, it also reveals that at least one of these families, whose members probably worked in the local textile mills, was keeping chickens in order to contribute to the family income or diet. Photograph by Lewis Hine for the National Child Labor Committee, November 1912. Library of Congress, Prints and Photographs Division, National Child Labor Committee Collection, LOT 7483, v. 2, no. 3216. Reproduction Number: LC-DIG-nclc-04806.

Immigrants from rural Europe often distrusted industrial processed food. A close observer of Italian immigrants to America in the 1930s wrote, "Here, as in Italy, the peasant wants his food as fresh as possible.... He believes that the commercial method [of canning] removes all the goodness from food."[180] (By contrast, Lithuanian and Russian immigrants were identified as heavy users of commercial canned foods.)[181] Apart from culture, working-class people may have enjoyed the work or wanted the flavor that only homemade food could provide.

Working-class people also put in hard labor to produce their own food because it offered an alternative to the cash economy. Scarce wages were needed for rent; women who couldn't or wouldn't work for wages instead sought to feed their families without spending cash. Home food products could also be used for local barter; immigrant families in Johnstown who attended ethnic churches offered milk, butter, eggs, and fruit to pay the pastor or parochial school fees. In these families, home-produced food saved 40 to 50 percent of the food budget.[182]

One important material factor seems to have been residential density, which is related to the amount of open space, land values, rents, and neighborhood structure. To produce food at home, it helped to have access to a yard or other outdoor space. Even in crowded cities, certain neighborhoods had outdoor spaces in the form of vacant lots, yards attached to rented houses, or a communal yard or courtyard. Families that had access to an outdoor space had a distinct advantage. First, a yard meant more space in which to do laundry and prepare food as well as more space for the children to play. Second, access to a yard meant the opportunity to grow vegetables or fruit and to raise poultry or other small livestock. People who had yards or access to other shared space could practice the type of home food production described above. As a result, residents of New York City, for example, did far less home food production than residents of either Chicago or Pittsburgh, as the city's density and its lack of open space worked against large-scale projects.

The material circumstances of city life affected family and individual decisions about what to eat and how to get it. Women who lived in close proximity to bakeries, delicatessens, restaurants, and pushcarts selling ready-to-eat food must have at least considered using them more often. Families who had access to yards and the know-how to smoke meat or make wine used those resources.

FOUR

Between Country and City

FOOD IN RURAL MILL TOWNS
AND COMPANY TOWNS

THE YEAR 1918 WAS TRAGIC for the family of John Morris, a coal miner in Scranton, Pennsylvania. The family was one of thousands interviewed for the Department of Labor's massive survey on the consumption habits of working-class families. An eight-page form about the family's members, incomes, and expenditures provides a glimpse of their lives. Two of the family's four children, a two-year-old and a three-month-old, had died during the year, possibly from the influenza epidemic that had ravaged the country that year, or perhaps from another common childhood disease. But the budget form reveals economic success as well as emotional loss. The family kept a cow and calf and raised hens and vegetables. From the Morrises' annual income of $1,248 the family spent only $565, or 45 percent, on food, and their garden brought in food worth $139 for the year. Mrs. Morris did not work for wages, instead staying home to care for the children and keep the garden and livestock in a four-room house with running water and a shared privy. Although Scranton was a fairly large town in 1918, the lives of the Morris family members resembled those of the millions of working-class Americans who lived and worked in mill towns, mining company towns, and other industrial villages of this era. Unlike their counterparts in big cities like New York and Chicago, they did industrial work in a rural setting, giving them opportunities and choices for getting food that were slightly different from those of their urban counterparts.

The earliest industrial workers in American lived and worked in rural settings. In the early nineteenth century, water-powered mills were placed at the "fall point" of a river or large stream, often far from towns and cities. Water-powered mills soon hired more workers, creating towns like Lowell, Massachusetts, in places that had been isolated countryside before. After the mid-nineteenth century, industry was increasingly located in already-established cities and large towns. As some factories began using steam engines for motive power, they no longer had to be located near rivers or streams. More factories were set up in the growing cities, where there were plenty of workers, and where supplies and finished goods could be easily shipped by railroad.

But many industries remained or grew in the countryside. Extractive industries were tied to a specific place, and the workers had to go where the resource was. Coal-mining towns sprang up in various regions where coal was found, and workers toiled in isolated camps in other extractive industries like metals mining and lumbering. Some manufacturers intentionally moved their factories away from cities and towns in the early twentieth century in search of workers who weren't unionized and would accept lower wages. For instance, the textile industry in nineteenth-century Philadelphia depended on a pool of skilled (and relatively well-paid) workers in that city to manufacture a variety of cloth. However, as the industry became more mechanized and skill became less important, its manufacturers began setting up factories in the rural South, where unskilled workers could be hired very cheaply.[1] Extractive industries joined manufacturers in search of cheap, docile workers to create thousands of industrial communities in rural settings.

Rural industrial workers did work that was similar to that of their urban counterparts: it was hot, heavy, repetitive, and often dangerous. However, instead of living in neighborhoods of brick and stone, they were surrounded by fields and forest, garden patches, and the mills and yards of their workplaces. They had easier access to land for food production than urban workers, but they sometimes lacked the time or labor required to grow any food, even when they desperately needed extra nutrition in their diets. Their homes and kitchen facilities were just as inefficient and outdated as those of their urban cousins. Rural workers were often isolated in their small communities, and the company loomed large in their lives, often providing not only wages but also housing, food, transportation, churches, and more. Although they did not suffer from the crowding of urban communities, they also did not enjoy urban advantages such as a plethora of retail choices, the opportunity to open small businesses, and the chance to buy prepared food. Ultimately, as they were tied to a single employer and uniquely dependent on the company for both their livelihood and living conditions, their lives were even more constrained than those of urban workers. Those constraints meant they had all the same food struggles as urban workers, but fewer opportunities.

The isolation of rural workers means that even less information was recorded about them than about the urban working class. At the time, most people thought of industrial workers as immigrants living in crowded cities like New York or Chicago, not as small pockets of workers dotted through the Appalachians, the Piedmont, and the western mountains. The Progressive reformers who have provided us with so much information about urban workers paid less attention to workers in industrial villages. There was great concern about the well-being of women and children in these towns, and about the high cost of living, which created the potential for labor strikes that would paralyze the country. But rural workers were more difficult to study. They were, in a sense, invisible to much of the country, especially the people who most often wrote books and newspapers. Anyone who lived in a city saw its workers on the street, on public transportation, and in the working-class neighborhoods that were still interspersed with those of the wealthy and poor. But only people who lived or traveled in the countryside saw the workers in small company towns.

Southern textile mill villages and coal-mining villages provide two good case studies through which to study food in rural industrial towns, precisely because they were among the few groups to be studied in depth. There were many other kinds of industrial villages, such as logging camps in the North, mining camps in the West and Southwest, and cannery workers in the midst of fields and orchards or on shores. However, most studies focused on textile and coal towns. In 1907–8, the United States Bureau of Labor compiled a long report entitled *Report on the Condition of Woman and Child Wage-Earners in the United States.* The nineteen-volume study focused on industries that used the labor of women and children, a group that included the southern textile mills. As in other studies, including the famous Pittsburgh Survey underway during the same years, investigators sought to understand workers' lives both inside and outside the mill. Volume 16 of the study, *Family Budgets of Typical Cotton-Mill Workers,* reported on workers in Atlanta, Georgia, and Burlington and Greensboro, North Carolina, with information on family income from all sources and expenditures on all purchases. The investigators also wrote short narratives about each family explaining their circumstances, which often involved repeated illnesses or other forms of bad luck that left families struggling.[2]

More information on rural industrial workers comes from a massive Department of Labor survey in 1918 on the cost of living, which gathered information from working-class families in industrial cities and towns across the country, including textile mill towns like Huntsville, Alabama, and coal-mining towns like Scranton, Pennsylvania.[3] Finally, in 1922 the United States Coal Commission was appointed by President Warren Harding to gather information on working and business conditions in the coal industry. More than five hundred people on the commission gathered information on work-ers' homes, family lives, income, housing, and communities.[4] The resulting series of reports, although certainly freighted with the assumptions of the investigators, offers a way to understand how mill families acquired food and fed themselves in myriad ways.

MILL TOWN, INDUSTRIAL VILLAGE, OR COMPANY TOWN?

Industrial workers in isolated areas lived in a variety of different industrial towns.[5] In the nineteenth century, some manufacturers and mill owners were already accustomed to providing housing for their workers, either free or at a low rent. The owners of mills far from towns had to build houses for workers if there were no houses nearby for them to rent. Some manufacturers tried to provide good-quality housing to attract skilled workers, who could afford to be picky about jobs. Others offered housing to encourage entire families to come and work in the mills, as in the southern textile mills. But firms in rural areas did not always build and control housing for their workers. Workers might be responsible for finding their own housing. However, in very rural areas where there was simply no stock of housing nearby for work-ers to rent, it was most practical for the company to construct housing for its workers who could not afford to commute. The Du Pont Company, just out-side Wilmington, Delaware, built homes for its workers, who were largely Irish immigrants, so they could live right next to the black powder works. One worker remembered the houses, saying, "I'll tell you what the houses were like. Just four walls, no conveniences. They were comfortable. They had the privies in the backyard—and they were good substantial houses, good and warm."[6]

In the late nineteenth century, more factory owners became interested in planning entire communities for workers near their factories or mills. They did so for a variety of reasons. Some were motivated by paternalism, the desire to take care of (and control) workers like a family, as if the mill owner were the father. In these villages the mill's management might provide schools, churches, and medical care for workers, prohibit alcohol, or even enforce a nighttime curfew or church attendance. Owners believed that happy, comfortable workers would work more efficiently, or they hoped that happy, comfortable workers would refrain from drinking, joining unions, and going on strike. These owners landscaped their factories and towns, set up community halls, organized baseball leagues and other recreation, and set up profit-sharing plans in addition to renting new, high-quality homes to workers. Owners hoped that these efforts, dubbed "welfare capitalism," would reduce worker dissent and also forestall legislation to improve workplaces and working conditions. Some factory owners were particularly concerned about "Americanizing" their immigrant workforce, so they offered night classes in the English language and lessons on how to cook and keep house in the "American style." For instance, the Pelzer model cotton-mill town in South Carolina featured a subsidized grade school, a lending library, concerts and lectures, a baseball league, a brass band, classes in sewing and cooking, a daycare center, and a stock-sharing program.[7]

Companies that built model towns were influenced by the "industrial betterment" movement around the turn of the twentieth century. Progressive social reformers had urged manufacturers to improve living conditions, warning that bad housing bred family disorder and social revolution, as well as reduced productivity through illness. Improved worker housing offered a means for social engineering, "transforming slum dwellers and factory workers into respectable American citizens," as historian Margaret Crawford put it.[8] One of the best-known and earliest builders of a model company town was George Pullman, who built the town of Pullman to house workers in his train car works in 1883. Pullman tried to eliminate the "bad influences" in his workers' lives, from drinking to labor organizing, by building and organizing a tightly controlled environment.[9] The town of Pullman was widely praised for its beauty, and city planners and other manufacturers watched its growth with great interest. Pullman maintained strict order in his town. He prohibited alcohol, limited smoking, and established a curfew for all residents. Pullman considered himself a landlord as well as an employer and expected a 6 percent return on his investment. His failure to reduce rents during slowdowns and layoffs ignited the strikes he had tried so hard to avoid.[10]

By 1930 more than two million people lived in company towns, built, owned, and operated entirely by their employers.[11] Most were not model towns and never received the publicity that Pullman's did. Although some employers attempted to construct self-sustaining communities, others simply

FIGURE 9. This photograph of company houses in the coal town of Kempton, West Virginia, was taken by John Vachon in May 1939 for the Farm Security Administration. The photograph captures the hasty construction and bleak environment of most company towns. Photograph by John Vachon for the Farm Security Administration, May 1939. Library of Congress, Prints and Photographs Division, U.S. Farm Security Administration / Office of War Information Collection. Reproduction Number: LC-USF33-T01–001357-M2.

provided bare-bones accommodations. And carefully planned communities were greatly outnumbered by shoddy and haphazard work camps and temporary villages.[12]

In general, housing built for workers of a factory or mill was better constructed and longer lasting than housing built for workers in extractive industries such as lumber or coal. Since the lumber or coal might last for only five or ten years, companies saw no reason to build sturdy homes. And, since most towns were built to quickly provide housing in an out-of-the-way place at the lowest possible cost to employers, they offered few amenities and presented a drab face to the few outsiders who ventured there. Workers' homes clustered around factories, textile or lumber mills, coal or copper mines, or canneries in isolated, rural areas. Some of these settlements were very small and rough, like Dollar Camp, a lumber camp in Oregon. Historian Leland Roth describes it thus: "Located at the end of a single rail line extending up the Calapooia River from Sweet Home, Oregon, the camp had ten to twelve dwellings, some with four to five rooms for families; others were simple two-room houses, little more than shanties, for single men."[13] Other company towns were built to last, like Viscose Village, built for workers at the American Viscose Plant in Marcus Hook, Pennsylvania. The houses featured full cellars, gas lighting, indoor plumbing, and hot-water heating, and the community offered a central plaza, dining and recreation facilities, and a workers' dispensary.[14]

Company stores proved controversial in rural company towns. Initially provided as a service for workers who lived far away from any shops, the company store could quickly become a way for unscrupulous managers to exploit their workers. Sometimes the only source of food and supplies for miles, company stores often charged high prices or high interest. In 1920, mining families who were limited to shopping at a company store paid 4 to 11 percent more for their food than those who had access to independent retailers.[15] Some employers preferred to pay workers in scrip rather than cash, which could be redeemed only at the company store, or perhaps redeemed for cash at a reduced value. Workers were thus fed and clothed, but they found it very difficult to save any of their earnings. Compared to urban industrial workers, then, rural workers lacked the opportunity to shop around for cheaper food prices or specific types of food. They paid more for fewer choices. In urban areas recent immigrants could often choose to purchase food from members of their ethnic community in order to get traditional foods or simply to deal with someone who spoke their language. Rural workers tied to a company store, however, did not have that option.

FIGURE 10. This company store, in the coal town of Caples, West Virginia, was photo-graphed by Marion Post Wolcott in September 1938 for the Farm Security Administration. Though it could be exploitative, the company store was also an important social gathering site in a small, isolated town. Photograph by Marion Post Wolcott for the Farm Security Administration, May 1939. Library of Congress, Prints and Photographs Division, U.S. Farm Security Administration / Office of War Information Collection. Reproduction Number: LC-USF33–030102-M1.

The company store system could also be openly exploitative. Employers who experienced high turnover often attempted to retain workers via the company store, keeping them in chronic debt to the employer and forcing them to continue working to pay for the goods they had already used. Sometimes the scrip system was imposed on minority workers but not whites. Historian Margaret Crawford found that in New Mexico mining villages, "mine operators often imposed a 'half-pay, half-goods' system on their Mexican workers, paying part of their wages with credit at the company store."[16] In 1930, federal investigators researching abuses found workers who had received no cash wages for fifteen years.[17] In an urban community with many retail and employment options, it was simply not possible to enslave people in this way. In an isolated industrial village, it was all too easy.

Despite the disadvantages and injustices, rural workers continued to accept work in industrial villages, usually because of a lack of other options. The southern textile industry drew its workers directly from the dislocations in American agriculture that made it increasingly hard for small farmers to support their families. Southern textile mill workers represented a first generation of industrial workers, people who left farm work behind to struggle under the poor conditions of mill life.

SOUTHERN TEXTILE MILL VILLAGES

Textile workers in mill villages throughout the South lived suspended between rural and industrial life. Throughout the late nineteenth and early twentieth centuries, low crop prices and poor living conditions forced families to abandon farming and take up "public work," as they called it. Textile mills sprang up to take advantage of water power and low-wage workers, especially in the Carolinas, Georgia, and Alabama. By one estimate, in 1905 one out of every five whites in South Carolina lived in a mill village.[18] Without a tradition of industrial work, mill families struggled to incorporate their rural survival habits, including those related to housekeeping and food, into the new demands of living in small villages and working in an industrial setting.

Textile mill workers in the new South came to the mills from agricultural work along a variety of paths. Most families who went to work in mills had been farming, as sharecroppers or tenants, but some had owned their land. Many turned to mill work after repeated agricultural depressions prevented their families from prospering on the farm. Others came when the loss of a husband's labor to illness, death, or abandonment made survival impossible. Still others came lured by mill agents who traveled the countryside promising inducements such as steady high wages and comfortable homes for families who promised to come and work.[19] People moved back and forth between farming and mill work during the year or during their lifetime, or they combined the two, or they split family members between farm and mill.[20]

People who migrated to mill villages hoped to better their material lives, but they didn't always succeed. About 90 percent of mill workers in the new South lived in company housing, where rent was free or nominal for employees and their families.[21] Conditions in the mill villages to which workers migrated changed over time. Families in early mill villages were expected to live in one-room cottages, a step down from the usual tenant farmer or sharecropper's dwelling, which had at least two rooms.[22] By the time of the 1907 Bureau of Labor study, four-room houses were more usual, with only one family per house.[23] In late nineteenth-century villages, houses were placed

FIGURE 11. A farming family of the type that often turned to textile mill work in their home near Wilde, Kentucky, in 1916. This family lived in an unpainted, run-down home with water obtained from a pump in the yard. Conditions in textile mill villages would be more crowded but otherwise not much different. Photograph by Lewis Hine for the National Child Labor Committee, August 1916. Library of Congress, Prints and Photographs Division, National Child Labor Committee Collection, LOT 7475, v. 2, no. 4436. Reproduction Number: LC-DIG-nclc-00485.

too close together and the communities lacked drainage, safe water supplies, and community facilities apart from a single company-owned store. By 1915, however, "village welfare work" had improved conditions with better sanitation, fly screens, churches, schools, stores, fenced yards that provided more privacy, improved streets, and landscaping. Conditions in mill villages, although poor, were not necessarily worse than those experienced by sharecroppers and tenant farmers, although mill villages were more crowded.[24]

Mill families' housing generally combined the backward technology of rural homes with the negative effects of urban crowding. The homes of mill workers lagged behind those of urban industrial workers in terms of household amenities, tools, and labor-saving devices. In 1907 some mill workers were still using open hearths, at least twenty-five years after most northern urban workers had acquired more efficient stoves for heating and cooking, and at a time when urban elites were beginning to get gas stoves that kept the

FIGURE 12. A textile mill town street in Macon, Georgia, in 1909. The homes are similar in size to the farmer's home but the surroundings are different. The homes probably lack storage, so items, such as mattresses put out to air, are piled on the porches. Notice the chickens running in the street. Photograph by Lewis Hine for the National Child Labor Committee, January 1909. Library of Congress, Prints and Photographs Division, National Child Labor Committee Collection, LOT 7479, v. 1, no. 0516. Reproduction Number: LC-DIG-nclc-01609.

kitchen much cooler. In Grace Lumpkin's *To Make My Bread,* a novel about textile mill workers in early twentieth-century North Carolina, a mill recruiter promises that workers in the mills would have "a house with windows and cook on a real stove."[25] But when mill workers did have stoves, they were subpar. A 1911 government report on living conditions found that in one home housing a family with eight children and a disabled grandfather, "the kitchen is furnished with a stove, a few cooking utensils, a table, and benches. The stove is so small that blocks are placed under the legs to make it high enough to be used comfortably in cooking."[26] A description of a North Carolina mill family's kitchen from 1938 reads like a description of urban working-class homes thirty years earlier: "Cooking utensils hung on the wall. An old granite boiler hung in the middle and on its left two frying pans. On the right the biscuit pan hung. There was a table in the kitchen too, upon which the food left over from dinner was bunched close together and covered over with a bleached flour sack cover. Against the far wall an oilstove leaned."[27] The oil stove would have been smelly, inefficient, and dangerous. Mill workers lighted their home with kerosene and drew water from outdoor wells or pumps, carrying every drop needed into the house and back out again.[28] None of the families studied in 1907 had indoor toilets. Only two of the twenty-one were connected to the city water. The others had outdoor pumps or a well. In 1918, most mill families in Huntsville, Alabama, still drew water from a pump in the yard or a hydrant in the street that was shared with other families.[29]

The houses were poorly insulated and hard to keep warm. The 1907 investigators wrote, "It costs the Southern cotton-mill worker more to heat his house than it does the worker who lives in Fall River, Mass., and moreover, the house in the North is warm, while that in the South is not."[30] Wood was used for cooking and heating, meaning that someone in the house had to split and carry in wood and carry ashes out again.

Mill families suffered from living conditions that were less sanitary than farm conditions because of the greater density of settlement. Although poor folks in the South widely lacked access to flush toilets, in densely populated mill villages this lack spread hookworms and drew flies. Combined with illness from nutritional deficiency, workplace injuries, and women's poor health from repeated childbirth without medical care, it is not surprising that some mill families studied spent up to 15 percent of their income on doctors' bills and medicines.[31] Mill houses were as crowded as the towns. As the authors of the 1907 study pointed out, "Overcrowding is as likely, or even more likely, to occur in a family with a large income than a family with a small income, for large incomes usually mean a large family, always a large number of workers."[32] Keeping a house clean, preparing dinner, and doing laundry must have been much more difficult in cramped, unsanitary conditions.

Housekeeping was particularly difficult for the many women who combined it with wage work. In mill towns married women usually worked at the mill for at least part of their lives. The majority of all mill households in the late nineteenth century were headed by females. Mill work offered an opportunity, though a grim one, for women with families and no husband. A single woman could hardly manage a farm by herself, but she could support her family in the mills, either by her own work, or by the work of her older children.[33] Married women with young children usually stayed home with them, unless they had a mother or sister to help with child care. They would sometimes go back to the mill once the children reached a certain age (they were old enough either to spend their days in school or to begin work themselves), but if there were enough older children, the mother would stay home to keep house while the children all went to work. The housework required in a large family of wage earners was serious enough that it could not be entirely neglected for wage work. Unmarried young women living at home were expected to continue the housework, helping their mothers or feeding and cleaning up after fathers, brothers, or younger siblings.[34] Many mill women married young as a way to escape the constant work required of daughters, only to find their workload rapidly increasing in their new home as babies began to arrive.[35]

Married women who went out to work faced long, exhausting days combining housework and wage work. In an oral history recalling the early twentieth century, Edna Hargett remembered mixing biscuits for her children to bake after she'd gone to work. "I'd get up at five o'clock in the mornings . . . and I'd make up the dough and have biscuits for my children, so whenever they got up they'd put it in the oil stove oven and cook them."[36] Perhaps the double shift, split between the home and the mill, is why women between the ages of twenty and forty were very often ill, worn down by childbearing, poor nutrition, and constant work.[37]

Many married women also earned money outside the mill when they could. As historian I. A. Newby writes, "They kept boarders, tended gardens and milk cows, raised chickens and pigs, took in sewing and sometimes washing and ironing." Three-quarters or more of textile mill women earned money from one or more of these sources.[38] Like urban women, married women living in textile mill towns seized every opportunity to contribute to their family income while still giving time to housework and child care and thus respecting the social custom that married women didn't "go out" to work.

Some mill families earned cash by taking in single people as boarders. This group included both families who casually took in only a few boarders and women entrepreneurs who ran full-scale businesses. When Betty Davidson's family first arrived to work in the mills of Burlington, North Carolina, they stayed at a boardinghouse run by a Miss Denny, who had African American maids and cooks helping to feed a dozen boarders, who ate at staggered meal times that accommodated all the mill shifts.[39] Stable or well-off white mill families could hire black women at low wages for household help. In an oral history, Flossie Moore Durham remembered that when she was young, her mother kept house while the rest of the family worked in the mill. Her mother could have hired an African American maid for five dollars a month as other white mill families did. "I know several families done that. They had

FIGURE 13. This family worked in the Tifton Cotton Mill in Tifton, Georgia, in 1909. Lewis Hine noted that the mother and five of the children worked in the mill. After the father died, the mother moved to the mill town to support her family. Caring for nine children while working in the mill must have been exhausting, but both her labor and her oldest children's was necessary to keep the family fed. Photograph by Lewis Hine for the National Child Labor Committee, January 1909. Library of Congress, Prints and Photographs Division, National Child Labor Committee Collection, LOT 7479, v. 1, no. 0487. Reproduction Number: LC-DIG-nclc-01580.

a big family, and like I say, they could get help for almost nothing and felt like they was able to do it and they did it."[40] For white women, help could be bought cheaply; for African American women, household work was readily available, offering a small but necessary addition to household income.

Gardening and keeping livestock appealed to mill families (as it did to urban working people) as a way to earn cash or supplement the family diet. The care of small livestock was traditionally women's work in rural households. LuAnn Jones describes the growing importance to southern rural women in the early twentieth century of keeping chickens as a means of supplementing—and, in some cases, surpassing—their husband's income from cash-crop farming.[41] Naturally, some mill families wanted to transfer this rural practice to their new mill homes as a way of generating extra food or cash income for the family. Jacquelyn Dowd Hall and the other historians who wrote *Like a Family,* a monumental 1987 work on mill workers, explain,

FIGURE 14. These houses in the coal town of Caples, West Virginia, suggest that miners' families could garden and even keep cows. Photograph by Marion Post Wolcott for the Farm Security Administration, September 1938. Library of Congress, Prints and Photographs Division, U.S. Farm Security Administration / Office of War Information Collection. Reproduction Number: LC-USF33–030059-M4.

"Gardening and husbandry skills helped mill families survive on meager wages," and they refer as well to other forms of work that had been transferred from the farm to the mill town by women, such as quilting, making sauerkraut, and shucking corn.[42]

About half the families studied by the Bureau of Labor in Huntsville, Alabama, in 1918 kept chickens, and most of them kept gardens, growing from four to a dozen different kinds of vegetables and fruit.[43] Some mill towns offered garden plots or pasturage for free to mill workers, presumably at a very low cost to the mills, which operated mostly in rural areas. These might be cleared gardens or simply the space for workers to clear and plant one themselves. In fact, many mill owners considered this part of the compensation system that made up for low wages.[44]

The irregularity of mill work was conducive to livestock raising and garden work. Mill hands worked long hours but at a fairly relaxed pace, and it seems they were often able to go back and forth from work to home throughout the day, allowing them to complete husbandry chores at home. Workers may have felt comfortable taking days off to do farm work. "'I can remember my Daddy,' Vinnie Partin said of his cotton-mill father in the early twentieth century. 'He would always get off from the mill on the day we were going to kill hogs.'"[45] Other workers left work in the spring, summer, or fall to help on a family farm or tend their own crops.[46] Elizabeth Engelhardt points out that almost anyone, including women who worked for wages or were single mothers, "could grow a patch of corn without too much physical or social difficulty" to make their family's cornbread.[47]

Families who could afford to keep livestock generally had a higher standard of living than others, as livestock contributed both to a family's income and their nutrition and variety of diet. Not everyone, however, could take advantage of this strategy. In the 1907 study, less than half of the families studied produced food at home. Only six of twenty-one families studied kept cows. Five kept pigs, and thirteen grew some "garden stuff."[48] In Huntsville in 1918, most families kept a garden, and a smaller number raised chickens. One woman remembered that, growing up in the mill village in Tryon, North Carolina, "Ours was the best house in the village; we had the very first bath room ever put in, and our house was furnished with the best, no cheap stuff like some folks buy. Pa always had a big garden, a cow and chickens. (The law don't 'low no hogs). There were garden flowers too, that is, as long as Ma lived."[49]

Gardens were cheaper to maintain than livestock and required less daily attention, but they could not the extra protein that most desperately needed in their diets. The Lebman family of Huntsville spent only $2.30 in supplies to net a $12 profit from their garden in 1918 (with the profit counted in the value of produce they ate). However, they spent $6 to raise chickens in 1918, with a net profit of $30 from the eggs and meat they ate or sold.[50] The higher standard of living was both cause and effect. Families who could afford to keep livestock were healthier and earned extra income; families who were healthier and had extra income to invest could more readily take on the challenges of raising livestock. By contrast, families who could not manage to keep livestock were noticeably poorer and tended to stay that way. The 1907 Bureau of Labor study revealed a connection between livestock and diet, reporting that "unless the family owned a cow milk does not appear in the diet, not even for coffee."[51] For many families who desperately needed that extra nutrition, the initial investment or the maintenance may have been too expensive. The government investigators reported that many families aspired to keep a cow, but in villages with no communal or company-provided pasturage, cows ate purchased feed, usually cottonseed meals and hulls "imported from the north and west." One family, working in a mill near

Atlanta in 1907, paid $2 of its $16 weekly income to feed its cow, a price too high for many families living close to the bone. The same family used to pay $1.60 a week for butter and milk. The family may have had better nutrition than many others, but it came at a high price.[52]

Another Atlanta-area family studied in 1907 demonstrated the hard choices it was necessary to make between investing in livestock and paying for other family expenses. The family "seemed to have some definite ideals," according to the government investigators, and were "very desirous to educate their children." The oldest boy, fourteen at the time of the survey, had been working since age eleven to help support the family. The parents took in a boarder so that they could afford to send him back to school (he returned to second grade with his eight-year-old brother). However, the family then bought a cow for $32 and found they could not afford the weekly installment payments unless the boy returned to work, so he did. Despite this family's ideals, the investment of a cow was more important than their son's education.[53]

How did the transition from farm life to industrial work change mill families' diets? One of the most important effects of industrialization on the diet of all rural southerners, and especially on mill workers with poor diets, was the loss of nutrients caused by refining grains. By 1907 the flour and cornmeal that had previously been stone-ground in small local mills was being milled by large commercial roller mills and refined to remove all the germ and bran. The resulting refined flour or meal was extremely popular but caused an epidemic of pellagra. A vitamin deficiency disease caused by a lack of whole grains, lean meat, dairy, and fresh vegetables, pellagra hit the poorest folks hardest because they lacked a varied diet and depended almost entirely on the refined flour and cornmeal as a source of calories. Pellagra was also worse among the nonworking members of mill families—mothers, young children, and old people—because they received a smaller share of the family's food. Married women, for example, suffered from pellagra more than single women or married men did, and women overall made up 69 percent of pellagra deaths.[54] Pellagra also increased because southerners had begun cooking their dried beans with baking soda, which sped up the long cooking time but stripped the beans of nutrients.[55] In this instance, an attempt to spend less time (and fuel) on cooking resulted in an unseen loss of nutrition.

Pellagra also related to the food economy in a particular neighborhood or district. Researchers studying pellagra in South Carolina in the 1920s found that one textile mill village in Oconee County, in a region of diversified farming, with a local grocery that sold fresh produce and meat, had almost no cases. Another village in Spartanburg County was surrounded by farmers growing only cotton; there was little local supply of produce or meat, and the village had the highest incidence of pellagra in the study.[56]

Mill families had the potential to eat a less monotonous diet than families on farms did, but they often didn't achieve it. Food on the farm was limited to what the family raised, what was in season or had been preserved, and what was available from the local store or provision agent. Mill families might have more access to industrially processed food such as canned fruit and vegetables and a wider range of meats, and they might have a choice of retail grocers if the company store did not impose a monopoly.[57] However, they didn't necessarily have the cash to buy a variety of foods, nor did they inevitably seek variety in their diet even if it was available.

Unlike urban industrial workers, who had access to a variety of retail options, prepared foods, and other ethnic cuisines, textile workers seem to have had a very plain and unchanging diet, not very different from those they followed as tenant farmers or croppers. Newby suggests that the diet of white "plain folk" in the South was universally monotonous, regardless of access to resources like a garden, a store, or more money. People limited their diet to quick breads, fatty meat, and boiled vegetables for cultural reasons, not economic ones. A 1901–4 survey conducted by the Department of Agriculture in Tennessee and Georgia compared country and town, farm and nonfarm, and poor and working-class people and found that "there was enough difference in their circumstances and income to permit meaningful variation in their food consumption, yet investigators were struck by the remarkable sameness of the dietaries of all the families."[58] The investigators calculated that three-quarters of their diet was based on cornmeal, wheat flour, and fatty cured pork, with only a few vegetables added.

A few sample dietaries help us to imagine mill workers' daily food. The 1907 Bureau of Labor's *Condition of Woman and Child Wage-Earners* records weekly menus and grocery lists of some of the families studied. Diets were composed of biscuit or cornbread for every meal, with syrup and coffee plus vegetables (cabbage, beans, greens, or potatoes) boiled with fat pork for seasoning. Families who could afford meat ate it fried or stewed for breakfast and supper. Dinner was commonly just vegetables and bread.

The first menu is from a family described by the investigators as representative of "the aristocratic element" among mill families, composed of a mother with three married daughters (and their husbands) and two more adult children working in the mill. One of the daughters was married to the son of the mill superintendent. With adult children working, the family had a high income. They rented their home privately, not from the mill. Their diet for two days in January 1909 was listed as follows:

Friday

Breakfast: Pork, rice, biscuit, butter, coffee, sugar.

Dinner: Peas, bacon, butter beans, sweet potatoes, fried pork, onions, pickles, corn bread, biscuit, coffee, sugar.

Supper: Ham, cheese, biscuit, butter, coffee, sirup, sugar.

Saturday

Breakfast: Pork and rice, biscuit, butter, sirup, coffee, sugar.

Dinner: Collards, bacon, Irish potatoes, sweet potatoes, corn bread, biscuit, coffee, sugar.

Supper: Oyster stew, fried pork, biscuit, butter, sirup, coffee, sugar.[59]

Winter vegetables, preserves, and beans enlivened the meat, biscuit, and corn bread base of the diet. Even in this prosperous household, vegetables appeared at only one meal of the day, and they consumed very little dairy.

Another family, this one with two parents, two children working at the mill, and another in school, was in significant debt. "With three wage earners," the authors noted, "this was due to misfortune rather than extravagance." The father, mother, and two wage-earning children had all been ill in the last year and lost several weeks of work. Two days of their diet were as follows:

Monday

Breakfast: Fried bacon, biscuit, sirup, Postum, oatmeal.
Dinner: Collards and peas with bacon, corn bread, Postum.
Supper: Fried bacon, biscuit, sirup, Postum.

Tuesday

Breakfast: Fried pork, biscuit, sirup, Postum.
Dinner: Fried pork, biscuit, sirup, Postum.
Supper: Fried meat, biscuit, sirup, Postum.[60]

The rest of the week was very similar. This family ate nearly the same thing every day. This diet, like the previous one, was recorded in January, when few fresh vegetables would have been available, but cabbages, white and sweet potatoes, and onions would have been relatively cheap. During the summer they may have had more access to fresh fruits or vegetables, or perhaps they would have eaten the same monotonous diet year-round. They ate almost no dairy products or eggs, no preserves, mostly flour biscuits, and no meat apart from bacon and fried (salt) pork.

The investigators noted that the diets of the poorest mill families were lower in quality and quantity than that of Atlanta prisoners studied at the same time.[61] In late November 1909 the Atlanta prisoners ate the following menu.

Monday

Breakfast: Wieners, grits, bread, butter, coffee.
Dinner: Pork and beans, raw onions, bread, butter, water.
Supper: Sweet potatoes, bread, butter, coffee.

Tuesday

Breakfast: Potatoes, bread, butter, coffee.
Dinner: Beef, collards, bread, water.
Supper: Prunes, bread, butter, coffee.

The prisoners consumed more calories and protein (as well as more vegetables and fruit and a wider variety of meats) than the mill workers.

Family circumstances rather than cultural differences had the greatest effect on family diets. Two Huntsville, Alabama, families, the Cruses and the Acklens, both studied by the Bureau of Labor in 1918, had very different diets. In the Acklen family, the husband (aged fifty-two) and two of his children (ages eighteen and twenty-one) worked in the cotton mill; one of the sons actually earned more than his father did. Another daughter was in school, and one son was epileptic. The family earned $1,950 per year, of which $548 (28 percent) was spent on food. This large family ate well: 1,248 pounds of self-rising flour and 1,250 pounds of cornmeal made the family's biscuits and cornbread for the year. They ate beef and pork, as well as some canned salmon and sardines, and they hunted rabbits. The mother didn't work for wages, so she probably spent part of her time working in the family's garden, in which she grew ten different vegetables. This family also had the advantage of living in a company house without paying rent since it was more than a mile from the mill; this might also have meant a larger yard for the garden. In contrast, in the Cruse family, only the father (aged thirty) worked for wages. His wife stayed home with their eight- and three-year-old children. The family earned only $725 a year, of which $361 (49 percent) was spent on food. The family did not keep a garden and ate a much smaller variety of vegetables: only sweet and white potatoes, cabbage, onions, and small amounts of string beans and corn. They bought fruit when they could and ate a lot of dried beans.

Families in the later stages of their lives like the Acklens, who had adult wage-earning children still at home, were often the most comfortable members of the working class.[62] Even while caring for an epileptic child, Mrs. Acklen had time to cultivate a large and productive garden, and as a result her family ate better and used a smaller percentage of their income for food. Mrs. Cruse's young family badly needed a greater variety of vegetables, but she evidently lacked the time, the inclination, or the resources to raise vegetables at home. The family spent half its small income on food and still ate poorly.[63]

The choice of quick breads over yeast breads reveal some of the conditions of material life in mill towns. Serving quick breads like biscuits and corn-bread (which can be cooked on top of the stove) rather than yeast bread reduced the time that an oven would be heating up the house. However, quick breads go stale quickly, meaning that someone had to mix and bake biscuits or corn bread for nearly every meal. Betty Davidson remembered that as a child she was responsible for making bread, either biscuits or corn-bread, three times a day for the family.[64] Households in 1918 in the Huntsville mills bought between three hundred and twelve hundred pounds of corn-meal a year to keep the family in cornbread. They also bought a thousand pounds or more of self-rising flour for biscuits, but they purchased very little baker's bread, crackers, or pastry.[65]

Unlike urban industrial women, mill women probably had little opportu-nity to buy food ready-made, but they may have had more opportunities to do so than farm women. The Acklens, for example, could supplement tradi-tional salt pork and game with some store-bought canned fish. Groceries sold loaves of bread, but mill women, like most southern women, seem rarely to have made their own yeast bread, preferring quick breads made fresh for every meal.[66] Author Harriett Arnow remembered that, as a child in Burnside, Kentucky, a lumber mill town, her family always had biscuits and cornbread for breakfast and lunch. "Loaf bread," yeast bread bought on occasion from the store, was eaten much less frequently. One day at the store, Harriet remembered, "I said, 'I want a loaf of loaf bread, please,' and somebody behind me tittered."[67]

Housekeepers also had to feed workers both at home and away. In the late nineteenth century, when textile mills were mostly located small, isolated villages, mill workers went home to lunch, or small children or others who didn't work would tote lunches to family members at the mill.[68] Later on, workers might have had more opportunity to buy food rather than pack a lunch from home. Eunice Austin, who worked in a hosiery mill in North Carolina in the 1930s, could buy sandwiches from a cart on her lunch break.[69] As mill towns grew, they increasingly resembled industrial cities, with plenty of opportunities to buy prepared food to lighten cooking tasks. In the early years, however, isolation was the rule and prepared food was rarely an option.

Textile mill workers made enough to keep body and soul together, but just barely. The most important factor in their economic lives was the number of able-bodied workers in the family. Households with several adults bringing in income ate a greater variety of food and could supplement their diet with inexpensive and nutritious home-produced food. With enough resources and some luck, they could produce food at home for better variety and health. Households with only one or two wage earners, or those brought down by sickness, got by on a grim, monotonous, and unhealthful diet, and even thrifty home food production was beyond their reach.

COAL MINING TOWNS

Unlike in the textile industry, it was the nature of the work rather than the need for cheap workers that led to isolated living conditions for coal miners. Coal miners worked in conditions that were more traditionally "industrial" than the casual, on-again-off-again work of textile mill hands. In a dirty, dangerous extractive industry, they labored under difficult conditions to bring a valuable resource to the surface, and they had to live wherever the coal was found. They had a different response to the problem of food from textile workers, because, although there were some similarities in their lives, coal-mining families often had fewer opportunities for women to contribute to the family economy with wages, and more opportunities to raise their own food.

Coal mines were the subject of government inquiry in the Progressive era, but the primary reasons for the government's interest were the appalling record of mine safety and the frequent strikes that convulsed the industry. By 1918, however, the Bureau of Labor included several coal-mining communities (as well as some western metals and mineral mining towns, like the copper town of Bisbee, Arizona) in its massive study of living conditions. More evidence about coal towns in Pennsylvania comes from extensive oral histories collected as the industry began to wane in the later twentieth century, and from archaeological studies conducted in former mining towns.

Coal mining exploded in the late nineteenth century, as more Americans bought coal to heat their homes and cook their food and coal was increasingly used to power railroads and industrial steam engines. Coal of varying grades is found in six U.S. regions: the eastern, interior, Gulf, northern Great Plains, Rocky Mountain, and Pacific Coast regions. The eastern region contains the large anthracite and bituminous coal fields of Pennsylvania and Appalachia. Anthracite coal is hard and shiny, with a higher carbon content; bituminous coal is softer and burns with more smoke. In the United States, anthracite coal is found only in Pennsylvania, and deposits become progressively softer and more ligneous as one proceeds west.[70] In some coal fields, farm or other industrial settlements preceded coal mining, and there was already a stock of housing available. But when new coal deposits were discovered and mined, new settlements popped up, usually built by the mining company to attract workers. By 1920 there were more than half a million coal miners in the United States, and 61 percent of bituminous coal miners (the majority of miners) lived in company housing.[71]

Although company towns were always built with profits in mind, coal communities seemed particularly designed to benefit the company first. These communities were planned for obsolescence. A particular coal seam would only last so long before being "mined out," and up until the early twentieth century, coal companies could not predict how long it would last. So they built the cheapest possible houses for workers, designed to survive only for the life of the mine. The companies were not concerned with the resale value of the houses they built, since there would be no demand for a house next to a tapped-out mine. This all contributed to bare-bones construction and few comforts.[72] The few amenities built—fenced yards, sidewalks—were intended to attract "a better class of men," less transient and unlikely to join unions.[73] Coal mine towns were drab and polluted because of the mining operations. In "coke towns," mined coal was heated to make coke (a processed form of fuel) in ovens that blasted soot and noxious fumes into the air around the clock, killing local vegetation.[74] In the model town of Windber,

Pennsylvania, the air was filled with rotten-egg odor from mine waste, shrill whistles signaling shift changes, the rumble of coal cars, and thick smoke from steam generators.[75] Cave-ins were a constant threat, as coal was often mined from the area directly underneath the town. Walls cracked and buckled as the ground shifted, and houses and roads sometimes fell into the sinkholes created as mines subsided. Mining companies generally disavowed any legal responsibility for these events.[76]

Unlike southern textile workers, coal workers had a history of labor organization, and some of the bitterest labor disputes of the period took place in coal and other mining towns. As a result, coal companies sought to manage towns in order to thwart labor organization. The threat of eviction effectively discouraged union membership. In the isolated towns, evicted workers could find no other housing and would have to leave both their jobs and the community. In Pennsylvania, state law required thirty days' notice for eviction, but coal companies sought and received a legal exception, so they could evict workers with only ten days' notice.[77] Paul Vrobel, a miner in Mather, Pennsylvania, recalled that when miners went on strike in 1922, sheriffs "would load all your furniture up on this wagon and haul it out to a country road some place, and take it and throw it off the wagon and leave it there."[78] Since coal towns were entirely company-owned, in effect, there were no public places. The company could ban labor organizers from the company store and even from passing through town since the road was private property.[79]

Coal town housing expressed the social hierarchy of the town, from managers through American-born workers down to foreign-born workers. Most of the managers and highly paid skilled workers in coal mining were born in the United States or Britain. Non-British immigrant workers were categorized as "unskilled," paid less, and offered few amenities. Sixty percent of coal workers nationally were foreign-born.[80] Many immigrants from southern and eastern Europe were recruited directly. They "arrived at the mines with nothing more than the clothes on their backs and their name and the name of the mine or company pinned to their shirts."[81] In Helvetia, a mining town in western Pennsylvania operated by the Rochester and Pittsburgh Coal Company, housing was segregated by skill and ethnicity. White, native-born, or British managers and foremen lived in single-family houses. Austrian, Polish, and Russian mine workers lived in two-family double houses.[82] Coal companies built houses with different levels of amenities for native- and foreign-born workers. Architect Leslie Allen, writing in *Industrial Housing*

Problems of 1917, suggested that skilled American workers needed bathtubs, closets, cellars, and screens, but that unskilled immigrant workers did not. Allen wrote, "We do want to house the lowest-paid man in a sanitary and hygienic home, but it is not necessary that this home be furnished with all the conveniences and appurtenances that are considered necessary in the American home."[83]

Historian Meg Mulrooney characterizes mine town houses as "uncomfortable, crowded, stuffy, and poorly lit."[84] In Pennsylvania coal regions, the double house was common, with two attached wood-framed homes that shared a porch and yard. In southern Appalachian coal towns, homes were built on raised brick piers, similar to homes in textile mill towns. In the South, miners lived in shotgun houses that were one room wide and three rooms deep. Company houses in a coal-mining town generally lacked running water; families got water from a pump in the yard or street and used a privy in the yard. Coal homes were commonly separated by large lots, which both served as firebreaks and allowed the occupants space for gardening.[85] The same Progressive reform trends that brought improvement to textile towns also led to improved coal towns. After 1915, coal housing was generally built to a slightly higher standard, with running water and indoor toilets and modest amenities like closets and screens on windows.[86] Allen's 1917 handbook for coal company housing gives some idea of a standard mining-house kitchen. He wrote that the kitchen should be big enough to contain a six-foot coal or wood stove, a five-foot sink and drainboard, a storage cupboard or hutch, an icebox, and a table with four to six chairs. This amounted to a room from ten to twelve feet square.[87] With no separate dining room, families ate in the kitchen, just like their urban counterparts.

Housing in coal mine towns was poorly insulated, hot in the summer and cold in the winter. One woman from a Pennsylvania mine town remembered, "You'd be scrubbing your kitchen floor and the first thing you knew, before you got one place wiped, the place where you just scrubbed would be frozen ice."[88] Tom Crop, from Helvetia, Pennsylvania, remembered that when his family first moved into a house with thin walls and no indoor plumbing in 1928, "it was cold. And we used to use the old slop jar or thunder mug, as it was called, and the urine would freeze at night in that big jar. . . . That's how cold it was." The family kept warm with quilts. The cooking and heating stoves were on the first floor, and a hole cut in the ceiling allowed the heat up to the second floor. The house was never truly warm until, years later, the company shingled the walls and put on new roofs.[89] The Crops' house was not unusual in its lack of indoor plumbing. In 1920 less than 3 percent of company-owned dwellings had bathtubs, showers, or flush toilets at a time when these amenities were common in even cheap urban homes.[90] Like those of textile mill workers, coal miners' homes lagged behind those of urban workers.

Coal company houses weren't well maintained by the company. In the coal town of Eckley, Pennsylvania, a company housing survey reported of one home, "The general condition of this house is poor. The plaster is cracked, broken, and in many places falling from the wall. The clapboards are cracked, broken, and in many places missing. The floors are badly worn and sag in places. The roof leaks in places." And yet the survey concluded, "This building serves its purpose."[91]

One benefit of coal housing was that coal was free or cheap to miners. Even in towns where miners had to pay for coal, children could scavenge spilled coal near the mine to reduce the bill. Mining towns often had electricity as well, since mines had a power plant to which houses could be connected. Hence Tom Crop's home had no toilet, but it had electricity, like two-thirds of coal mine homes nationwide, long before other working-class Americans had power.[92]

In these shabby homes, miners and their families, like other members of the working class, ate food that was shaped in part by their ethnic heritage and in part by their circumstances. Families from northern and eastern Europe ate soups, stews, some roasted meats, and plenty of vegetables, with potatoes and bread at every meal. In southwestern Pennsylvania, Slavic miners carried sandwiches of homemade bread with bacon or ham, while locally born "mountain folk" might bring fried or roasted squirrel or rabbit.[93] The company stores carried canned food and usually butchered meat, including steaks and chops, as well as larger joints that could be cooked slowly and served for several meals. Poorer miners, and those in southern mining regions like West Virginia and Alabama, clung to the rural "meat, meal, and molasses" diet of sharecroppers and textile mill workers. As the Unites States Coal Commission phrased it in the 1920s, miners purchased "food that appeased hunger at least cost. . . . Cereals and fats were eaten excessively."[94] In northern mining communities, however, diet was shaped by two important factors: home food production, and the fact that miners' wives could get no wage work and almost always worked at home.

Coal miners gardened extensively, and did more so than textile mill workers. Unlike urban workers, mine workers had plenty of outdoor space in the form of back lots, long fenced yards that were usually shared by two houses and filled with privies, coal sheds, clotheslines, bake ovens, animal pens, and gardens. In Helvetia, Tom Crop's family raised seventeen bushels of potatoes a year in their back lot, along with tomatoes, peppers, cabbage, carrots, cucumbers, rhubarb, beets, and dill. His mother canned vegetables, pickles, ketchup, and juice for the family's use.[95] Various residents of Helvetia remembered that mine families ate all of their own produce, with no surplus to sell, and that the gardens were so large that they took up the entire yard.[96] About half of the coal-mining families studied in the larger town of Scranton in the 1918 study kept gardens. Interestingly, keeping a garden did not particularly affect the food costs of these families. All the families spent roughly 25 to 50 percent of their income on food.[97] Perhaps families who grew food might have otherwise spent much more, or eaten a less varied diet.

Gardens were much more common than livestock. As in textile towns, livestock required a larger initial investment and more time and expense to maintain, and miner families seem to have been unable or unwilling to do this work, even for the prospect of better nutrition. Most miner households in Helvetia in the 1890s kept a garden, and many kept chickens, but only 16 percent of residents owned a cow, and no one owned more than one. Cows in Helvetia could wander freely until the 1930s, when the mine supervisor put an end to the mess by fencing a cow pasture and charging $1 a month to keep a cow there.[98] Cows were probably scarcer because they were expensive to acquire and keep. Chickens were the most common, because they could be fed on insects and scraps; cows required more substantial feed. Even small livestock represented a substantial investment. In 1918 the Cawley family of Scranton had a net loss of $27.85 on the chickens they raised—a heavy blow for a family that earned only $991 that year and spent $482 (49 percent) of their earnings on food.[99]

Gardening and livestock keeping combined with other forms of home food production to improve the variety and nutrition, as well as the taste, of miners' food. As in Tom Crop's family, women preserved as much produce as they could for winter use. Vegetables were canned, dried, pickled, or stored in the root cellar. Eastern European mining families made sauerkraut. One woman remembered that in her childhood in a southeastern Pennsylvania mining town, "We always made a fifty-gallon barrel of sauerkraut. My dad would get a mountain of cabbage heads late in the fall . . . and cut it up on our cabbage shredder." The children stomped down the cabbage in the barrel with their bare feet. When the cabbage fermented, "you could smell it a mile off."[100] Families preserved meat as well: sausage patties could be canned in jars, which were then sealed with grease. Men butchered hogs, made kolbassi sausage, and smoked hams.[101]

Mining families could also take advantage of their rural surroundings by hunting and foraging for food. Foraging was work for children, who searched for berries, mushrooms, and dandelion greens in the woods and fields.[102] Men and boys hunted rabbits, groundhogs, and squirrels. In archaeological evidence from former mining towns, the bones from butchered cattle or pigs were found alongside those of rabbits and fish.[103]

It made economic sense for mining families to rely on home food production, which was the only available means of economic support apart from the all-powerful mining company. With no sources of outside income, families depended on garden produce to see them through work stoppages, strikes, and injuries to wage workers. Home-produced food could also be used for community barter to conserve cash.[104] Married women and daughters in coal towns didn't have any local options for wage work, as there were no jobs for women in the mines and few other businesses in town would hire them. In 70 percent of mining households nationwide in 1920, the father was the sole breadwinner. Women's and children's labor was far less common than in textiles.[105] The most common way for women to earn cash was through keeping boarders. One household in Helvetia contained sixteen members, including six daughters and eight boarders. Without any sons to enter the mines, this household turned the wife and daughters' labor into income by running a boardinghouse.[106] Other women found occasional work in town as maids or secretaries for mine managers or foremen, but most women could only contribute to the family's resources with home production, by tending gardens or livestock or by processing food at home rather than buying it.

Women's labor in the household was irreplaceable in mining towns (unlike in urban industrial neighborhoods) because there were few opportunities to buy prepared food. Family members of Pennsylvania miners baked yeast bread rather than making quick bread or biscuits, as southern textile workers did. Tom Crop's mother baked thirteen loaves a week for her family in the 1920s. To keep the house cool in summer, she used a kerosene stove on a side porch, with a box on top for baking. (The smelly, dangerous kerosene stove was probably best kept out of the house.) Some families built freestanding bake ovens of stone or brick in their yards to keep the house cooler while baking—possibly an Italian or Greek tradition.[107] Women also packed lunches for mine workers, canned and preserved food, and bought necessities every day from the company store. By the 1920s and '30s, however, some women took the opportunity to buy canned food from the store rather than canning it themselves.[108]

Like textile mill towns, coal towns often featured a company store. This was both a necessity for workers, who, especially in coal-mining towns, might live miles from the nearest settlement, and a source of profit for the company, which could charge high prices with no competition. Miners were sometimes paid in scrip redeemable only at the company store, and food prices kept pace with wage increases.[109] In 1877, some company stores were found by government investigators to be charging prices 160 percent higher than independent dealers. Even when there were competing retailers, miners did not have complete freedom to shop around. In towns with both company stores and independent retailers, miners quickly learned that if they failed to shop at the company store, they would be subtly penalized with harder work assignments in the mine. Historian Harold Aurand calculated that for Pennsylvania mine workers, "shopping at a company store deprived the mineworker of between 10 to 15 percent of the purchasing power of his income."[110] Larger mining towns offered other retail options. In Colver, Pennsylvania, for example, three grocers in the so-called "Jewtown" offered delivery and credit, but they required prompt payment on payday.[111]

Women in mine towns supplied only by a company-owned store had no opportunity to shop around for low prices. Women may have been glad to avoid the hard work of shopping for bargains that was required in urban settings, but the isolation of the company town also constrained their choices. As the Coal Commission wrote in the early 1920s, "The mine-worker's wife is thus ... relieved of the responsibility of making current living expenses equal income. . . . But a system which *prevents* shifting most of the burden of spending the family income results in enervation. It is much easier to go to conveniently located company commissaries and to succumb to the prices asked in such depots than it is to shop around to locate the store which charges lowest prices."[112]

Despite the rural setting of their workplaces and homes, workers in industrial villages and company towns had much in common with urban industrial workers, and all procured their food under difficult conditions. For textile mill families, life was most affected by the need for as many wage earners as possible, which squeezed women into a double shift. Cooking and other housework couldn't be ignored; it simply had to be done on top of an exhausting workday. For coal-mining families, the company loomed large, providing noticeably subpar housing that made cooking more difficult. For both kinds of rural industrial workers, gardening and other kinds of home food production made the difference between comfort and privation. Those families who could manage to raise some vegetables or livestock with a bit of capital and labor from family members were more stable and comfortable than those who couldn't afford the money or the time to do so. As for urban workers, the living conditions, job opportunities, and neighborhood conditions of rural workers affected their food choices at least as much as tradition and taste.

FIVE

"A Woman's Work Is Never Done"

COOKING, CLASS, AND WOMEN'S WORK

PROVIDING FOOD FOR A WORKING-CLASS family required cooperation from everyone, whether through wages, marketing, producing food through garden and livestock chores, acquiring cooking tools, or bringing in extra income by keeping boarders or a family business. However, cooking was inextricably linked to women's identities. In popular thought and culture, cooking defined the identities of women, especially married women, who were expected to provide physical as well as emotional nurture for their families. As a central feature of femininity, cooking was seen as a test of moral character as well. Good women cooked well and were happy to do it; bad women complained or shirked their duty. Reformers who studied working-class foodways from the 1880s through the 1910s in an attempt to help poor families eat and live better saw cooking through a heavily gendered and moral perspective. This perspective colored the questions they asked and the evidence they collected, as well as the solutions they offered to the problem of food.

Any question about cooking was also a question about women's role in society. Did housework—women's work—"count" as real economic activity, or should it be kept separate from economy and commerce and considered strictly an act of love? In an industrial society, should women's work change with the times, or should it stick to the time-tested, old-fashioned techniques? Women's work, like men's, was increasingly done outside the home. Could cooking could ever leave the house entirely and be taken over by collective enterprise or industry, as had butchering, soap making, weaving, and other preindustrial arts? Could the traditional family survive if this most basic of nurturing tasks was removed from the home? As the old adage said, a woman's work was never done. What, then, was a woman

FIGURE 15. Women's social identity was heavily tied to feeding, from breastfeeding and beyond. This Chicago mother was visited and photographed by the Infant Welfare Committee sometime between 1910 and 1920. Here tools for cooking, feeding, childcare, washing, and other household tasks are jumbled closely together in a small space. Breastfeeding Chicago 1910–20 Infant Welfare #9 ICHI 03852. Chicago History Museum.

without work to do? What would happen to women's character if they were freed from this exhausting, rewarding, demanding, and inherently "womanly" work? Alternately, could women ever be truly modern if they continued to cook? Could women ever achieve full citizenship and a place in public life without getting off the treadmill of preparing and serving three meals a day?

Ultimately, these questions about cooking and gender were also inseparable from questions about class. From the perspective of those who offered solutions to the problems of poverty, working-class women seemed to have a special obligation to be "good women," that is, to perform their role by devoting all their time and energy to proper housewifery. Reformers sensed the great importance of women's traditional work in the working-class household. They knew that women's work was important, but their understanding revolved around virtue rather than economy.

Women's work in the household has often not been counted as "real work" because it is unpaid and because there are so many cultural and emotional wrappings around it. Yet some historians and economists have recognized what working-class people already knew: housework had major economic value and was vital to a family's survival. In her research on antebellum working-class women, Jeanne Boydston calculates the value of women's labor, including cooking, cleaning, laundry, the production of clothes, scavenging, gardening, and child care, and finds that women added more to the family economy than they took out, and more, in fact, than they could ever earn in wages. "A wife working without pay at home may have been more valuable to the family maintenance than a wife working for pay—inside or outside the home," she suggests.[1] Women's labor continued to be essential to family survival into the twentieth century, especially in times and places when married women rarely worked for wages. Historian Ewa Morawska estimates that the immigrant women of Johnstown, Pennsylvania, who kept boarders and produced much of their family's food, added about twenty dollars a month to their family's income, the equivalent of two-thirds to three-fourths of their husbands' earnings in the mill in the years before World War I.[2] The 1918 Department of Labor study used a multipage survey form to accurately capture family income and expenditure patterns. There were six categories for family income: earnings, board and lodgings, net from gardens and chickens, gifts of money, food, and clothing, net from rents and interest, and fuel picked up. Some married women contributed cash earnings from wages, but many more families included calculated income (in cash or in kind) from the "women's work" of keeping boarders, raising food, and scavenging for fuel.

Scott Nearing, a radical economist of the early twentieth century, recognized the great economic importance of women's household work at a time when many other economists did not. He wrote that, especially for low-income families, "If the family is not to suffer, the mother must be a woman of rare ability. She must know how to make her own and her children's clothing; she must be physically able to do all of the household work, including the washing. And she must know enough to purchase with her allowance food that has the proper nutritive value." He concluded that a man who was employed to perform this level of skilled management work in a factory would be highly paid, but poor women had to do it to ensure family survival.[3]

Nearing was concerned that most low-income women were poorly educated for these complex and vital tasks.

In times of economic depression or family crisis women worked even harder, and many took on again labor such as laundry and cleaning that they might otherwise have paid for. Historian Lois Rita Hembold found that during the Great Depression, "when cash income declined, housewives replaced purchasing with subsistence production. Whether they planted gardens, canned food, remade old clothing, made do with less heat, or moved into poorer housing which required extra effort to keep clean and comfortable, women worked harder."[4] A study of South Bend, Indiana, in the 1930s found that families were "less likely to rely on financial strategies such as using up their savings, taking out loans, going into debt for unpaid bills, or cashing in insurance policies. Rather, they depended on additional work from women as their first line of defense."[5]

The nature of industrial capitalism demanded hard work from women. Marxist historians as well as Socialists like Nearing argued that women's labor at home, including cooking and other kinds of housework, was a necessary complement to men's wage work under industrial capitalism. Men could not truly support themselves and their families on their wages without a wife to "reproduce" their labor. Women produced food, washed the laundry, and maintained the household so that men could return to work day after day. Men's wages could be artificially low because women's unpaid work at home made up the deficit in the cost of living. The cultural association of women with cooking thus supported the economic structure. Women had to do the work of cooking (and cleaning, and food production) in order to reproduce their family's labor, and to ensure family survival when wages were low.[6] It was impossible for working-class families to survive without women's work.

Although Marxists pointed to a close connection between men's wage work and women's work at home, most people in the nineteenth century tended to think of them as separate worlds. Wage work outside of the home was defined as "masculine" (although clearly many women worked for wages). The home and all its tasks were defined as "feminine," reinforcing the idea that cooking was the natural task of woman (although men still participated in some home food production tasks and other housework). The gendered division of labor had not always been so inflexible. Household work had been increasingly feminized over the course of the nineteenth century. Historian Ruth Schwarz Cowan writes that in the colonial period, "the work processes of cooking required the labor of people of both sexes; cooking itself may have been defined as women's work (which it was), but cooking could not be done without prior preparation of tools and foodstuffs, and a good deal of that prior preparation was, as it happens, defined as men's work."[7] That is, men built the fireplace and chopped the firewood and made the iron pots and raised the wheat that women cooked. But during the nineteenth century, "in almost every aspect of household work, industrialization served to eliminate the work that men (and children) had once been assigned to do, while at the same time leaving the work of women either untouched or even augmented."[8] Men were released from household work to wage work; women remained behind with their traditional tasks, which were lightened but not materially changed by urban amenities.

The ideology of "separate spheres"—the belief that men belonged in commerce and women belonged in household work—converted this economic reality into the defining characteristics of masculinity and femininity. The ideology was most powerful among middle-class women, whose husbands usually worked outside the home in business, managerial, or professional work. Barred from the professions and socially discouraged from wage work, these women were most in need of an identity. Although their housework was lighter than it had been in the past, and they could employ servants (in a period of low wages, even lower-middle-class families could hire some), housework and the judicious management of the household was still a palpable contribution to the family economy.

In fact, women of all classes were never truly isolated from the market. Farm women took a keen interest in selling their eggs, milk, and other farm produce, and their "egg money" was often vital to family survival. Married working-class women took on wage work even while doing their own housework by taking in laundry, sewing garments or assembling small items by the piece, keeping boarders, or selling cooked food. Middle-class women who were pinched for money could take on more genteel work, such as teaching or fine sewing. Millions of women in the middle and working classes played an active part in their husbands' businesses, or ran businesses themselves.[9]

However, the idea of the existence of separate spheres was a powerful one, and it shaped the way that people, and especially middle-class women, wrote and talked about housework. Men belonged in the world of politics, capitalism, and commerce; women belonged in an opposing world of children, home, and love where commerce should not enter. To abandon one's proper sphere suggested immorality. A woman who neglected her housework or paid others to do it was as immoral as a man who neglected his business and loafed all day. For example, women whose families chose to live in boardinghouses, which included room and board (and allowed freedom from housework) were lambasted as "selfish, lazy, extravagant, and poorly trained in the art of domestic management"; boarding represented "wifely insubordination."[10] But, in a display of the disconnect between ideology and practice, millions of families lived in boardinghouses for short or long periods despite the attending moral pressure.

Middle-class and educated women in the late nineteenth century spent a lot of time thinking and writing about the meaning of their primary function in the home, and their thoughts influenced the public discourse on cooking. The most prominent writers on the subject sought to glorify housework, not eliminate it. Catherine Beecher, one of the earliest and best-known writers on domestic economy and housework in the nineteenth century, devoted her career to raising the status of housework by emphasizing its skilled nature and its social importance. Though unmarried, childless, and never a homeowner herself, she spent her life teaching and writing about the home arts and praising domesticity from the perspective of married, middle-class American mothers.

Beecher believed that because housekeeping was considered low-status "drudgery," women were inclined to neglect it, causing illness through bad food and unhealthy homes. Rather than being elevated by entering the public sphere and having political power outside the home, she argued that women should derive social and (indirect) political power through the traditional female tasks of housekeeping. Beecher combined practical advice and plans for more efficient and sanitary kitchen and home plans with reflections on the uplifting nature of housework. Housekeeping wasn't drudgery; it was work of the highest social importance, sanctified by moral power. As historian Nicole Tonkovich points out, to Beecher, the simple act of making bread demonstrated a mastery of household science (through an understanding of the mechanism of raising), artistry (because making bread well was difficult but rewarding), Christian devotion (because bread provided symbolic sustenance, as at the Last Supper), and patriotism (because bread provided strength for citizens of the republic). And, since Beecher's imagined audience would supervise servants rather than knead the bread themselves, teaching a servant how to make bread properly was described as an act of education and loving charity.[11] Done well, housekeeping could improve the nation's health, happiness, and spirituality, and it was much easier when done systematically.

Beecher never wavered from the perspective of middle-class women, who expected servants to do much of the heavy housework. Beecher imagined the mistress's role as that of a benevolent and well-informed supervisor. Although she did argue that servants should be treated and paid well, she frequently slipped into the use of stereotypes, describing the clumsy, oafish "Biddies," or Irish immigrant servants, who were supposedly difficult to train and oblivious to aesthetic niceties. Unlike later Progressive reformers, she seemed to have little interest in the domestic problems of poor and working-class women, who had no relief from the heaviest housework (and, in fact, often worked a double shift, doing paid housework or other work on top of fulfilling their own family responsibilities).[12] Further, working-class women had little opportunity to lighten their work by remodeling the kitchen or moving into a better-designed home, like the ones she recommended.

Later writers on housework were inspired by Beecher's practical suggestions for a more systematic and rational approach to the work. Home economists like Ellen Richards (who created the field and spent her life advocating for the place of women in university sciences) sought to bring science and efficiency to housework, not only in order to make it both easier and more rewarding for housewives, but also to provide opportunities in the sciences for professional women. The home economists promoted a more public, secular version of Beecher's vision. Better-kept homes meant a healthier, happier nation, with less disease, better-raised children, more nutritious food, and a more rewarding public role for women.[13]

Neither Beecher nor the home economists, however, challenged the idea that cooking was women's work. They sought to make it a more rewarding job with better results, and argued that it was so important a job as to warrant higher social status for women, but they never suggested that women stop cooking or find alternatives. In fact, their project to uplift housework magnified its moral importance. Writers on housework who followed Beecher were uncomfortable with what they saw as working-class attempts to shirk housekeeping duties like cooking. Such important work must be studied and perfected, not left to commerce.

Some social theorists around the turn of the twentieth century did, however, suggest that cooking and other forms of household production were better turned out of the house altogether and addressed as collective enterprises. Some Socialist thinkers, more radical than either Beecher or the home economists, argued that women needed to be freed from housework, either by community-based voluntary cooperation or by commercial services, in order to pursue careers outside the home. Their intellectual forerunners in America were the Fourierists and other utopian groups, who gathered together to create ideal communities by reimagining men's and women's social roles and the nature of their work. Unlike Beecher, Socialist thinkers didn't consider housework particularly uplifting or rewarding, but rather as a set of dull but necessary tasks critical to social survival. Socialists wanted to use the tools of modern mass production to relieve women from the back-breaking, endless, and inefficient labor of home food production. Marxist Socialists advocated cooperation, arguing that women's oppression was linked to the institution of private property, and that they could only be freed when all property (and all housework) was made collective.[14] A writer for the *Chicago Daily Socialist* in 1906 made a connection between Socialist goals and the improvement of women's condition. In a Socialist society food would be prepared centrally, freeing women from drudgery. Responding to the claim that socialism would "break up the home" (and refuting those who saw women's household labor as "natural"), the writer asked, "If your bread was made by a system that takes THIRTY SECONDS to make and bake a loaf, as is now done in large establishments, instead of your wife broiling all day over a hot stove to bake six loaves, would that break up the home?"[15]

Socialists disagreed among themselves on many subjects, but in general they shared the "producerist" belief that labor was the source of all wealth, and therefore all labor was important. Only a few Socialist thinkers expanded this definition to encompass even the unpaid home labor of women.[16] Socialist women were also more likely to perceive that women's labor, both inside and outside the home, was a necessary part of the "reproduction" of proletariat labor, vital to the continued oppression of industrial capitalism. They saw very plainly that cooking was subject to the same exploitation and inequality as any other sort of capitalist labor.[17] The Socialist critique of food and cooking stood out from those of all the other reformers and activists who were interested in food because only Socialists saw food as a purely material issue. Nearly everyone else viewed cooking through a prism of gender and morality that obscured the nature of cooking as labor.

A wide variety of activists, more or less radical, took up the call for coop-erative housekeeping in the late nineteenth and early twentieth centuries. Historian Dolores Hayden labels these activists "material feminists." Many of them embraced Socialist theories as well as related ideas like the Nationalism espoused by followers of Edward Bellamy and his plan for a peaceful revolution and an egalitarian society.[18] Charlotte Perkins Gilman was the best known of those who advocated centralized, commercial services to replace housework. Instead of individual women toiling over individual stoves in poorly designed individual kitchens, families could simply pay to have their meals prepared in a professional kitchen by trained cooks, delivered hot and fresh, and the dirty dishes whisked away afterward. But Gilman was most concerned with freeing middle- and upper-class women from "drudgery" and was glad to shift it onto low-paid but efficient professional cooks and servants.[19] Other reformers seized on the idea that nutritious food could best be prepared centrally and sold at low cost to working-class women. The New England Kitchen's organizers sought both to offer good-quality "quick food" like soup, mush, and boiled beef as an alternative to saloon lunches and cheap pies, and to "educate the palates" of their customers by teaching them to prefer what the reformers considered simpler, more wholesome food. These reformers accepted the idea that the function of cooking might leave the home in an industrial society; indeed, they thought that mass-produced food would be more efficient and more sanitary than home cooking. The founders of the New England Kitchen merely wanted to make sure the food was healthy, affordable, unadulterated, and "honest" in a way that commercial pies could not be. Others, especially the home economists who began working for the food industry, testing and endorsing new food products, thought that public opinion (along with careful supervision by trained home economists) would soon produce commercial food that was better and cheaper than home cooking for everyone.[20]

The Progressive reformers of the early twentieth century drew ideas from both home economists and Socialists. Although the term encompasses a sprawling and complex movement, the Progressives were unified by their interest in the connection between the home and the wider society. Michael McGerr argues that the Progressive project to remake people and their environments in the mold of the middle class was even more central to the movement than the better-known campaign to control corporate power.[21] Progressives held complicated ideas about the connections between women and food. Although they often advocated a greater role for women outside the home and insisted that the public was responsible for the private matter of food, reformers still evinced a particular concern for the moral perils surrounding home cooking.

McGerr points out that Progressives showed compassion for the poor, and that their emphasis on the power of the environment refocused blame from the individual to the society.[22] Indeed, after 1900 many Progressives devoted their careers to publicizing and correcting the material conditions in homes and neighborhoods that made good cooking difficult, like a lack of clean running water, filthy conditions, and contaminated food.[23] They sought to address problems associated with food with methods such as tenement reform, journalism, school lunch programs, cooking classes, and home visits. But, although their methods were progressive, focused on correcting the home environment, their language betrayed a lingering tendency to equate cooking with morality. To an extent, Progressive reformers understood and sympathized with the problems of cramped kitchens, poor utilities, and long work hours, but, ultimately, cooking was too closely linked to gender performance and virtue to let women off the hook.[24]

HOUSEWORK AND VIRTUE

For many of those who studied the food problems of the poor, cooking seemed to express virtue, and virtue seemed especially important for poor women to maintain. Cooking, the heavenly ordained task of women, was considered their primary contribution to their family's health, and to neglect or reject cooking was seen as a sinful shirking of responsibility and an indication of bad character. Even wealthy and middle-class women, who were never expected to do all the heavy work of cooking, were criticized if they left their cooks unsupervised and untrained. The many poor and working-class women who bought their way out of the job with baker's bread, delicatessen food, or other kinds of prepared food came under heavy criticism. Attempts to lighten the load of cooking by buying prepared food or paying for cooking services were interpreted, by both men and other women, as evidence of bad moral character. In Harlem around 1910, in a middle-class preacher's family in which the mother did heroic amounts of cooking, it was considered "a disgrace to bring in bread from a store, and, for that matter, anything that was already baked."[25] As late as the 1940s a Chicago housewife captured the social stigma of purchasing bakers' bread: "Women who go running out to the bakeshops are lazy no-goods who don't care anything about the health of their families."[26] Similarly, married working women who relied on cooked food from the delicatessen were called lazy, frivolous, or bad managers. By contrast, the labor of cooking was often portrayed as a virtue.

The humble lunch pail often functioned as a symbol of a loving wife's care and affection for her husband, demonstrated through skillful cooking and a neat, tidy presentation. Working-class men, if they did not work near a saloon or cheap restaurant or couldn't afford to buy lunch, took lunch pails to work each day. Lunch pails (also called dinner pails), which were made of a light metal, such as tin, had covers and were sometimes divided into two or more interior compartments stacked in layers. A "three-story pail" would have a bottom section for tea or other liquid, a middle section for sandwiches, and a top section for pie.[27] Sometimes there were small separate tins that fit inside to hold condiments or wet items. Other lunch pails were simple covered buckets, which could double as "growlers" to carry beer home from the saloon. Lunch pails were usually filled with sandwiches of some kind, eggs, fruit, and cake or pie. Cookbook author Mary Hinman Abel suggested packing a lunch pail for a winter's day with "bread, cold boiled pork, cold baked beans with mustard and vinegar, doughnuts, apple pie, cold coffee."[28] The lunch pail was so ubiquitous that it could function as a political statement. In 1900 President McKinley's reelection campaign slogan promised workers a "full dinner pail."[29]

In journalism and fiction the lunch pail was a symbol of home, and of a wife or mother's devotion. In the early twentieth century Progressive journalist Margaret Byington, who wrote about steelworkers' wives in Pittsburgh, was impressed with their hard work and resourcefulness. She described how each would "take great pains" with her husband's lunch-pail meal "to make it appetizing, especially by adding preserves in a little cup in the corner of the bucket. They try to give the man what he likes the most."[30] A tragic story published in the Socialist *Daily People* in 1911 told a pathetic tale of a worker killed on the job. His neat appearance, with clean and patched clothing, and his carefully packed lunch indicated his devoted wife (now widow) at home: "Here is his lunch basket. Who'll take it home to the woman who patched those overalls? Let's see what she put in this morning. A bottle of coffee first; a napkin of snowy white; one egg, two thick sandwiches—that is to say, the slices of bread were thick, the meat was very thin—and a piece of home-made apple pie. That's all."[31] Although the family could not afford thick slices of meat, still the lunch pail expressed his wife's virtue. The napkin was kept as clean as his clothes, and its whiteness suggested her pure moral character. The pie was homemade instead of purchased at the store, reflecting her willingness to work hard at home rather than pay someone else to cook for her. The wife's dedication highlighted the tragedy of her husband's needless death.

Another wife, this one entirely fictional, assented to the loving duty of making lunches only gradually. A 1910 story in the *Craftsman* (a journal dedicated to the Arts and Crafts movement that also praised the dignity of honest labor) told the story of a young department store salesgirl who marries a clerk, hoping to rise into gentility. However, when her husband loses his desk job and cheerfully takes a laborer's job "in the yards" (the stockyard or the rail yard), she is crushed. She particularly resents his new habit of carrying a lunch pail (instead of buying his lunch), which she regards as a degrading mark of manual labor. She refuses to make his lunch, forcing him to fill his pail with his own "thick, clumsy" sandwiches. Eventually, she regains respect for her husband and demonstrates it by surprising him with a well-packed lunch she makes herself. The lunch pail was a symbol of working-class life, but also of a wife's pride in her husband.[32] Only a complaining, selfish woman would refuse to perform the wifely duty of packing a nice lunch.

That women's home cooking carried heavy moral weight can also be glimpsed in the Progressive reformers' general distaste for "handouts," like those offered at charity soup kitchens. By 1900, some reformers argued that the old tradition of feeding the poor at soup kitchens bred "generation after generation" of paupers. A charity publication claimed that by handing out soup, "mendicancy is bred; vagrancy is encouraged; entire neighborhoods are degraded and pauperized."[33] Handing out food for free, they argued, caused these moral and social problems. If women didn't cook, the whole neighborhood went to pot, so to speak. The new, more modern style of philanthropy took the form not of charity handouts, but rather enabling (and, indeed, requiring) women to cook for themselves. Ironically, although settlement workers and home economists were themselves engaged in carving out new fields of endeavor for women in public life, they repeatedly argued that most women must devote all their time and energy to being better housekeepers, for the good of the family, for the good of society, and for their own good. The future of the industrial city depended on housewives' hard work and self-discipline.

School lunch programs became another battlefield for conflicts about women's home cooking. Until the early twentieth century, schools did not generally offer lunches. Children either brought a lunch, went home for food, went without, or bought inexpensive snacks on or near the school premises from vendors who offered candy, pastries, and other items, usually made from cheap materials.[34] Progressive reformers, interested in the diet of the poor and newly aware of the importance of nutritious food for growing children, were dismayed that children survived on nasty, nonnutritive, and possibly adulterated sweets sold by suspicious-looking, unregulated vendors.[35]

Around the turn of the twentieth century, social settlements in poor neighborhoods began to tackle the school lunch problem as a way simultaneously to help children and to educate families about nutrition. The Starr Centre settlement house in Philadelphia is a good example of the types of programs that sprang up in major cities such as Boston, New York, and Chicago. Beginning in 1894, the Starr Centre offered "penny lunches," prepared by settlement house workers or volunteers and sold to children on school grounds. The penny lunches offered a variety of foods at one penny for each serving. Children could thus put together a meal with any amount of money they had, aided by some gentle nutritional guidance by the volunteers. In 1909 the menus included graham wafers, pretzels, milk biscuits, coffee cakes, tea buns, a variety of fresh and stewed fruit, shredded wheat biscuit, milk, cocoa, hominy, rice pudding, bean soup, and meat sandwich.[36] (The options betrayed the early nutritionists' fondness for carbohydrates as a cheap source of nutrition.)

The penny lunch program had a dual purpose: to alleviate children's hunger immediately at small cost without providing a morally degrading free lunch, and to teach nutrition and good food choices by example. The 1908 Starr Centre annual report proudly announced that, as a result of the "habits of neatness and cleanliness enforced by our helpers," "the recess is more quiet; there are fewer quarrels; and a perceptively less amount of surreptitious cigarette smoking, as well-fed boys do not crave cigarettes as hungry ones do."[37] The Starr Centre also sent an investigator to the homes of children who consistently had little or no money for lunch, or who seemed half-starved. The investigator sought to learn whether children were underfed "because of poverty, ignorance, or neglect."[38] Mother's "ignorance"—of the right foods to choose and the right ways to cook them—seemed as likely as poverty or neglect to cause underfeeding.

The center's penny lunch program was successful, as were school lunch programs elsewhere. Giving children a few cents for lunch was no doubt easier for parents than packing a lunch or preparing a hot one; the competitors who had sold children snacks were casual peddlers who could not or would not defend their commercial turf; and the food sold (especially the buns, biscuits, and cakes) seems to have been similar enough to students' usual fare to be accepted by the children. So the penny lunch program thrived. In several cities, settlement school lunch programs evolved into hot lunches organized and funded by the school district. This was an instance in which reformers offered institutional cooking to replace the lack of home cooking and as an alternative to the unregulated commercial alternatives.

By 1911, however, organizers at the Starr Centre had developed a nagging uncertainty about the lunch program. "Does [the program] remove a responsibility from the home which could be kept where it belongs?" the trustees asked in their annual report. "If so, it is mistaken philanthropy."[39] No matter how much the penny lunches might contribute to children's health, they still should not stand in the way of the mother's fundamental responsibility to provide nutrition for her family. To have mothers actively tend to their children's nutrition was the ultimate goal; moving that responsibility out of the home was only a temporary solution. Eliminating or minimizing home cooking might contribute to the breakdown of family life.

At the same time that the Starr Centre philanthropists began to feel uncomfortable with offering mothers a pass from cooking, pioneering home economist Ellen Richards was struggling with the place of cooking in an industrial society. As in so much else in her pathbreaking life, she stood at the forefront of a shift away from the old-fashioned domesticity of Catherine Beecher. Richards strongly believed that there was a right and a wrong way to cook. The New England Kitchen she helped develop offered cooked food as both a solution to inadequate kitchens and a template for the right kind of cooking. She was one of the creators of the home economics movement, which sought to bring science, efficiency, and thereby legitimacy to housework. Richards dismissed the idea that housework was naturally "uplifting," as Beecher had argued. As she wrote in 1900, all of the personally rewarding productive tasks had been removed from the home by industrialization, leaving only cooking and cleaning, which were much less than satisfying. "What is cooked one hour is eaten the next; the cleaning of one day must be repeated the next, and the hopelessness of it all has sunk into women's souls. It is like sweeping back the sea or digging the sand in face of the wind—nothing to show for it."[40]

Richards recognized that many middle-class women had eliminated cooking and other housework from their lives by living in boardinghouses or hotels. She thoroughly disapproved of this development but conceded that, ultimately, cooking at home could be at least partly replaced by mass-produced food for middle-class people. Since we already accept other mass-produced goods, she argued, "Why cannot bread made by the yard and pies by the hundred, be in like manner accepted?" In fact, she looked forward to the cleaner and more efficient production of food: "When housekeeping is reorganized on a business basis the present waste and drudgery and dirt in the house-kitchen will be abolished, and along with the soap-making will go the soup- and bread-making—the heavy kettles and greasy dishes. The cleaning of fowls, the trimming of vegetables will be done out of the house." In 1900 she envisioned "the home of 1920," in which the kitchen would be connected by pneumatic tubes to a supply station that would distribute prepared foods.[41]

However, Richards revealed a lingering distaste for consumerism and the place of commerce in household work. She believed that the home was the basis of civilization, and thus she felt it should remain a place of moral and personal development. Cooking at home, though heavy, repetitive work, was educational, and women's labor was the glue that held together their families. "In sociological work is it not considered a great step when a family is persuaded to gather as a unit about the table instead of each taking from the bakeshop or the cupboard that which will serve to keep body and soul together?"[42] Women must understand the work of cooking as a test of management skills, and the act of dining together as a school for children's social and moral development. Although cooking and eating outside the home might be more efficient, Richards argued, it was not always worth the loss in moral education.

If cooking was discipline, then "consuming" cooking (by buying cooked or convenience food) was a dangerous extravagance. By the early twentieth century the United States had completed its transformation into a consumer culture, one in which most people bought everything they used, and in which possessions as much as family, work, race, or religion defined individuals and groups. Critics of consumerism often charged that the ability to buy household services rather than doing the work degraded virtue, especially among the women on whose labor the household most depended. Richards wrote with vehemence about the self-indulgence and profligacy caused by consumption. She believed that to buy household services instead of doing the work turned the home from "a nursery of good citizens" to "a place of selfish ease, of freedom amounting to license, a receiving all and giving nothing."[43] According to Richards, "luxuries" like consumer goods, abundant food, and labor-saving devices had turned the home into a place of selfishness and wastefulness instead of a place where citizens learned to be frugal and sober. Richards was torn between the efficiency of bread baked by the yard and the unpleasant spectacle of bakery food (with its old connotations of lazy, selfish women) replacing the family meal. Home economists in later years, like Christine Frederick, would wholeheartedly embrace consumption and work closely with food manufacturers to promote easier cooking and housekeeping for everyone. The efficient mass-prepared food to which Richards looked with wariness was the wave of the future for working-class and middle-class women alike.

MAINTAINING BOUNDARIES: WOMEN AND DOMESTIC SPACES

To people who believed that cooking expressed moral character, the organization of working-class kitchens could be troubling indeed. Richards's discomfort with commerce in the home was not unique. To late nineteenth-century middle-class Americans, a well-ordered home indicated a well-ordered family.[44] The social world (indicated by the parlor) should be entirely separate from the work spaces (the kitchen). Like their husbands, middle-class women were supervisors, not manual laborers. The lady of the home oversaw maids, cooks, laundresses, and others who did the difficult, dirty, and heavy work in specific workrooms (the kitchen and the basement or cellar). Meanwhile, she instructed her children, maintained the family's social networks, and did light, attractive handwork in the parlor, dining room, and bedrooms.[45]

Even more importantly, the world of the family was to be a refuge from the public world, and therefore entirely free from any suggestion of commerce. In homes that employed servants, this meant that hired workers must be kept separate from family members. A model home designed in 1897 featured a kitchen that was "in every way separated from the main part of the house by two doors. . . . The servants also go directly to their rooms by the back stairway without at any time entering the main parts of the house."[46] In a well-designed middle-class home, housework was almost invisible.

Naturally, in many families that considered themselves middle class, there was not quite enough money to effect a complete separation between worker and supervisor. Most middle-class women did some of the cooking and other heavy tasks themselves (and a fair proportion did almost all of it), and the work spaces may have been in extremely close proximity to the social spaces. But "respectable" women at least tried to keep them separate.[47] They sought to have their home free from cooking odors when guests arrived in order to preserve the division between work and social areas. They also tried to hire maids who would be unobtrusive and "know their place," so that the wage-earning members of the household would be properly distanced from the family. Even a woman who "did her own work" (a euphemism for lacking a servant) would try to cover up the evidence of it when company came, so that her work as housekeeper would be distinct from her identity as mistress of the home. In an 1871 novel, a woman and her daughter are forced to fire their maid and begin doing their own cooking. In order to maintain the appearance of gentility, they put the cookstove in the dining room, tucked behind a green screen. The resulting "art kitchen" was kept sparkling clean and pleasant. Because they worked to keep everything perfectly tidy, no odors or smoke betrayed their embarrassing and inappropriate labor to the guests.[48]

Because women were the embodiment of the home, a disorderly home reflected badly on them personally. A woman who let her housekeeping spill over into the home's public spaces, without regard for boundaries, was considered lazy and slatternly.[49] When middle-class observers looked at working-class homes as they attempted to solve social problems like poverty, they were bothered by the lack of clearly established boundaries between work and leisure, between commerce and family life, and between individual family members' private lives. The crowded multiuse rooms of workers' housing seemed to carry moral consequences. In an 1896 dietary study, nutritionists W. O. Atwater and Charles Woods described the home of a very poor family.

> The bedrooms were so small that there was only room for the bed. Two of the children slept on mattresses on the floor of the front room. There were set tubs and a sink in the kitchen. The kitchen served as a dining room. The table was not set and the family did not sit down together to eat their meals. There were no regular meals, the table serving more as a lunch counter where each one went and helped himself. No meal was prepared at noon.[50]

This report focused on the lack of clearly defined sleeping and eating areas and an orderly family schedule. There was no spatial distinction between the family's working, eating, and sleeping areas, and the family lacked set meal times. Improper spaces resulted in improper behavior. The implication was that family life would necessarily be degenerate in a home where activities were not clearly organized and where spaces were so jumbled. The disorder showed most clearly in the family's eating habits, where commerce had been allowed to creep into the sacred family sphere. "The oldest daughter contributed to a 'common spread' with her shopmates, and the children were given 5 cents each per day with which they bought cakes and fruits at the open stands on the street."[51] The mother didn't pack lunches; instead, the father ate at his restaurant job and the children purchased prepared food outside the home. The family's kitchen was even compared to a commercial lunch counter. According to Atwater and Woods, "The great trouble here, as in most of the cases studied, is in the lack of management."[52] It was not the family's essential poverty, or the need for all members to work for wages, or the cramped conditions in their rented rooms that was the problem. The problem was the mother's mismanagement, which was manifested by disordered spaces and the reliance on consumption rather than production.

According to the nutritionists, this kind of family disorder could be cured through improvements in the family's living space and through the mother's renewed attention to her "proper" tasks. An update written some months after the initial dietary survey reported that the family's situation had initially gotten worse. The mother became too sick to work, and much of the furniture was pawned. But then their lives began to improve, starting with a new apartment. The mother got a job as a tenement housekeeper (cleaning the halls and common areas of the building they lived in) and in exchange paid reduced rent on a better apartment (with the same number of rooms, but sunnier).[53] The major change was in the mother's work patterns, as she now gave more time to homemaking. According to the update, "The family have improved in their way of living. The table is now set with a white cloth and the family sit down together.... When it is necessary for the girls to carry a lunch the mother prepares it for them, and it costs less than a third of what it would otherwise."[54] The table suggested a clearly defined dining area, and the white cloth was emblematic of the mother's new ability to keep a clean house. The mother cooked regular meals and packed lunches (presumably on top of her duties cleaning the tenement house) instead of allowing her family to promiscuously and wastefully pay for someone else's labor to cook meals. Although it is impossible to tell exactly how the mother herself felt about these changes, she seemed to have embraced the chance to keep a tidier house and to use her own labor to provide better food for her family. She, too, liked the idea of a white cloth and a family meal, even if it came at the cost of more labor. From the nutritionists' perspective, a disorderly family had become orderly simply through an improved separation of spaces and the "correct" use of the mother's time.

Cooking was certainly heavily gendered—but it was also perceived through the lens of class. From the perspective of upper-class observers trying to offer solutions to the problem of food and poverty, working-class women needed to adhere even more strongly to their traditional feminine role. Richards, the settlement-house workers, and the nutritionists unconsciously held the working class to middle-class standards of behavior in regards to women's roles. To them, if working-class women could be more like middle-class women—managers as well as workers, able to devote all their time to housewifery, and committed to separating domestic and commercial life—then they would enjoy the undoubtedly more comfortable, stable life of the upper class.

When femininity was defined in middle-class terms, working-class women could not but fail to be truly feminine. Buying food rather than cooking it, allowing their husbands and children to buy food, performing their cooking tasks half-heartedly or without love, and failing to keep commerce out of the home were seen as grave errors by reformers around the turn of the twentieth century. Yet most of these same reformers seemed intent on rejecting the economic importance of housework. Though they sensed that cooking was vital to family survival, they explained its importance through concepts of womanliness and virtue rather than economics.

We know much less about how working-class women understood their own lives and identities because so much of the information available about them was recorded by outsiders. Yet it seems clear that, despite criticism from reformers, working-class women—as they sought to show love through cooking but also juggled wage work with housework, cooked sometimes and bought prepared food sometimes—were the wave of the future, more so than the middle-class women who controlled the mainstream discourse about housework. For their part, working-class women continued doing what they needed to do for their own and their family's survival whether it met the middle-class criteria of "womanly virtue" or not.

Intense reform efforts centered on home cooking began to fade in the 1920s, although working-class people continued to struggle to make ends meet in that decade and beyond. The home economics movement that had begun in the late nineteenth century to rationalize home work had shifted much of its energy to supporting the food industry. Home economists parlayed their degrees and expertise into jobs with food processors, helping to develop, test, and promote new processes and packages of food. Rather than encourage women to produce plain, nourishing food at home, home economists now urged them to take advantage of industrial shortcuts, try new products and new recipes, and otherwise consume the fruits of the industry. Christine Frederick, who wrote a guide for advertisers called *Selling Mrs. Consumer,* exemplified the new direction of home economists.[55] The "bread by the yard" that Richards envisioned did come about, as bakery bread finally edged out homemade bread for everyone, not just the working class. At the same time, her critique of consumption faded and was replaced by other voices that cheerfully endorsed new products as "modern," not extravagant or sinful. Home economists talked less about virtue and more about how to maximize the household budget with careful buying rather than careful cooking.[56] The shift from morality to consumption foreshadowed the immense expansion of the food industry and its effects on all Americans in the remainder of the twentieth century.

SIX

What's for Dinner Tonight?

FOOD CHOICES ARE NEVER SIMPLE, and they do not exist in a vacuum. In the late nineteenth and early twentieth centuries, every part of working-class people's lives affected what they ate: their cultural and ethnic heritage, but also their jobs, their family structures, their neighborhoods, the tools and utilities available to them, and the size of their kitchens. The process of industrialization transformed all these aspects of daily life, constantly changing the struggle for food. Individual preferences about what to eat were always constrained by material circumstances, and especially so for people with difficult lives and fewer choices. That is to say, class mattered. But when people—and especially those who sought to offer solutions to problems related to food—talked about food, they preferred to avoid class issues and instead framed the problem in terms of gender. Working-class foodways were created at the intersection of class and gender. Today, although our lives and the ways we get food have been further transformed, class and gender still inform the way we think about our own food problems.

With great resourcefulness, working-class people grappled with their material constraints while also discovering solutions and even opportunities. As new kitchen technology promised to lighten cooking tasks, working-class people were able to acquire second-hand tools, but they often lacked the new urban utilities. Unlike middle-class people, members of the working class couldn't and didn't separate the kitchen from the rest of the house. Their kitchens were inefficient, hot, and cramped, but they were also central to family life. Buying and cooking food in urban working-class neighborhoods presented its own set of challenges and rewards. Shopping was tiring, complicated work that needed to be performed daily, but there were many opportunities to buy cooked food from bakeries, delis, small restaurants, and saloons rather than cook at home. Buying cooked food, whether in small or large quantities, allowed workers to live in nontraditional families, freed homes from the heat of the cookstove, and permitted women to take wage work to contribute to the family income. The same urban density that discouraged home cooking and hampered food production for most offered opportunities for entrepreneurship to others. When urban working-class people bought "convenience" food, it was produced locally, probably in the same neighborhood, and thus was fundamentally different from the mass-produced convenience foods we buy today. In rural industrial villages, home food production divided the haves from the have-nots: the poorest families lacked the resources to even start food production, even though they needed extra nutrition the most. Home food production represented capital and labor, and it helped distinguish between those who were comfortable and those who were poorer.

The Progressive legacy of public interest in food still affects the way that we think about cooking and class. Progressives brought awareness of food as a private matter with public consequences, and therefore one deserving of public solutions, including government regulation, better education, and local political activism. But the Progressives also brought a moral argument to the table. Cooking was so strongly identified with women that proposed solutions to the problem of food were heavily gendered. Middle-class reformers and scholars wanted to keep women's work in the home separate from commerce, and hence they disapproved of women who bought prepared foods. Cooking was imagined as the way women best exemplified femininity and morality, and so although there were various suggestions to take cooking out of the home via government, collective, or commercial organization, they tended to break upon the rocks of gender. The moral imperative was even stronger when gender and class intersected. Poor women had a special responsibility to make the right choices, avoiding the temptations of prepared food.

The world of food that working-class people created for themselves irrevocably shaped our food choices today. Foods that originated with immigrants—pizza, spaghetti with meatballs, bagels, hoagies, pretzels, pierogies—have become regional or mainstream American cuisine and our most easily identifiable culinary exports. These foods are "100 percent American" in a way that their immigrant sponsors could never be. Their popularity is due in part to the thousands of immigrant entrepreneurs who established food businesses to sell the foods they knew best in order to support their families.[1] Our kitchens are the central rooms of our homes, and we expect to eat, work, and socialize there, just as workers did in their cramped tenements and mill town houses. Although we enjoy spending time in our kitchens, we think nothing of eating on the go or buying some prepared food to ease the task of home cooking. As in so many working-class families at the turn of the century, the majority of married women today expect to work, although many are lucky enough to work voluntarily at careers rather than at grueling industrial jobs out of necessity. In many ways, today we cook and eat like the working class did at the turn of the twentieth century.

Like the Progressives, we feel a sense of public responsibility for the food problems of the poor; also like the Progressives, we disagree about the right way to solve these problems. Those who advocated efficient centralized food systems at the turn of the twentieth century could scarcely have dreamed of the scale of food processing and manufacturing today. Food manufacturers large and small have transformed American food in the twentieth century. Through advertising, they have shaped our dialogue about cooking and who should do it. In this new and bewildering world, we still grapple with the problem of food—how best to feed ourselves when resources are limited, and how to help others do the same—and there are no easy answers.

As I've tried to show, working-class people used a variety of strategies to feed themselves and their families. Some stuck to the old ways, producing food at home whenever possible. They raised vegetables, kept chickens, baked bread, canned fruit, rolled noodles, preserved eggs, and used old family recipes to turn the cheapest ingredients into filling, nourishing food. They bought everything locally because imported food was expensive; they bought little mass-produced food, because they couldn't afford it or distrusted it. Their lifestyle looked remarkably similar to the one promoted by foodie gurus like Michael Pollan, who urge a rejection of industrial food system and a return to a more traditional style of cooking and eating. As Pollan writes about avoiding heavily processed foods, "Don't eat anything your great-great-grandmother wouldn't recognize as food."[2]

Other working-class people—or sometimes the same ones at different times and places in their lives—sought a different solution. They lived in dense cities or towns where they could buy cooked, processed, or imported food and they happily bought it. Some of these foods, like Italian olive oil and cheese, were imported to serve ethnic traditions. Others were new and cheap processed foods: canned meat from Chicago, canned tomatoes from New Jersey, canned peaches from Georgia. Some of it was ready-to-eat, like bread and pies from a compatriot's bakery, or sausage from the delicatessen, or a hot lunch from the saloon. This solution—buying rather than cooking, consuming rather than producing—has undoubtedly been the dominant legacy from a century ago, and the more problematic one.

In the early twentieth century Americans were slowly adopting mass-produced packaged and ready-to-eat foods. Working-class people ate out or used convenience food more than middle-class people. Most of the "fast food" they bought was not mass-produced nor advertised nationally. Usually it was produced locally by small business owners and ethnic entrepreneurs—people much like themselves. Still, at the time even working-class people were beginning to recognize and buy brand-name foods: Coca-Cola, Armour meat, Campbell's soup.

At first mass-produced packaged foods were least successful among the middle-class full-time housewives who could most easily afford them. Middle-class women enjoyed the time and resources necessary for home cooking, and they based their status (as both women and members of the middle class) on being conscientious home cooks. Processed foods represented a kind of deskilling and were considered to rob women of the chance to demonstrate their skills (even as they provided refuge for women who shamefully lacked those skills). Canned and frozen foods both faced resistance when they were first introduced because shoppers could not apply their traditional shopping skills to evaluate the quality of food. You can't squeeze canned peaches, nor smell frozen fish for freshness.[3] Similarly, such foods eliminate the opportunity to prove one's status or skill: opening a can of soup doesn't demonstrate culinary mastery. And besides, older convenience foods like canned soup and baker's bread were associated with the working-class women who had long been obliged to combine wage work with housework. Using quick food seemed not only unfeminine, but low-class as well.

As Americans enjoyed relative prosperity and greater income equality after World War II, food processors and manufacturers in search of greater profits realized that people could not eat much more than they already did. Historically, as incomes increased, the proportion of money spent on food decreased. People with higher incomes wouldn't buy more food, the way they bought more clothes or toys, but perhaps they could be convinced to spend more money on the same amount of food. To increase profits, food producers turned to either economies of production (cheap, mass-produced food products that required little human labor) or value-added products, products that were instant, quick-cooking, ready-to-eat, or claimed to save time. The profit margin on a cake mix, for example, is much higher than that on a bag of flour. In the years after World War II, almost everyone bought some of these processed foods, combining them with more traditional cooking. Married, unmarried, working, and stay-at-home women were equally likely to buy them.[4] In search of more processed foods to sell, food chemists developed a plethora of additives to assist in processing food and increase its shelf life. In a trend that had begun in the late nineteenth century, producers of relatively unprocessed foods like produce and meat changed their processes to increase profits and benefit from economies of scale. Fruit and vegetable growers planted hardy varieties developed at regional agricultural colleges that would better survive long-term storage and long-distance shipping. After World War II, fresh produce was increasingly sold trimmed and packaged as well.[5] Meat producers began using vitamins and antibiotics to reduce livestock disease while increasing production with intensive raising practices that crammed chickens, cows, and pigs into smaller spaces.[6]

Though pervasive advertising, food marketers presented processed food—once considered low-class and unfeminine—as modern, sophisticated, and efficient. Advertisers played up the difficulty and drudgery of traditional food preparation in comparison with the ease of preparing processed food. And they constantly linked the new foods to femininity to reassure women that they could be "real" wives and mothers while taking these cooking shortcuts.[7] As more middle-class women worked for wages, or stayed at home and simply chose to cook less, and as manufacturers busily advertised their modern, time-saving foods, the idea that women might reduce their cooking chores and still remain "good women" began to take hold in mainstream American culture. As Laura Shapiro writes, the new products made it possible to ask whether women *should* cook for their families if it could be done outside the home instead. Did women really enjoy cooking? "There was a glimmer of space between women and cooking, just enough to invite reflection."[8] Ads succeeded in decoupling home cooking from femininity.

Both working- and middle-class people increasingly ate out as the twentieth century wore on. As early as the turn of the twentieth century, urban white-collar workers began patronizing cafeterias, lunchrooms, and diners for lunch rather than commute back home for lunch or pack their own. Despite a nineteenth-century tradition that limited fine dining to elites, middle-class people pushed their way in, demanding to be accommodated with lower prices and less formal service. Middle-class cosmopolitans even made cautious but thrilling forays into "ethnic" food at Italian restaurants and Chinese "chop suey" houses.[9] Eating out became even more common during the 1920s and '30s, when the spread of automobiles promoted domestic travel and vacationing, and middle-class families began to visit roadside stands and chains like Howard Johnson's. In midcentury America countless sandwich shops, pizza parlors, and Chinese restaurants offered inexpensive meals to urban and suburban dwellers. In the 1950s and '60s, fast-food chains like McDonald's and Kentucky Fried Chicken catered to families, offering child-friendly tastes, a hangout for teenagers, and quick family dinners all in one. The same food-processing technology and economies of scale that produced cheaper food for home consumption also helped the new fast-food and casual dining restaurants serve a wide variety of food both quickly and cheaply.[10] Marketing hit the same notes as well: fast food was presented an easy, fun alternative to the drudgery of home cooking.

Twentieth-century food marketing has been so successful that today we tend to see cooking as a difficult, unpleasant task, and one that can easily be abandoned without loss of social or gender status. The time that Americans of all classes spend on cooking has declined continually since the beginning of the twentieth century. Few of us grow up watching our mothers cook every day, and so the process of cooking seems complicated and mysterious, better left to food manufacturers and restaurants. Meanwhile, cookbook authors find that recipes have to be written more simply than in the past, without using once-familiar terms like "sauté" or "fold in."[11] Food professionals complain about a general loss of cooking skills just as cooking teachers did in the late nineteenth century. Even as more people take up elaborate cooking as a hobby or watch chefs compete aggressively in "show cooking" on the Food Network, it seems less and less important to prepare everyday food from scratch.[12] One might also argue that the eagerness of food manufacturers to sell partially processed food (especially as a way to add value to fresh produce) has led to widespread deskilling. Squash is peeled, chopped, and sold in bags, potentially leaving the next generation unsure how to actually peel a whole squash. A consumer who has only ever prepared popcorn sealed in a microwaveable bag might assume that popping corn "from scratch" must be difficult.

As ever, images of women play a central role in food marketing. Women spend less time cooking than ever before, but they still spend more time on it than men do. Even stay-at-home mothers spend less time cooking than those of previous generations, in part because of the availability of processed and ready-to-eat foods. Yet no matter much the process of "making dinner" has been transformed, it still remains the job of women to make it, buy it, assemble it, or pick it up. Despite almost equal participation in the workforce, most women are still expected (and expect) to arrange their family's meals. Although many men do cook, both recreationally and routinely, many more expect women to do it.[13] Manufacturers imagine their consumers as women and advertise their products by suggesting that women are too busy (with jobs or parenting) to cook, or they lack the skills to do so.

Food manufacturers and advertisers have (quite ironically) seized on women's guilt about not cooking as the best marketing tool to sell packaged foods that don't require much cooking. In the imagery of television commercials, eating fast food or frozen lasagna at home using the family's dishes, cutlery, cloth napkins, and dining table transforms it from lazy convenience food to family-appropriate fare. The cultural dialogue in these ads is an advertising fable about a mother's ability to resourcefully combine convenient manufactured foods in order to bring her family into happy, loving union around the table.[14] As Ellen Richards argued at the turn of the twentieth century, even if manufactured food is more efficient, women must still bring their families together through good management and virtue. In fact, the presence of women in the images provides a symbolic, old-fashioned guarantee of virtue to the long-derided choice to buy rather than cook. Women show their caring by making the right consumer choices: choosy moms choose Jif.

Manufacturers have a vested interest in making us believe that cooking is difficult. But we need not accept that home cooking is dull drudgery, or that it must be replaced by highly processed food. And, as we have increasingly become aware, processed industrial food is detrimental to both individual health and the environment. No wonder that food critics of all stripes, from chefs to nutritionists to the first lady, have encouraged us to turn back the tide of change that began more than a hundred years ago, when working-class people started to buy food rather than cook it. These critics have assailed the food industry, calling attention to bad practices and suspicious ingredients. They laud the working-class women and men who kept ethnic food traditions alive at home rather than succumbing to advertised products. And they assert, above all, that regular people can and should produce their own food.

Proponents of "alternative food" encourage us to turn our yards into vegetable gardens, as the wives of coal miners did; but cultivating our gardens will be a choice rather than a necessity.[15] As part of a trend that reaches back to the counterculture of the 1960s, they urge home cooks to make food rather than buy it: they suggest we bake bread, roll pasta, simmer sauces, and whisk dressings, or at least buy them premade from local artisans rather than from huge, faceless industries. Advocates of the old-fashioned style argue that food grown close to home and processed in the home is cheaper, better for our health, better for the environment, and better tasting. Some even suggest that home-produced food will help stave off disease and obesity. And many Americans of all classes have taken a step back from industrial food by cultivating gardens, buying from farmers' markets, or cooking dinner at home more often.

It is, however, possible to romanticize home food production as a solution to today's food problems. The Progressives often advised poor people to save money by cooking at home without a full appreciation of its costs. The women who found time to raise vegetables, make preserves, and bake bread may have done so with great enjoyment and satisfaction, or they might simply have been exhausted. As everyone who has had to feed himself or herself when tired, busy, or broke knows, cooking is work. It has become immeasurably lighter through the use of modern kitchens, tools, and utilities and the greater availability of ingredients, but it is still work—and work that usually falls on women's shoulders. There is a class dimension at work, too. Working-class people face real obstacles to home cooking, not to mention more laborious home food production. They work long hours and have little time to work the "second shift." They might not have easy access to retailers of fresh food. Working-class people are disproportionately single parents rather than married or partnered, and thus bear a heavier burden with fewer resources. Simply advising people to save money and their health by cooking at home does not take into account the difficulties of doing so.

Finally, advocating home food production, or small-scale local and organic food production, as a corrective to the problems of industrialized food runs the risk of transferring responsibility from society or industry back onto the individual, relying on a consumer "choice" that obscures inequality.[16] The idea of eating locally has developed in counterpoint to a complex global food system that is based on inequality. As Susanne Freidberg points out in her history of freshness, eating locally is easier in some locales than in others.[17] People in wealthy areas, with plenty of personal and community resources, have access to fresher, more sustainable, organic, tastier food; people in poorer communities must get what the system produces most cheaply. Just as it was at the turn of the twentieth century, the ability to produce food at home is sometimes out of reach for those who need it most. Everyone should have access to safe and sustainable food, not just those who can afford to raise it themselves.

The problem of food remains to be solved. And, as the Progressives realized, food problems cross class lines and affect us all. Food insecurity, poor nutrition, unsafe food, and unsustainable practices are social problems, not just individual ones. Can we find a way to bring back the rewards of home cooking without the moral pressure? Or can we find alternatives to home cooking that do not come at such a high social cost? If we want to improve the food we eat, we will also have to think seriously about class. We will have to stop focusing so intently on individual choices and think about the structural factors that create those choices—and ask whether we all have the same opportunities and means to eat well. We will have to accept what working-class people knew at the turn of the twentieth century. Food is everyone's problem, and your neighborhood and community—your home, your family, your job, and your local stores—matter as much as your palate.

NOTES

1. THE PROBLEM OF FOOD

1. Scott Nearing cites the 1903 Bureau of Labor Report and the 1907 Chapin study for an average of 40 to 45 percent of household income spent on food in working-class families. Scott Nearing, *Financing the Wage-Earner's Family: A Survey of the Facts Bearing on Income and Expenditures in the Families of American Wage-Earners* (New York: B. W. Huebsch, 1914), 50–51. In a 1918 Department of Labor survey, families spent between 30 and 60 percent of their income on food; families with lower incomes spent closer to the high end of the range. Department of Labor, Bureau of Labor Statistics, "Cost of Living Schedules for Urban Families, 1918–1919," Record Group 257, Bureau of Labor Statistics, Entry #36; Stack area 530, row 55, compartment 1, shelf 6, ff, Boxes 1–91; National Archives II, College Park, Maryland.

2. Sources for the section below include: Sophonisba Breckinridge, *New Homes for Old* (reprint, Montclair, NJ: Patterson Smith, 1971) ("coffee and bread" for breakfast, p. 131); Dennis F. Brestensky, Evelyn A. Hovanec, and Albert N. Skomra, eds., *Patch/Work Voices: The Culture and Lore of a Mining People* (Pittsburgh: University of Pittsburgh Press, 1978); Hasia Diner, *Hungering for America: Italian, Irish, and Jewish Foodways in the Age of Migration* (Cambridge, MA: Harvard University Press, 2001); Elizabeth S. D. Engelhardt, *A Mess of Greens: Southern Gender and Southern Food* (Athens: University of Georgia Press, 2011); Harvey Levenstein, *Revolution at the Table: The Transformation of the American Diet* (Berkeley: University of California Press, 1988); Karen Bescherer Metheny, *From the Miner's Doublehouse: Archaeology and Landscape in a Pennsylvania Coal Company Town* (Knoxville: University of Tennessee Press, 2007); Louise Bolard More, *Wage-Earner's Budgets: A Study of Standards and Cost of Living in New York City* (reprint, New York: Arno Press and the New York Times, 1971); I. A. Newby, *Plain Folk in the New South: Social Change and Cultural Persistence, 1880–1915* (Baton Rouge: Louisiana State University Press, 1989); Madelon Powers, *Faces along the Bar: Lore and Order in the Workingman's Saloon, 1870–1920* (Chicago: University of Chicago

Press, 1998); Moses Rischin, *The Promised City: New York's Jews, 1870–1914* (Cambridge, MA: Harvard University Press, 1962); Jane Ziegelman, *97 Orchard: An Edible History of Five Immigrant Families in One New York Tenement* (New York: Smithsonian Books, 2010).

3. United States Census Bureau, *Report on Transportation Business in the United States at the Eleventh Census 1890*, 4.

4. James R. Barrett, "Unity and Fragmentation: Class, Race, and Ethnicity on Chicago's South Side, 1900–1922," *Journal of Social History* 18, no. 1 (Autumn 1984): 37–55. On wages, see Lizabeth A. Cohen, *Making a New Deal: Industrial Workers in Chicago, 1919–1939* (Cambridge: Cambridge University Press, 1990), 29.

5. Eric Foner, "Why Is There No Socialism in the United States?," *History Workshop Journal* 17, no. 1 (1984): 57–58.

6. Nearing, *Financing the Wage-Earner's Family*, 15.

7. The Negro Population of Detroit, undated manuscript, Box 7, Detroit Urban League Papers, Michigan Historical Collections, Ann Arbor, Michigan; United States Bureau of the Census, Population, 1930, v. 3, pt. 1: 1147. Cited in Elizabeth Ann Martin, "Detroit and the Great Migration, 1916–1929," Bentley Historical Library, University of Michigan, http://bentley.umich.edu/research/publications/migration/ch1.php (accessed February 17, 2012).

8. Herbert G. Gutman, *Work, Culture, and Society in Industrializing America: Essays in American Working-Class and Social History* (New York: Alfred A. Knopf, 1976), 40.

9. Ibid., 40.

10. John Bodnar, *The Transplanted: A History of Immigrants in Urban America* (Bloomington: Indiana University Press, 1985), 64.

11. Ibid., 52–53.

12. Diner, *Hungering for America*.

13. Andrew P. Haley, *Turning the Tables: Restaurants and the Rise of the American Middle Class, 1880–1920* (Chapel Hill: University of North Carolina Press, 2011).

14. Nearing, *Financing the Wage-Earner's Family*, 19.

15. Ibid., 28.

16. Harold W. Aurand, *Coalcracker Culture: Work and Values in Pennsylvania Anthracite, 1835–1935* (Selinsgrove, PA: Susquehanna University Press, 2003), 67–68.

17. Werner Troesken argues that blacks died from typhoid, for example, at twice the rate of whites until local municipalities began extending water and sewer utilities into black communities in order to prevent epidemic disease. Troesken, *Water, Race, and Disease* (Boston, MIT Press, 2004).

18. J. D. Burks, "Clean Milk and Public Health," *Annals of the American Academy of Political and Social Science* 37 (1911): 443; Suellen Hoy, *Chasing Dirt: The American Pursuit of Cleanliness* (New York: Oxford University Press, 1995), 109.

19. Frank E. Wing, "Thirty-Five Years of Typhoid: The Fever's Economic Cost to Pittsburgh and the Long Fight for Pure Water," *Charities and the Commons*, February 6, 1909, 923–39.

20. Ibid., 930.

21. United States Senate, *Report on the Condition of Woman and Child Wage-Earners in the United States. Vol. 16, Family Budgets of Typical Cotton-Mill Workers,* Senate Document No. 645, 61st Cong., 2d. sess. (Washington, DC: Government Printing Office, 1911), 61.

22. Harry M. Marks, "Epidemiologists Explain Pellagra: Gender, Race, and Political Economy in the Work of Edgar Sydenstricker," *Journal of the History of Medicine and Allied Sciences* 58, no. 1 (January 2003): 34–55.

23. Lawrence B. Glickman, *A Living Wage: American Workers and the Making of Consumer Society* (Ithaca, NY: Cornell University Press, 1997), 43.

24. Lois Rita Helmbold, "Beyond the Family Economy: Black and White Working-Class Women during the Great Depression," *Feminist Studies* 13, no. 3 (Fall 1987): 629–55

25. W. Elliot Brownlee, *Dynamics of Ascent: A History of the American Economy* (New York: Alfred A. Knopf, 1974), 223. Economists disagree about whether the cost of living rose more quickly than wages or whether they rose in tandem. On the controversy among economists, see Peter Shergold, *Working-Class Life: The "American Standard" in Comparative Perspective, 1899–1913* (Pittsburgh: University of Pittsburgh Press, 1982), 7–15.

26. Willard Wesley Cochrane, *The Development of American Agriculture: A Historical Analysis* (Minneapolis: University of Minnesota Press, 1979), 94.

27. Shergold, *Working-Class Life,* chapter 7.

28. For instance, at least three cookbooks published in the 1910s promised thrifty meal options and techniques for cooking low-cost food: Marietta McPherson Greenough, *Better Meals for Less Money* (New York: H. Holt, 1917); Edith Gwendolyn Harbison, *Low Cost Recipes* (Philadelphia: George W. Jacobs, 1914); and Dora Morrell Hughes, *Thrift in the Household* (Boston: Lothrop, Lee, and Shepard, 1918).

29. Susan Porter Benson, "Living on the Margin: Working-Class Marriages and Family Survival Strategies in the United States, 1919–1941," in *The Sex of Things: Gender and Consumption in Historical Perspective,* ed. Victoria de Grazia and Ellen Furlough (Berkeley: University of California Press, 1996), 213.

30. Robyn Muncy has shown how reformers created a "female dominion" across various reform movements, with female communities and networks of power offering education and advancement for women. Muncy, *Creating a Female Dominion in American Reform, 1890–1935* (New York: Oxford University Press, 1991), especially chapter 1. Michael Katz points to the strength of reform movements centered around "child saving," attempts to use the state and private charity to improve the lives of mothers and children. Michael B. Katz, *In the Shadow of the Poorhouse: A Social History of Welfare in America* (New York: Basic Books, 1986).

31. Nancy Tomes, *The Gospel of Germs: Men, Women, and the Microbe in American Life* (Cambridge, MA: Harvard University Press, 1998), especially chapter 9.

32. Caroline L. Hunt, *The Life of Ellen H. Richards, 1842–1911* (reprint, Washington, DC: American Home Economics Association, 1958). In the course of a very

active life, Richards also helped found the Association of College Alumnae (later the American Association of University Women), was involved with numerous domestic science programs, and received an honorary doctorate in science from Smith College in 1910. Edward T. James et al., eds., *Notable American Women, 1607–1950* (Cambridge, MA: Belknap Press of Harvard University Press, 1971), 3: 143–46.

33. Lita Bane, *The Story of Isabel Bevier* (Peoria, IL: Chas. A. Bennett, 1955), 34.

34. On the home economics movement as a women's political movement, see Sarah Stage, "Ellen Richards and the Social Significance of the Home Economics Movement," in Stage and Virginia B. Vincenti, eds., *Rethinking Home Economics: Women and the History of a Profession* (Ithaca, NY: Cornell University Press, 1997).

35. See Tomes, *The Gospel of Germs.*

36. John Foster Carr, *Guide to the United States for the Jewish Immigrant: A Nearly Literal Translation of the Second Yiddish Edition* (New York: Connecticut Daughters of the American Revolution, 1913), 40–49 (emphasis in the original).

37. Levenstein, *Revolution at the Table,* 46–47.

38. W. O. Atwater, "Meat vs. Vegetables," *Harper's Weekly,* October 14, 1889, 1051. According to CalorieKing.com, four cups of whole milk has 586 calories; twelve ounces of lean sirloin has 640 calories, and five ounces of flour has 516 calories. www.CalorieKing.com (accessed July 20, 2012).

39. Mary Hinman Abel, *Practical Sanitary and Economic Cooking Adapted to Persons of Moderate and Small Means* (Rochester, NY: American Public Health Association, 1890), 14.

40. Abel, *Practical Sanitary and Economic Cooking,* 29.

41. "Stuff One Gets in Candy. Sulphurous Acid, Glue, and Shellac Some of It," *Daily People* (New York), February 21, 1910.

42. Rima D. Apple, *Vitamania: Vitamins in American Culture* (New Brunswick, NJ: Rutgers University Press, 1996), 17.

43. Laura Shapiro, *Perfection Salad: Women and Cooking at the Turn of the Century* (New York: Farrar, Straus and Giroux, 1986), 76–82, 87–88.

44. Robert Coit Chapin, *The Standard of Living among Workingmen's Families in New York City* (New York: Charities Publication Committee, 1909), 3–12.

45. Daniel Horowitz, *The Morality of Spending: Attitudes toward the Consumer Society in America, 1875–1940* (Baltimore, MD: Johns Hopkins University Press, 1985), 16.

46. The Bureau of Labor was initially established in the Department of the Interior in 1884. It was incorporated into the Department of Commerce and Labor in 1903 and transferred to the Department of Labor in 1913, when it was renamed the Bureau of Labor Statistics. Horowitz, *The Morality of Spending,* 16.

47. Chapin, *The Standard of Living,* 16–17.

48. See, for example, W. O. Atwater and Charles D. Woods, "Dietary Studies in New York City in 1895 and 1896," USDA Office of Experiment Stations, Bulletin No. 46 (Washington, DC: Government Printing Office, 1898).

49. Department of Labor, Bureau of Labor Statistics, "Cost of Living Schedules for Urban Families, 1918–1919."

50. Horowitz, *The Morality of Spending*, 24.

51. Department of Labor, Bureau of Labor Statistics. "Cost of Living Schedules for Urban Families, 1918–1919."

52. "The Rumford Kitchen Leaflets, No. 17: The Story of the New England Kitchen, Part II: A Study in Social Economics," in Ellen H. Richards, ed., *Plain Words about Food: The Rumford Kitchen Leaflets* (Boston: Home Science Publishing, 1899), 151.

53. Glickman, *A Living Wage*. Glickman argues that working men's ideology contrasted a "living wage" with "wage slavery" or "prostitution"—a loss of personal freedom and of masculine identity (see especially chapters 1 through 4).

54. Michael McGerr, *A Fierce Discontent: The Rise and Fall of the Progressive Movement in America, 1870–1920* (New York: Free Press, 2003), 79.

55. Margaret F. Byington, *Homestead: The Households of a Mill Town* (reprint, Pittsburgh: University Center for International Studies, University of Pittsburgh, 1974), 65.

56. Daniel Horowitz discusses the "bourgeois emphasis on self-help and personal discipline" that was implicit in the questions and categories of budget investigators. Horowitz, *The Morality of Spending*, 61–62.

2. FACTORIES, RAILROADS, AND ROTARY EGGBEATERS

1. Susanne Freidberg's *Fresh: A Perishable History* (Cambridge, MA: Belknap Press of Harvard University Press, 2009) is a fascinating account of the transformation of "freshness" through the nineteenth and twentieth centuries.

2. Harvey Levenstein, *Revolution at the Table: The Transformation of the American Diet* (New York: Oxford University Press, 1988), 30–32; R. Douglas Hurt, *American Agriculture: A Brief History* (Ames: Iowa State University Press, 1994), 184–85; Richard J. Hooker, *Food and Drink in America: A History* (Indianapolis: Bobbs-Merrill, 1981), 229–32.

3. Many of the farmers who moved to the Great Plains had incorrectly believed that there was sufficient rainfall, or that "rain would follow the plow." This did not prove to be the case, and farmers were forced to adapt to the dry environment with different farming technologies. New crops, including drought-resistant strains of wheat and sorghum rather than thirstier corn, were the key. Gary D. Libecap and Zeynep Kocabiyik Hansen, "'Rain Follows the Plow' and Dryfarming Doctrine: The Climate Information Problem and Homestead Failure in the Upper Great Plains, 1890–1925," *Journal of Economic History* 62, no. 1. (March 2002): 86–120; Hurt, *American Agriculture*, 179.

4. Hurt, *American Agriculture*, 195–200.

5. Ibid., 179.

6. William Cronon, *Nature's Metropolis: Chicago and the Great West* (New York: W. W. Norton, 1991), chapter 3.

7. Roger Horowitz, *Putting Meat on the American Table: Taste, Technology, Transformation* (Baltimore, MD: Johns Hopkins University Press, 2006), 30.

8. Cronon, *Nature's Metropolis,* 243.

9. Hooker, *Food and Drink in America,* 224–26.

10. Freidberg, *Fresh,* 203–18; Harvey Levenstein, *Fear of Food: A History of Why We Worry about What We Eat* (Chicago: University of Chicago Press, 2012), chapter 2.

11. Hooker, *Food and Drink in America,* 229.

12. Ibid., 237.

13. Maria Parloa, *Miss Parloa's New Cook Book and Marketing Guide* (Boston: Estes & Lauriat, 1880), 48.

14. Freidberg, *Fresh,* 94–96.

15. "Food Preservation in New York," *Harper's Weekly,* July 4, 1891, 508. The facilities stored fabrics and tobacco as well as food: "Woolens and fine dress goods keep best at about 50° Fahr., furs and pelts at about 45°, tobacco of the better grades at 42°, eggs at just above the freezing-point, and fish just below that standard. Poultry, game, and meats are best when kept frozen; fine Philadelphia chickens and capons, Boston ducks, New York turkeys, and venison are best when kept at a temperature of between 15° and 20° above zero. Each room is devoted to one class of goods, and is kept at one temperature."

16. Lee A. Craig, Barry Goodwin, and Thomas Grennes, "The Effect of Mechanical Refrigeration on Nutrition in the United States," *Social Science History* 28, no. 2 (Summer 2004): 325–36.

17. William T. Elsing, "Life in New York Tenement-Houses as Seen by a City Missionary," in Robert A. Woods et al., *The Poor in Great Cities: Their Problems and What Is Doing to Solve Them* (New York: Charles Scribner's Sons, 1895), 61. The unsigned foreword to the book states that the articles were written in 1891–93.

18. Mark W. Wilde, "Industrialization of Food Processing in the United States, 1860–1960," PhD diss., University of Delaware, 1988, chapters 3 and 4.

19. On bread, see William G. Panschar, *Baking in America: Economic Development. Volume I* (Evanston, IL: Northwestern University Press, 1956), chapter 3. For ham, see Horowitz, *Putting Meat on the American Table,* chapter 3. For pasta, see Donna Gabaccia, *We Are What We Eat: Ethnic Food and the Making of Americans* (Cambridge, MA: Harvard University Press, 1998), 68.

20. James H. Collins, *The Story of Canned Foods* (New York: E. P. Dutton, 1924), 38.

21. United States Bureau of the Census, *Historical Statistics of the United States: Colonial Times to 1970* (Washington, DC: U.S. Government Printing Office, 1975), 164.

22. Hooker, *Food and Drink in America,* 215; Joseph R. Conlin, *Bacon, Beans, and Galantines* (Reno: University of Nevada Press, 1986), 118–26.

23. In the first half of the nineteenth century, food was "canned" in glass jars or tin cans by a tedious hand process. The tin cans were made by skilled tinsmiths and sealed by hand with solder. Tinsmiths, who had been highly paid, skilled, organized

workers, were driven out of the industry with the development of machinery to make and seal the cans in the late nineteenth century. Filling and closing the cans also became mechanized, with the development of the "sanitary can" in 1897, which required no solder but was crimped closed. Collins, *The Story of Canned Foods,* 36. Well into the twentieth century, low-paid women and girls still did the tedious work of preparing food for canning: shucking corn or oysters, shelling peas or peeling tomatoes, and feeding the prepared food into the small fill holes in the tin cans. In the late nineteenth century the canning industry succeeded in developing machinery to perform these tasks, culminating in such triumphs as the mechanical pea-podder and the "iron chink" salmon gutter, so named because it replaced Chinese immigrants in the salmon-packing industry. Levenstein, *Revolution at the Table,* 32.

24. At a time when cookbooks instructed cooks to boil fresh young peas for half an hour (longer for older peas), canned peas were probably not so different in texture from fresh. The Women's Centennial Executive Committee's *The National Cookery Book. Compiled from Original Receipts, for the Women's Centennial Committees of the International Exhibition of 1876* (Philadelphia: Women's Centennial Executive Committee, 1876) suggested that "fresh and young" peas and asparagus should be boiled for an hour (150–51). Fannie Merritt Farmer's *Boston Cooking School Cook Book* (Boston: Little, Brown, 1896) suggested from twenty to sixty minutes of boiling for green peas (34). By contrast, a cookbook published in 1730, *The Frugal Housewife,* advocated cooking vegetables only until crisp-tender: cauliflower must be taken out of the pot "before it loses its crispness, for colliflower is good for nothing that boils till it becomes quite soft." The taste for very soft vegetables was peculiar to the nineteenth century. Jean McKibin, ed., *The Frugal Colonial Housewife* (reprint, Garden City, NY: Dolphin Books, Doubleday, 1976), 34.

25. Fannie Merritt Farmer, *What to Have for Dinner* (New York: Dodge, 1905).

26. Robert Coit Chapin, *The Standard of Living among Workingmen's Families in New York City* (New York: Charities Publication Committee, 1909), 156.

27. United States Bureau of the Census, *Historical Statistics of the United States,* 329–31.

28. "Italian Housewives' Dishes," *New York Times,* June 7, 1903, 28; Hasia Diner, *Hungering for America: Italian, Irish, and Jewish Foodways in the Age of Migration* (Cambridge, MA: Harvard University Press, 2001), 62.

29. Christine Frederick, *Selling Mrs. Consumer* (New York: Business Bourse, 1929), 162.

30. Scientific management expert Lillian Gilbreth promoted the idea that a middle-class woman could easily do her own housework if her home, especially her kitchen, was well designed and efficient. She used photographs and motion studies to determine the "best way" to do household tasks and published them in *The Quest for the One Best Way* (1925) and *The Homemaker and Her Job* (1927). Sarah A. Leavitt, *From Catharine Beecher to Martha Stewart: A Cultural History of Domestic Advice* (Chapel Hill: University of North Carolina Press, 2002), 54.

31. Lizabeth A. Cohen, "Embellishing a Life of Labor: An Interpretation of the Material Culture of American Working-Class Homes, 1885–1915," *Journal of American Culture* 3, no. 4 (Winter 1980): 752–75.

32. Susan Williams, *Savory Suppers and Fashionable Feasts: Dining in Victorian America* (New York: Pantheon Books, 1985), 56–57.

33. Margaret F. Byington, *Homestead: The Households of a Mill Town* (reprint, Pittsburgh: University Center for International Studies, University of Pittsburgh, 1974), 56.

34. Louise Bolard More, *Wage-Earner's Budgets* (New York: Henry Holt, 1907), 132–34.

35. Katherine Grier discusses the construction and use of lambrequins in *Culture and Comfort: Parlor Making and Middle-Class Identity, 1850–1930* (Washington, DC: Smithsonian Institution Press, 1988), 144–45.

36. Susan Strasser, *Never Done: A History of American Housework* (New York: Pantheon Books, 1982), 100.

37. Byington, *Homestead,* 54.

38. Edith Abbot, *The Tenements of Chicago, 1908–1935* (Chicago: University of Chicago Press, 1936), 59–61.

39. Sophonisba P. Breckenridge, *New Homes for Old* (reprint, Montclair, NJ: Patterson Smith, 1971), 60.

40. Robert S. Lynd and Helen Merrell Lynd, *Middletown: A Study in Modern American Culture* (San Diego: A Harvest Book, Harcourt Brace, 1957), 97.

41. "Tenement Number Six," *Daily People* (New York), August 11, 1911.

42. S.J. Kleinberg, "Technology and Women's Work: The Lives of Working-Class Women in Pittsburgh, 1870–1900," *Labor History* 17, no. 1 (Winter 1976): 62.

43. Ibid., 63.

44. Ibid.

45. S.J. Kleinberg, *The Shadow of the Mills: Working-Class Families in Pittsburgh, 1870–1907* (Pittsburgh: University of Pittsburgh Press, 1989), 92.

46. "Bathtubs are being introduced gradually and set tubs are being included as a matter of course." Mary Kingsbury Simkhovitch, *The City Workers' World in America* (New York: Macmillan, 1917), 37.

47. Betty Smith, *A Tree Grows in Brooklyn* (n.p.: Everybody's Vacation Publishing, 1943), 115.

48. Ibid., 95.

49. Mary Hinman Abel, "A Study in Social Economics: The Story of the New England Kitchen," in Ellen H. Richards, *Plain Words about Food: The Rumford Kitchen Leaflets* (Boston: Home Science Publishing, 1899), 137–38. The account did not describe how, exactly, the people got the hot water back to their homes, but it was probably carried in buckets. Customers of the New England Kitchen had to bring their own containers for food (commonly buckets, basins, and jars), and most working-class families would have had a metal bucket in which to carry water, lunches, or beer.

50. V.G. Kirkpatrick, "War-Time Work of the Visiting Housekeeper," in the *Yearbook of the United Charities of Chicago* (Chicago: United Charities of Chicago, 1917), 18.

51. Strasser, *Never Done,* 71; "Tenement Number Six."

52. Leonard Covello and Guido D'Agostino, *The Heart Is the Teacher* (New York: McGraw-Hill, 1958), 46.

53. Agnes Daley, "Life in a New Tenement House," *Charities: The Official Organ of the Charity Organization Society of the City of New York* 5, no. 28 (December 8, 1900): 3.

54. Alvan Francis Sanborn, *Moody's Lodging House and Other Tenement Sketches* (Boston: Copeland and Day, 1895), 100. From the Immigrant in America microfilm collection, Historical Society of Pennsylvania, reel 69, no. 160.

55. Oral history respondent number S-12-A, pages 48–49 of transcript, in "Women, Ethnicity, and Mental Health: A Comparative Oral History Project, 1975–1977," Archives of Industrial Society, Hillman Library, University of Pittsburgh.

56. Oral history respondent number S-1-A, page 15 of transcript, in "Women, Ethnicity, and Mental Health."

57. Strasser, *Never Done,* 55.

58. See Priscilla J. Brewer, *From Fireplace to Cookstove: Technology and the Domestic Ideal in America* (Syracuse, NY: Syracuse University Press, 2000), for an excellent account of cookstoves.

59. Jerome Davis, *The Russian Immigrant* (New York: MacMillan, 1922), 62.

60. Stove price from *1897 Sears, Roebuck Catalogue* (reprint, Philadelphia: Chelsea House, 1968), 119. Wages from Paul H. Douglas, *Real Wages in the United States, 1890–1926* (Boston: Houghton Mifflin, 1930). Wages calculated from table 73, page 205; hourly earnings for all industry extrapolated to yearly and then to weekly by assuming full employment, 2,080 hours per year.

61. Mabel Hyde Kittredge, *Housekeeping Notes: How to Furnish and Keep House in a Tenement Flat* (Boston: Whitcomb and Barrows, 1911), 1.

62. Maurice Fishberg, *Health and Sanitation of the Immigrant Jewish Population of New York* (New York: Press of Philip Cowen, ca. 1902), 13.

63. At least one domestic advisor and cookbook author, Mary Hinman Abel, acknowledged the difficulty of learning this sort of sense-based traditional technique: "One housekeeper says 'hot enough so that you can hold your hand in until you count twelve,' another 'until you can county thirty,' and the puzzled novice can only inquire 'how fast do you count?'" *Practical Sanitary and Economic Cooking Adapted to Persons of Moderate and Small Means* (Rochester, NY: American Public Health Association, 1890), 95.

64. Brewer, *From Fireplace to Cookstove,* 170.

65. Strasser, *Never Done,* 41.

66. Brewer, *From Fireplace to Cookstove,* 229.

67. *Sears, Roebuck Catalogue,* 115.

68. Helen Campbell, *Prisoners of Poverty: Women Wage-Workers, Their Trades and Their Lives* (reprint, Westport, CT: Greenwood Press, 1970), 119.

69. Abraham Cahan, "A Woman of Valor," in Moses Rischin, ed., *Grandma Never Lived in America: The New Journalism of Abraham Cahan* (Bloomington: Indiana University Press, 1985), 406.

70. "Burned by Gas Explosion," *Daily People* (New York), November 6, 1905. It is possible that this and other mentions of gas stove explosions are actually referring to *gasoline* stoves, which were cheap but notoriously flammable and prone to explosion.

71. Brewer, *From Fireplace to Cookstove*, 238.

72. Oral history respondent number I-5-A, in "Women, Ethnicity, and Mental Health."

73. Lynd and Lynd, *Middletown*, 98.

74. Ellen M. Plante, *The American Kitchen 1700 to the Present* (New York: Facts on File, 1995), 104.

75. *Sears, Roebuck Catalogue, 1897*, 130–32.

76. That is, one dozen forks, one dozen silver spoons, one dozen large knives, one dozen glass tumblers, two dozen wine glasses, one dozen soup plates, and four dozen plates. Williams, *Savory Suppers and Fashionable Feasts*, 81. The list is from Catharine Beecher, *Miss Beecher's Domestic Receipt Book Designed as a Supplement to Her Treatise on Domestic Economy* (New York: Harper & Brothers, 1852), 237.

77. Williams, *Savory Suppers*, 81–87.

78. Kittredge, *Housekeeping Notes*, 7.

79. Angelo Di Domenico's *Graded Lessons in English for Italians: An Aid in Americanization* (Boston: Christopher Publishing House, 1922), an English primer for immigrants, contained a number of sample conversations. In the "conversation at the house furnishing store," the presumed immigrant orders the items mentioned on this list (p. 49). The salesman then suggests a number of other items (an egg-beater, nutcracker, saucepan, funnel, colander, and "a box of tooth picks"), all of which the immigrant gamely agrees to buy as well. Although it is possible that this is simply an exercise in vocabulary, naming all possible kitchen utensils, I have mentioned in my text only the ones the immigrant asked for. Interestingly, the list contains flour and a bread box, but no bread pans or other baking pans.

80. "Mrs. Palontona," December 1911; Call Number: LOT 7481, no. 2711; Reproduction Number: LC-DIG-nclc-04111; National Child Labor Committee Collection, Library of Congress, Prints and Photographs Collection, Library of Congress.

81. "Family of Dometrio Capilluto," December 1911; Call Number: LOT 7481, no. 2689; Reproduction Number: LC-DIG-nclc-04089; National Child Labor Committee Collection, Library of Congress, Prints and Photographs Collection, Library of Congress.

82. Oral history respondent number S-3-A, page 12 of transcript, in "Women, Ethnicity, and Mental Health."

83. "America's Homes Get Bigger and Better," *Good Morning America*, December 27, 2005.

3. FOOD AND COOKING IN THE CITY

1. Louise Bolard More, *Wage-Earner's Budgets: A Study of Standards and Costs of Living in New York City* (New York: Henry Holt and Co., 1907), 226.

2. Ibid.

3. In *Building a Housewife's Paradise: Gender, Politics, and American Grocery Stores in the Twentieth Century* (Chapel Hill: University of North Carolina Press, 2010), Tracey Deutsch explains in detail why food shopping was so physically and emotionally difficult: shoppers faced long treks and long lines to get good prices, which was made more difficult by the need to bargain shrewdly; shoppers often suspected they were being cheated; and there was social conflict between buyers and sellers of different ethnic groups. See particularly chapter 1 of Deutsch's book.

4. Susan Strasser, *Satisfaction Guaranteed: The Making of the American Mass Market* (Washington: Smithsonian Institution Press, 1989), chapter 3.

5. Ibid., 70–71; Chicago Municipal Markets Commission, "Preliminary Report to the Mayor and Aldermen of the City of Chicago by the Chicago Municipal Markets Commission" (Chicago, April 27, 1914), 23–24. Most retailers seem not to have put any limits on delivery: they would deliver any amount of goods, of any value, to customers as many times a day as they were requested.

6. Chicago Municipal Markets Commission, "Preliminary Report," 23.

7. Richard S. Tedlow, *New and Improved: The Story of Mass Marketing in America* (New York: Basic Books, 1990), especially chapter 4.

8. Strasser, *Satisfaction Guaranteed*, 204–5 and 224–25.

9. Tedlow, *New and Improved*, 226–33.

10. Strasser, *Satisfaction Guaranteed*, 229–30. Strasser notes, "As late as 1923, over two-thirds of American retail business was still done through general stores and small, single-unit stores selling one line of goods" (230).

11. Peter R. Shergold, *Working-Class Life: The "American Standard" in Comparative Perspective, 1899–1913* (Pittsburgh: University of Pittsburgh Press, 1982), 125 ff.

12. Helen Tangires, *Public Markets and Civic Culture in Nineteenth-Century America* (Baltimore, MD: Johns Hopkins University Press, 2003), especially chapter 8.

13. James D. McCabe, *New York by Sunlight and Gaslight: A Work Descriptive of the Great American Metropolis* (Philadelphia: Douglass Brothers, 1882), 665.

14. Shergold, *Working-Class Life*, 126.

15. In the summer of 1913, for example, 30 percent of Pittsburgh's fruit and vegetables were bought from hucksters' wagons. Ibid.,127.

16. Daniel Bluestone, "The Pushcart Evil," in *The Landscape of Modernity: Essays on New York City, 1900–1940*, ed. David Ward and Olivier Zunz (New York: Russell Sage Foundation, 1992), 290.

17. Rischin, *The Promised City: New York's Jews, 1870–1914* (Cambridge, MA: Harvard University Press, 1962), 56.

18. Thomas Bell, *Out of This Furnace* (reprint, Pittsburgh: University of Pittsburgh Press, 1976), 144.

19. Peter Morton Coan, *Ellis Island Interviews: In Their Own Words* (New York: Facts on File, 1997), 389.

20. Bluestone, "The Pushcart Evil."

21. Konrad Bercovici, *Around the World in New York* (New York: The Century Co., 1924), 127–28.

22. Rischin, *The Promised City*, 55–56.

23. In a 1938 article from the WPA Federal Writers' Project Collection, Terry Roth reported that, although they were not as numerous as they had been in previous years, street peddlers were still plentiful in New York, where they sold hot food, fruits, vegetables, and fish and bought rags and junk. Terry Roth, "Street Cries and Criers of New York," November 3, 1938, Library of Congress, Manuscript Division, WPA Federal Writers' Project Collection, at "American Life Histories: Manuscripts from the Federal Writers' Project, 1936–1940," http://memory.loc.gov/ammem /wpaintro/wpahome.html (accessed March 14, 2011).

24. Strasser, *Satisfaction Guaranteed*, 70–71.

25. Alvan Francis Sanborn, *Moody's Lodging House and Other Tenement Sketches* (Boston: Copeland and Day, 1895), 111. From the *Immigrant in America* microfilm collection, HSP, Reel 69, no. 160.

26. Dominic A. Pacyga, *Polish Immigrants and Industrial Chicago: Workers on the South Side, 1880–1922* (Columbus: Ohio State University Press, 1991), 79.

27. Sophonisba Breckinridge, *New Homes for Old* (reprint: Montclair, NJ: Patterson Smith, 1971), 126–28.

28. Strasser, *Satisfaction Guaranteed*, 64–68.

29. On ethnic hostility, see Deutsch, *Building a Housewife's Paradise*, 14. On black consumers, see Lizabeth Cohen, *Making a New Deal: Industrial Workers in Chicago, 1919–1939* (Cambridge: Cambridge University Press, 1990), 152.

30. Mabel Hyde Kittredge, *Housekeeping Notes: How to Furnish and Keep House in a Tenement Flat* (Boston: Whitcomb and Barrows, 1911), 37.

31. J. W. Sullivan, *Markets for the People: The Consumer's Part* (New York: Macmillan Company, 1913), 24.

32. Marcus T. Reynolds, *The Housing of the Poor in American Cities* (reprint, College Park, MD: McGrath, 1969), 117.

33. Abraham Cahan, "A Woman of Valor," June 29, 1902, in Moses Rischin, ed., *Grandma Never Lived in America: The New Journalism of Abraham Cahan* (Bloomington: Indiana University Press, 1985), 402.

34. Ibid.

35. Roger Horowitz, *Putting Meat on the American Table: Taste, Technology, Transformation* (Baltimore, MD: Johns Hopkins University Press, 2006). See especially chapters 2 and 6. See also Caroline French Benton, *Living on a Little* (Boston: Page, 1908), 174.

36. Reynolds, *The Housing of the Poor in American Cities*, 117–18.

37. Deutsch, *Building a Housewife's Paradise*.

38. See, for example, Harvey Levenstein, *Revolution at the Table: The Transformation of the American Diet* (New York: Oxford University Press, 1988), chapter 13, "A Revolution of Declining Expectations."

39. Sidney Mintz, *Sweetness and Power: The Place of Sugar in Modern History* (New York: Viking, 1985), 128.

40. Data from the *Abstract of Census of Manufactures, 1919*, in Hazel Kyrk and Joseph Stancliffe Davis, *The American Baking Industry, 1849–1923, As Shown in the Census Reports* (Stanford, CA: Stanford University Press, 1925), 82. Population figures from the U.S. Census Bureau are at www.census.gov/population/censusdata /table-2.pdf.

41. The population density figures are from www.census.gov/population /censusdata/table-2.pdf.

42. G. A. Stephens, "Baking Industry," *Encyclopedia of the Social Sciences,* 6: 305, cited in Margaret G. Reid, *Food for People* (New York: John Wiley & Sons, 1943), 28.

43. Robert S. Lynd and Helen Merrell Lynd, *Middletown: A Study in American Culture* (San Diego: Harcourt Brace, 1929), 155.

44. William G. Panschar, *Baking in America: Economic Development. Volume I* (Evanston, IL: Northwestern University Press, 1956), 95.

45. Ibid., 68.

46. Sanborn, *Moody's Lodging House,* 111.

47. Levenstein, *Revolution at the Table,* 32.

48. Isabel Bevier, "Nutrition Investigations in Pittsburg *[sic]*, Pennsylvania, 1894–1896," USDA Office of Experiment Stations, Bulletin No. 52 (Washington, DC: Government Printing Office, 1898), 16.

49. W. O. Atwater and Charles. D. Woods, "Dietary Studies in New York City in 1895 and 1896," USDA Office of Experiment Stations, Bulletin No. 46 (Washington, DC: Government Printing Office, 1898), 22.

50. Cahan, "A Woman of Valor," 402.

51. Margaret F. Byington, *Homestead: The Households of a Mill Town* (reprint, University Center for International Studies, University of Pittsburgh, 1974), 68–76.

52. Department of Labor, Bureau of Labor Statistics, "Cost of Living Schedules for Urban Families, 1918–1919"; Record Group 257, Bureau of Labor Statistics, Entry #36; Stack area 530, row 55, compartment 1, shelf 6, ff, Boxes 1–91; National Archives II, College Park, Maryland. The 1918 bread prices were probably slightly higher than usual because of the wartime wheat shortages and substitution requirements.

53. All consumer price index calculations from *EH.Net: Economic History Services,* ed. Samuel H. Williamson (www.eh.net) and its very useful "Measuring Worth: Seven Ways to Compute the Relative Value of a U.S. Dollar Amount," with a variety of comparative economic value calculators. Dollars for 2009 are the most recent available. See www.measuringworth.com/uscompare/ (accessed February 21, 2011).

54. "Bread Sold by Weight," *Daily People* (New York), September 12, 1913.

55. Florence R. Faxon, "Shall Bread Be Made in the Home?" *American Kitchen Magazine* 12, no. 3 (December 1899).

56. Cahan, "A Woman of Valor," 402.

57. Robert Coit Chapin, *The Standard of Living among Workingmen's Families in New York City* (New York: Charities Publication Committee, 1909), 154–61.

58. Atwater and Woods, "Dietary Studies in New York City in 1895 and 1896," passim.

59. Daniel Horowitz, *The Morality of Spending: Attitudes toward the Consumer Society in America, 1875–1940* (Baltimore, MD: Johns Hopkins University Press, 1985), 120–21.

60. Department of Labor, Bureau of Labor Statistics, "Cost of Living Schedules for Urban Families, 1918–1919." I recognize the difficulty in comparing pounds of flour with pounds of bread. On average, each pound of today's "white" wheat flour baked commercially yields 1.5 pounds of bread. However, given the variations in bread types (yeast bread with or without eggs, quick breads such as biscuits and corn bread) and the other uses for flour (for desserts, for thickening, for battering, etc.), it is impossible to say with certainty whether this ratio was accurate for the families represented in the budget studies. I choose simply to assume that if households bought less flour than bread, then they mostly depended on store-bought bread.

61. W. O. Atwater and A. P. Bryant, "Dietary Studies in New York City in 1896 and 1897," USDA Office of Experiment Stations, Bulletin No. 116 (Washington, DC: Government Printing Office, 1902). The study mentions coffee cake, corn cake, currant loaf, jelly cake, sweet cake, fruit cake, sugar buns, sweet buns, hot cross buns, doughnuts, crullers, and apple, custard, and lemon pies.

62. Louise Marion Bosworth, *The Living Wage of Women Workers: A Study of Incomes and Expenditures of Four Hundred and Fifty Women Workers in the City of Boston* (Philadelphia: American Academy of Political and Social Science, 1911), 43–44.

63. Byington, *Homestead*, 76.

64. Atwater and Woods, "Dietary Studies in New York City in 1895 and 1896," 10.

65. Ibid., 25.

66. Mary Hinman Abel, in *Practical Sanitary and Economic Cooking Adapted to Persons of Moderate and Small Means* (Rochester, NY: American Public Health Association, 1890), 16, stated that flour was much cheaper than purchased bread. She acknowledged the difficulty of purchasing the ingredients and equipment for baking bread at home for urban American women, but it was still a better choice, she claimed, than paying too much for poor-quality baker's bread.

67. Faxon, "Shall Bread Be Made in the Home?"

68. Reynolds, *The Housing of the Poor in American Cities*, 121.

69. Faxon, "Shall Bread Be Made in the Home?"

70. S. J. Kleinberg, *The Shadow of the Mills: Working-Class Families in Pittsburgh, 1870–1907* (Pittsburgh: University of Pittsburgh Press, 1989), 23.

71. Bevier, "Nutrition Investigations in *Pittsburg [sic]*," 25.

72. Atwater and Bryant, "Dietary Studies in New York City in 1896 and 1897," 29.

73. Lynd and Lynd, *Middletown*, 155.

74. Bevier, "Nutrition Investigations in Pittsburg *[sic]*," passim.

75. Ken Albala, *Food in Early Modern Europe* (Westport, CT: Greenwood Press, 2003), 96.

76. Panschar, *Baking in America*, 35.

77. Atwater and Woods, "Dietary Studies in New York City in 1895 and 1896," 55.

78. Chapin, *The Standard of Living among Workingmen's Families*, 132.

79. Abel, *Practical Sanitary and Economic Cooking*, 17, mentions the use of commercial bakery ovens in Germany to bake homemade pies, cakes, joints, and mixed dishes for one to two cents.

80. Tracy N. Poe, "The Labour and Leisure of Food Production as a Mode of Ethnic Identity Building among Italians in Chicago, 1890–1940," *Rethinking History* 51, no. 1 (2001): 131–48.

81. Dolores Hayden, *The Grand Domestic Revolution: A History of Feminist Designs for American Homes, Neighborhoods, and Cities* (Cambridge, MA: MIT Press, 1981).

82. Abraham Cahan, "The Bake Shop Count," originally published February 8, 1902, reprinted in Rischin, ed., *Grandma Never Lived in America*, 245–46.

83. Rischin, *The Promised City*, 57.

84. Beaten biscuits are a hard, crisp version of baking-powder biscuits, made by beating the dough for up to forty-five minutes with a heavy object. They are served split, with a thin slice of ham, for a popular southern appetizer.

85. Elizabeth S. D. Engelhardt, "Beating the Biscuits in Appalachia: Race, Class, and Gender Politics of Women Baking Bread," in *Cooking Lessons: The Politics of Gender and Food*, ed. Sherrie A. Innes (Lanham, MD: Rowman and Littlefield, 2001), 160.

86. Benjamin Franklin recorded in his autobiography that when he first arrived in Philadelphia, disheveled and low on funds, he bought three large puffy rolls or loaves for three cents. L. Jesse Lemisch, ed., *Benjamin Franklin: The Autobiography and Other Writings* (New York: Signet Classic, 1961), 38.

87. Mary Kingsbury Simkhovitch, *The City Workers' World in America* (New York: Macmillan Company, 1917), 97.

88. Faxon, "Shall Bread Be Made in the Home?"

89. Chapin, *The Standard of Living*, 145.

90. Department of Labor, Bureau of Labor Statistics, "Cost of Living Schedules for Urban Families, 1918–1919."

91. On the origins of pepper pot soup, see Evan Jones, *American Food: The Gastronomic Story* (New York: E. P. Dutton, 1975), 70–71.

92. Mark Kurlansky, *The Big Oyster: History on the Half Shell* (New York: Ballantine Books, 2006), 157–62, 214.

93. See Richard J. Hooker, *Food and Drink in America: A History* (Indianapolis: Bobbs-Merrill, 1981), chapter 10.

94. European-style restaurants offered rich interiors, fine wines, and a self-consciously Continental cuisine, with menus of French and German dishes that were written in French.

95. On restaurant history, see Hooker, *Food and Drink in America;* also Harvey Levenstein, *Revolution at the Table* and *Paradox of Plenty: A Social History of Eating in Modern America* (New York: Oxford University Press, 1993). On restaurants and

the middle class, see Andrew P. Haley, *Turning the Tables: Restaurants and the Rise of the Middle Class, 1880–1920* (Chapel Hill: University of North Carolina Press, 2011).

96. Hooker, *Food and Drink in America,* 278–79.

97. Thomas Burgess, *Greeks in America: An Account of Their Coming, Progress, Customs, Living, and Aspirations* (Boston: Sherman, French, 1913), 36–37.

98. Hasia Diner, *Hungering for America: Italian, Irish, and Jewish Foodways in the Age of Migration* (Cambridge, MA: Harvard University Press, 2001), 196.

99. Quoted in Ailon Shiloh, ed., *By Myself I'm a Book! An Oral History of the Immigrant Jewish Experience in Pittsburgh* (Waltham, MA: American Jewish Historical Society, 1972), 44.

100. Recording of oral history with Herman Gordon, National Council of Jewish Women, Oral History Project, Archives of Industrial Society, University of Pittsburgh Library.

101. Recording of oral history with Louis Arenson, National Council of Jewish Women, Oral History Project.

102. See various articles translated by the Chicago Foreign Language Press Survey, including "The United Hebrew Trades" (*The World,* January 8, 1916); "Bakery Bosses Demand Right and Justice through Arbitration" (*Daily Jewish Courier,* April 29, 1918); "Why Was the Price of Bread Raised?" (*Daily Jewish Courier,* March 9, 1922); "Bakery Owners Declare Guerilla War against Their Workers" (*Forward,* December 19, 1920); "Jewish Bakers Win a Raise by the Bosses" (*Forward,* May 29, 1923); "Rosenthal and Stern the First to Sign Agreement with Jewish Waiters' Union" (*Forward,* June 26, 1923). Jewish, IK, Boxes 29 and 30, University of Chicago Special Collections.

103. "Jewish Women," *Daily Jewish Courier,* July 8, 1912. Translated for the Chicago Foreign Language Press Survey and filed in Jewish, IK, Box 30, University of Chicago Special Collections.

104. Marni Davis, *Jews and Booze: Becoming American in the Age of Prohibition* (New York: New York University Press, 2012).

105. Tracy Poe. "Food, Culture, and Entrepreneurship among African-Americans, Italians, and Swedes in Chicago," PhD diss., Harvard University, 1999, 62.

106. Poe, "Food, Culture, and Entrepreneurship," 56.

107. Tabb's Quick Lunch advertisement, *Chicago Defender,* February 22, 1919; J. A. Bell's advertisement, *Chicago Defender,* June 10, 1916.

108. Frederick Douglass Opie, *Hog and Hominy: Soul Food from Africa to America* (New York: Columbia University Press, 2008), 64.

109. Diner, *Hungering for America,* 40–41.

110. See "Unsanitary Factories," *L'Italia,* June 23, 1906. Translated by John Grotto, January 19, 1937, for the Chicago Foreign Language Press Survey, filed in Italian, I M: Attitudes / Health and Sanitation, box 26, University of Chicago Special Collections. See also "Italian Housewives' Dishes," *New York Times,* June 7, 1903.

111. Giovanni E. Schiavo, *The Italians in Chicago: A Study in Americanization* (Chicago: Italian American Publishing, 1928), 99–101.

112. Poe, "Food, Culture, and Entrepreneurship," 89.

113. "An Italian Family in America. Mildred Farber, Italian Backgrounds, School of Education, New York University," in Leonard Covello Papers, Historical Society of Pennsylvania, Box 67, folder 22—"Social Backgrounds—reference—Documents (marked unused), Assimilation of Italian Family from Social Backgrounds Course."

114. Diner, *Hungering for America,* 74- 79.

115. I. W. Howerth, "Are the Italians a Dangerous Class?," *The Charities Review: A Journal of Practical Sociology* 4, no. 1: 17-40.

116. Jerome Davis, *The Russian Immigrant* (New York: MacMillan Company, 1922), 80.

117. Hooker, *Food and Drink in America,* 259.

118. Broughton Brandenburg, *Imported Americans: The Story of the Experiences of a Disguised American and His Wife Studying the Immigrant Question* (New York: Frederick A. Stokes Company, 1904), 9–10.

119. Ibid., 11.

120. Howard P. Chudacoff, *The Age of the Bachelor: Creating an American Subculture* (Princeton, NJ: Princeton University Press, 1999), 126. Cites City Club of Chicago, "A Community Survey in the Twenty-First Ward," *City Club Bulletin* 6 (March 13, 1913), 94.

121. Louise Marion Bosworth, *The Living Wage of Women Workers: A Study of Incomes and Expenditures of Four Hundred and Fifty Women Workers in the City of Boston* (Philadelphia: American Academy of Political and Social Science, 1911). 40. On lodgers being allowed to cook in their rooms, see p. 43.

122. Diner, *Hungering for America,* 200.

123. Franklin J. Meine, *Stories of the Streets and of the Town: From the Chicago Record, 1893–1900* (Chicago: Caxton Club, 1941), 112, 120.

124. Paul Richards, *The Lunch Room* (Chicago: Hotel Monthly, 1916), 9.

125. Alvan Marlow, "Cheap Restaurants. Mysteries of the Caravanserais of the Wretched," *Daily People* (New York), August 6, 1900; Pasquale Russo, *Twelve O'Clock Lunch (The astonishing truth regarding the filthy and unsanitary conditions existing in the Hotels, Restaurants and Lunch Rooms)* (Chicago: Pasquale Russo, 1923), 22.

126. "Family Solidarity," in Leonard Covello Papers, Historical Society of Pennsylvania, Box 68, folder 1—"Social Backgrounds—reference—Documents and notes."

127. Roy Rosenzweig, *Eight Hours for What We Will: Workers and Leisure in an Industrial City, 1870–1920* (Cambridge: Cambridge University Press, 1983), 95.

128. Chicago business directory, 1901, listings for "Saloons," pp. 2521–2536, microfilm at the New York Public Library. Chicago population figure from Campbell Gibson, "Population of the 100 Largest Cities and Other Urban Places in the United States: 1790 to 1990," U.S. Census Bureau, www.census.gov/population /www/documentation/twps0027.html (accessed January 15, 2008).

129. Walter E. Lagerquist, "Social Geography of the Lower East Side," *New York Times,* April 3, 1910.

130. Davis, *Jews and Booze*, 86.

131. The "nickel beer" was a well-established standard, and saloonkeepers increased profits by selling a smaller glass or a lower-quality beer for the nickel price. This caused difficulties when the wholesale price of beer rose and saloonkeepers were forced to acquire new stocks of smaller glasses in order to maintain profits. Perry R. Duis, *The Saloon: Public Drinking in Chicago and Boston, 1880–1920* (Urbana: University of Illinois Press, 1983), 48.

132. Madelon Powers, *Faces along the Bar: Lore and Order in the Workingman's Saloon, 1870–1920* (Chicago: University of Chicago Press, 1998).

133. Upton Sinclair, *The Jungle* (reprint, New York: Barnes & Noble, 1995), 87.

134. "The Free Lunch Microbe," *New York Times,* July 31, 1904.

135. Marlow, "Cheap Restaurants."

136. Raymond Calkins, *Substitutes for the Saloon* (Boston and New York: Houghton Mifflin Company, 1901), 230.

137. Calkins, *Substitutes for the Saloon* (Boston: Houghton Mifflin, 1901), 15.

138. Royal L. Melendy, "The Saloon in Chicago, Part II," *American Journal of Sociology,* January 1901, 455.

139. Ibid.

140. Sinclair, *The Jungle,* 87.

141. Dorothy Richardson, *The Long Day: The Story of a New York Working Girl* (reprint, Charlottesville: University of Virginia Press, 1990), 257–59. Although Richardson presented the story as an autobiography, in fact she was a journalist and took a series of low-wage jobs for the purpose of investigation. The incident could therefore have been based in fact or entirely fabricated. Madelon Powers comments on this incident. Although the female characters interpret the men's actions as chivalrous ("It's dacent wurrkin'-men that comes here, and they knows a lady when they see her, and they ups and goes!"), Powers points out that the men in the saloon may have been uncomfortable or ambivalent about "sharing" the traditionally male saloon with working women. Powers, *Faces along the Bar,* 211–12.

142. Kathy Peiss reports that respectable working-class women would cross the street to avoid passing a saloon full of harassing loiterers. *Cheap Amusements: Leisure in Turn-of-the-Century New York* (Philadelphia: Temple University Press, 1986), 27.

143. "Roosevelt Quizzes Girl Dress Strikers," *New York Times,* January 22, 1913.

144. Perry R. Duis, *Challenging Chicago: Coping with Everyday Life, 1837–1920* (Urbana: University of Illinois Press, 1998), 161. Free lunches were outlawed in New Ulm, Minnesota, in March 1917, also as a war measure. Rae Katherine Eighmey, *Food Will Win the War: Minnesota Crops, Cooks, and Conservation during World War I* (St. Paul: Minnesota Historical Society Press, 2010), 161.

145. Richards, *The Lunch Room,* 1.

146. Duis, *Challenging Chicago,* 159.

147. Levenstein, *Revolution at the Table,* 187. Journalist George Ade estimated that around 1905, saloons were outlawed by local option in at least half of the United States. Ade, *The Old-Time Saloon: Not Wet—Not Dry, Just History* (New York:

R. Long & R. R. Smith, 1931), 18. Roy Rosenzweig reports that because of licensing laws in Rochester, New York, saloons often forbade the free lunch, but that saloons patronized by Polish, Lithuanian, Jewish, and Italian workers were most likely to offer the free lunch in defiance of the law. Rosenzweig, *Eight Hours for What We Will*, 188.

148. Reid, *Food for People*, 30.

149. Levenstein, *Revolution at the Table*, 185.

150. Richards, *The Lunch Room*, 78.

151. Rosenzweig, *Eight Hours for What We Will*, 9–10.

152. Hooker, *Food and Drink in America*, 294.

153. Diner, *Hungering for America*, 201.

154. "Making Housekeepers in the City Schools," *New York Times,* June 14, 1908.

155. "People Unmarried," *Daily People* (New York), September 21, 1913.

156. Mary Hinman Abel, "A Study in Social Economics: The Story of the New England Kitchen," in Ellen H. Richards, ed., *Plain Words about Food: The Rumford Kitchen Leaflets* (Boston: Home Science Publishing, 1899), 162; "School Luncheon Conference Report," December 3, 1910, Box 4, Folder 28, School Lunch Program records, Women's Educational and Industrial Union, Schlesinger Library, Harvard University.

157. "A Crusade for Health," *New York Times,* April 1, 1902.

158. Brandenburg, *Imported Americans*, 211.

159. Melendy, "The Saloon in Chicago, Part II," 456.

160. George Ade, "Vehicles Out of the Ordinary," in *Stories of the Streets and of the Town: From the Chicago Record, 1893–1900*, ed. Franklin J. Meine (Chicago: Caxton Club, 1941), 89–112; Duis, *Challenging Chicago*, 160.

161. Diner, *Hungering for America*, 50, 201.

162. See Strasser, *Satisfaction Guaranteed,* especially chapter 5, on marketing aimed at working-class people.

163. Oral history respondent number S-15-B, page 4 of transcript, in "Women, Ethnicity, and Mental Health: A Comparative Oral History Project, 1975–1977," Archives of Industrial Society, Hillman Library, University of Pittsburgh.

164. Oral history respondent number S-20-A, page 7 of transcript, in ibid.

165. Oral history respondent number I-1-A, page 12 of transcript, in ibid.

166. Diner, *Hungering for America*, 61.

167. Oral history respondent number I-3-A, pages 11–13 of transcript, in "Women, Ethnicity, and Mental Health."

168. Oral history respondent number I-19-A, pages 2–4 of transcript, in ibid.

169. Oral history respondent number I-7-A, page 5 of transcript, in ibid.

170. Edith Abbot, *The Tenements of Chicago, 1908–1935* (Chicago: University of Chicago Press, 1936), 80. The district under discussion—the Old Lumber Yards district—was canvased by University of Chicago students either in 1916–17 or in 1929.

171. Poe, "The Labour and Leisure of Food Production," 131–41.

172. Ewa Morawska, *For Bread with Butter: The Life-Worlds of East Central Europeans in Johnstown, Pennsylvania, 1890–1940* (Cambridge: Cambridge University Press, 1985), 134.

173. "Cost of Production: Iron, Steel, Coal, etc.," Sixth Annual Report of the Commissioner of Labor, 1890 (Washington, DC: Government Printing Office, 1891), 804–1164. These numbers are only suggestive. Information on gardens was gathered only anecdotally, and although some interviewers made regular notes that indicated the presence of a garden along with other measures of prosperity and respectability (sewing machine, organ, cornet, horses, family refined/not refined, in debt, drinkers, etc.), others made only very terse notes. Also, the report did not specify the towns or cities surveyed but only the industry (for example, bituminous coal) and the state. It is therefore hard to say just how rural or how urban these families were. Some were more obviously rural, such as the Pennsylvania iron ore workers, 93 percent of whom kept a productive garden or livestock (including a staggering number of pigs).

174. "Cost of Living in the United States," U.S. Department of Labor and the Bureau of Labor Statistics, Bulletin No. 357, May 1924 (Washington, DC: Government Printing Office, 1924).

175. "Italian Housewives' Dishes," 28.

176. Jane Ziegelman, *97 Orchard: An Edible History of Five Immigrant Families in One New York Tenement* (New York: Smithsonian Books, 2010), 113–15.

177. John Foster Carr, *Guide to the United States for the Jewish Immigrant: A Nearly Literal Translation of the Second Yiddish Edition* (New York: Connecticut Daughters of the American Revolution, 1913), 41.

178. Diner, *Hungering for America*, 62–63.

179. "Attitudes toward Italians—Isolation—Remembrance of B. Fish, 1941," in Leonard Covello Papers, Historical Society of Pennsylvania, Box 68, folder 3—"Social Backgrounds—reference—Documents and Notes."

180. Phyllis Williams, *South Italian Folkways in Europe and America* (New Haven, CT: Yale University Press, 1938), 64.

181. Breckenridge, *New Homes for Old*, 126, 130.

182. Morawska, *For Bread with Butter*, 134–35.

4. BETWEEN COUNTRY AND CITY

1. Edwin Scott Roscoe and George Lewis Thuering, *The Textile Industry in Pennsylvania.* (Engineering Research Bulletin B-74: Pennsylvania State University, College of Engineering and Architecture, University Park, May 1958), 2.

2. United States Senate, *Report on the Condition of Woman and Child Wage-Earners in the United States. Vol. 16, Family Budgets of Typical Cotton-Mill Workers*, Senate Document No. 645, 61st Cong., 2d. sess. (Washington, DC: Government Printing Office, 1911).

3. Because of the large size of the 1918 study, which included detailed twelve-page surveys for each of hundreds of families in perhaps fifty U.S. communities, I adopted

a sampling method. I studied twenty random families from each location in depth. Thus my conclusions are suggestive rather than conclusive. The survey is also limited by the selective nature of the criteria used by investigators in selecting families. The families selected were all two-parent families in which the husband was the major breadwinner; no recent immigrants, boardinghouse keepers, or "slum or charity" families were studied. These criteria meant that many types of households of interest to me are not represented in the survey, and the families surveyed skew toward the upper working class or "labor aristocracy." A husband who could support his entire family without the labor of his wife and children was likely a skilled worker. The survey also includes low-level salaried or "white-collar" workers, such as city officials or bookkeepers, who are not part of my conception of the working class. Nevertheless, the depth of detail makes the survey an invaluable source despite its limitations. The criteria for the family's inclusion in the study are printed on each survey sheet. Department of Labor, Bureau of Labor Statistics, "Cost of Living Schedules for Urban Families, 1918–1919"; Record Group 257, Bureau of Labor Statistics, Entry #6; Stack area 530, row 55, compartment 1, shelf 6, ff, Boxes 1–91, National Archives II, College Park, Maryland.

4. Edward Eyre Hunt, F. G. Tryon, and Joseph H. Willits, eds., *What the Coal Commission Found: An Authoritative Summary by the Staff* (Baltimore, MD: Williams and Wilkins, 1925), 17–21.

5. Historians of these towns, whether interested in architecture, the landscape, or industrial relations, make fine distinctions between company-owned and -controlled towns and "industrial villages" that simply sprang up to service an industry in an isolated area. Leland M. Roth, "Company Towns in the Western United States," in *The Company Town: Architecture and Society in the Early Industrial Age*, ed. John S. Garner (New York: Oxford University Press, 1992), gives an excellent and very detailed overview of the types and purposes of company towns. Margaret Crawford's *Building the Workingman's Paradise: The Design of American Company Towns* (London: Verso, 1995) is the standard work on the architecture and landscape of "model" towns. Historians of labor have particularly noted that a company's control of its workers' housing, social life, and leisure was of a piece with its ability to brutally crush labor organization. For the purposes of this study, the degree of a company's control over its workers is less important, simply because the activities in which I'm interested—cooking and eating—were generally of little interest to the company.

6. Glenn Porter, *The Workers' World at Hagley* (Greenville, DE: Eleutherian Mills–Hagley Foundation, 1981), 39.

7. I. A. Newby, *Plain Folk in the New South: Social Change and Cultural Persistence, 1880–1915.* (Baton Rouge: Louisiana State University Press, 1989), 275.

8. Crawford, *Building the Workingman's Paradise*, 48.

9. Ibid., 37.

10. Ibid., 42.

11. Ibid., 2.

12. Roth, "Company Towns in the Western United States," 175.

13. Ibid., 193.

14. Christine Tate, "Viscose Village: Model Industrial Workers' Housing in Marcus Hook, Delaware County, Pennsylvania," PhD diss., University of Pennsylvania, 2002, 66–84.

15. Hunt, *What the Coal Commission Found*, 152.

16. Crawford, *Building the Workingman's Paradise*, 136.

17. Ibid., 30.

18. David L. Carlton, *Mill and Town in South Carolina, 1880–1920* (Baton Rouge: Louisiana State University Press, 1982), 7.

19. Jacquelyn Dowd Hall et al., *Like a Family: The Making of a Southern Cotton Mill World* (Chapel Hill: University of North Carolina Press, 1987), 31–33, 36.

20. Newby, *Plain Folk in the New South*, 6.

21. Ibid., 222–23, 244.

22. Ibid., 250.

23. United States Senate, *Report on the Condition of Woman and Child Wage-Earners in the United States*, 27.

24. Newby, *Plain Folk in the New South*, 245–46, 250.

25. Grace Lumpkin, *To Make My Bread* (Urbana: University of Illinois Press, 1995), 39.

26. United States Senate, *Report on the Condition of Woman and Child Wage-Earners in the United States*, 67–68.

27. John Pierce, Federal Writers Project MS, untitled, September 23, 1938, Library of Congress.

28. Hall et al., *Like a Family*, 119.

29. Department of Labor, Bureau of Labor Statistics, "Cost of Living Schedules for Urban Families, 1918–1919."

30. United States Senate, *Report on the Condition of Woman and Child Wage-Earners in the United States*, 29.

31. Ibid., 31.

32. Ibid., 36.

33. Newby, *Plain Folk in the New South*, 237–38.

34. Beth English, "'I Have a Lot of Work to Do': Cotton Mill Work and Women's Culture in Matoaca, Virginia, 1888–95," *Virginia Magazine of History and Biography* 114, no. 3: 365–66.

35. Newby, *Plain Folk in the New South*, 290–91.

36. Hall et al., *Like a Family*, 157.

37. Ibid., 158.

38. Newby, *Plain Folk in the New South*, 238. Mill women were thus in line with rural women, who, according to recent historiography, were oriented toward the production of cash.

39. Interview with Betty Davidson by Allen Tullos, February 2 and 17, 1979, H-0019, in the Southern Oral History Program Collection, #4007, Southern Historical Collection, Wilson Library, University of North Carolina at Chapel Hill, transcript p. 33.

40. Interview with Flossie Moore Durham by Mary Fredrickson and Brent D. Glass, September 2, 1976, H-0066, in the Southern Oral History Program Collection, transcript pp. 25–26.

41. Lu Ann Jones, *Mama Learned Us to Work: Farm Women in the New South* (Chapel Hill: University of North Carolina Press, 2002).

42. Hall et al., *Like a Family,* 147, 151.

43. Department of Labor, Bureau of Labor Statistics, "Cost of Living Schedules for Urban Families, 1918–1919."

44. Newby, *Plain Folk in the New South,* 222.

45. Ibid., 171.

46. Hall et al., *Like a Family,* 40.

47. Elizabeth S. D. Engelhardt, *A Mess of Greens: Southern Gender and Southern Food* (Athens: University of Georgia Press, 2011), 66.

48. United States Senate, *Report on the Condition of Woman and Child Wage-Earners in the United States,* 24.

49. Adyleen G. Merrick, Federal Writers Project MS, untitled, October 10, 1939, Library of Congress.

50. Department of Labor, Bureau of Labor Statistics, "Cost of Living Schedules for Urban Families, 1918–1919."

51. United States Senate, *Report on the Condition of Woman and Child Wage-Earners in the United States,* 23.

52. Ibid., 50–51.

53. Ibid., 46–47.

54. Newby, *Plain Folk in the New South,* 365–70; Harry M. Marks, "Epidemiologists Explain Pellagra: Gender, Race, and Political Economy in the Work of Edward Sydenstricker," *Journal of the History of Medicine and Allied Sciences* 58, no. 1 (January 2003): 35.

55. Elizabeth W. Etheridge. *The Butterfly Caste: A Social History of Pellagra in the South* (Westport, CT: Greenwood, 1972).

56. Marks, "Epidemiologists Explain Pellagra," 47–48.

57. Holland Thompson, "Life in a Southern Mill Town," *Political Science Quarterly* 15, no. 1 (March 1900): 1–13. Thompson claimed that in the mill town he investigated, workers ate an "extravagant" diet of canned food, "choice steaks," and imported produce out of season. However, as Engelhardt suggests, he may not have distinguished between the food on the grocers' shelves and the food that actually made it onto workers' tables. Engelhardt, *A Mess of Greens,* 127.

58. Newby, *Plain Folk in the New South,* 367.

59. United States Senate, *Report on the Condition of Woman and Child Wage-Earners in the United States,* 41.

60. Ibid., 53. Postum was a roasted-grain coffee substitute first developed in 1895. The members of this particular family were Mormons, and thus abstained from caffeine, but Postum shows up in the diets of other mill families as well.

61. United States Senate, *Report on the Condition of Woman and Child Wage-Earners in the United States,* 25.

62. The classic study of working-class families' changing fortunes as members grew and aged is Tamara K. Hareven, *Family Time and Industrial Time* (Cambridge: Cambridge University Press, 1982).

63. Department of Labor, Bureau of Labor Statistics, "Cost of Living Schedules for Urban Families, 1918–1919." See the Acklen (#6) and Cruse (#9) family schedules.

64. Interview with Betty Davidson by Allen Tullos, February 2 and 17, 1979, H-0019, in the Southern Oral History Program Collection #4007.

65. Department of Labor, Bureau of Labor Statistics, "Cost of Living Schedules for Urban Families, 1918–1919."

66. United States Senate, *Report on the Condition of Woman and Child Wage-Earners in the United States,* 27.

67. Interview with Harriet Arnow by Mimi Conway, April 1976, Interview G-0006, in the Southern Oral History Program Collection #4007, transcript p. 9.

68. Newby, *Plain Folks in the New South,* 61.

69. Interview with Eunice Austin by Jacquelyn Dowd Hall, 2 July 1980, H-0107, in the Southern Oral History Program Collection #4007.

70. Margaret Mulrooney, *A Legacy of Coal: The Coal Company Towns of Southwestern Pennsylvania,* Historic American Buildings Survey / Historic American Engineering Record (Washington, DC: National Parks Service, 1989), 12.

71. Hunt, *What the Coal Commission Found,* 136; Mulrooney, *A Legacy of Coal,* 14.

72. Mulrooney, *A Legacy of Coal,* 14.

73. Karen Bescherer Metheny, *From the Miner's Doublehouse: Archaeology and Landscape in a Pennsylvania Coal Company Town* (Knoxville: University of Tennessee Press, 2007), 55.

74. Mulrooney, *A Legacy of Coal,* 35.

75. Mulrooney, *A Legacy of Coal,* 59.

76. Harold W. Aurand, *Coalcracker Culture: Work and Values in Pennsylvania Anthracite, 1835–1935* (Selinsgrove: Susquehanna University Press, 2003), 31.

77. Mulrooney, *A Legacy of Coal,* 25.

78. Dennis F. Brestensky, Evelyn A. Hovanec, and Albert N. Skomra, eds., *Patch/Work Voices: The Culture and Lore of a Mining People* (University of Pittsburgh, 1978), 21–22.

79. Mulrooney, *A Legacy of Coal,* 25.

80. Hunt, *What the Coal Commission Found,* 136. The commission noted that the local percentage of foreign-born workers varied greatly. For example, there were fewer than 4 percent foreign-born workers in Alabama mines, where native white and African American workers predominated.

81. Metheny, *From the Miner's Doublehouse,* 59.

82. Ibid., 62.

83. Leslie H. Allen, *Industrial Housing Problems* (Boston: Aberthaw Construction, 1917), cited in Mulrooney, *A Legacy of Coal,* 23.

84. Mulrooney, *A Legacy of Coal,* 27.

85. Ibid., 16–19.

86. Ibid., 21.

87. Allen, *Industrial Housing Problems*, 12, cited in Mulrooney, *A Legacy of Coal*, 21.

88. Brestensky, Hovanec, and Skomra, *Patch/Work Voices*, 41.

89. Metheny, *From the Miner's Doublehouse*, 124.

90. Hunt, *What the Coal Commission Found*, 143.

91. Harold W. Aurand, *Coalcracker Culture: Work and Values in Pennsylvania Anthracite, 1835–1935* (Selinsgrove, PA: Susquehanna University Press, 2003), 25. Aurand cites Lehigh Valley Coal Company and Coxe Brothers and Company, *Valuation of 1916*, vol. 38, Eckley Miner's Village Museum.

92. Hunt, *What the Coal Commission Found*, 144.

93. Brestensky, Hovanec, and Skomra, *Patch/Work Voices*, 58.

94. Hunt, *What the Coal Commission Found*, 158.

95. Metheny, *From the Miner's Doublehouse*, 128–29.

96. Ibid., 216–17.

97. Department of Labor, Bureau of Labor Statistics, "Cost of Living Schedules for Urban Families, 1918–1919."

98. Metheny, *From the Miner's Doublehouse*, 3, 133.

99. Department of Labor, Bureau of Labor Statistics, "Cost of Living Schedules for Urban Families, 1918–1919."

100. Brestensky, Hovanec, and Skomra, *Patch/Work Voices*, 62.

101. Ibid., 63–64.

102. Ibid., 61.

103. Metheny, *From the Miner's Doublehouse*, 129.

104. Ibid., 130. Around 1900 the prosperous miners of Frostburg, Maryland, were reported to keep horses: "The expense of keeping the horses is of course far below the city standard, such an important charge as shoeing, for instance, being paid for with a bushel of potatoes from the home garden patch." Katherine A. Harvey, *The Best-Dressed Miners: Life and Labor in the Maryland Coal Region, 1835–1910* (Ithaca, NY: Cornell University Press, 1969), 97.

105. Hunt, *What the Coal Commission Found*, 138.

106. Metheny, *From the Miner's Doublehouse*, 98.

107. Ibid., 29, 186.

108. Ibid., 135.

109. Ibid., 65.

110. Aurand, *Coalcracker Culture*, 105.

111. Mulrooney, *A Legacy of Coal*, 106.

112. Hunt, *What the Coal Commission Found*, 151.

5. "A WOMAN'S WORK IS NEVER DONE"

1. Jeanne Boydston, "To Earn Her Daily Bread: Housework and Antebellum Working-Class Subsistence," *Radical History Review* 35 (1986): 19; Elizabeth Blackmar, *Manhattan for Rent, 1785–1850* (Ithaca, NY: Cornell University Press, 1989).

2. Ewa Morawska, *For Bread with Butter: The Life-Worlds of East Central Europeans in Johnstown, Pennsylvania, 1890–1940* (Cambridge: Cambridge University Press, 1985), 130.

3. Scott Nearing, *Financing the Wage-Earner's Family: A Survey of the Facts Bearing on Income and Expenditures in the Families of American Wage-Earners* (New York: B. W. Huebsch, 1914), 85.

4. Lois Rita Helmbold, "Beyond the Family Economy: Black and White Working-Class Women during the Great Depression," *Feminist Studies* 13, no. 3 (Fall 1987): 629–55.

5. Ibid.

6. Bonnie Fox, ed., *Hidden in the Household: Women's Domestic Labour under Capitalism* (Toronto: The Women's Press, 1980).

7. Ruth Schwarz Cowan, *More Work for Mother: The Ironies of Household Technology from the Open Hearth to the Microwave* (New York: Basic Books, 1983), 24.

8. Ibid., 63–64.

9. Gamber's work on dressmakers and boardinghouse keepers illustrates the many ways nineteenth-century women engaged in business. See also Gamber, *The Female Economy: The Millinery and Dressmaking Trades, 1860–1930* (Urbana: University of Illinois Press, 1997).

10. Wendy Gamber, *The Boardinghouse in Nineteenth-Century America* (Baltimore, MD: Johns Hopkins University Press, 2007), 117, 122.

11. Nicole Tonkovich, foreword to *The American Woman's Home* by Catherine E. Beecher and Harriet Beecher Stowe (Hartford, CT: Harriet Beecher Stowe Center; Rutgers University Press, 2002).

12. Ibid.

13. Sarah Stage and Virginia B. Vincenti, eds., *Rethinking Home Economics: Women and the History of a Profession* (Ithaca, NY: Cornell University Press, 1997).

14. Sally M. Miller, "Social Democratic Millennium: Visions of Gender," in *Expectations for the Millennium: American Socialist Visions of the Future,* ed. Peter H. Buckingham (Westport, CT: Greenwood Press, 2002), 60.

15. *Chicago Daily Socialist,* November 26, 1906 (emphasis in the original).

16. On Socialist critiques of domestic life, see also Francis Robert Schor, *Utopianism and Radicalism in a Reforming America* (Westport, CT: Greenwood Press, 1997), especially chapters 1 and 2.

17. Kate Weigand, *Red Feminism: American Communism and the Making of Women's Liberation* (Baltimore, MD: Johns Hopkins University Press, 2001), 28.

18. Dolores Hayden, *The Grand Domestic Revolution: A History of Feminist Design for American Homes, Neighborhoods, and Cities* (Cambridge, MA: MIT Press, 1981), chapters 2 and 10.

19. Miller, "Social Democratic Millennium," 59; Mark W. Van Wienen, "A Rose by Any Other Name: Charlotte Perkins Stetson (Gilman) and the Case for American Reform Socialism," *American Quarterly* 55, no. 4 (December 2003): 603–34. Van Wienen points out that although Gilman repudiated much of her Socialist

activity during the 1930s, she lectured and published frequently on reform socialism during the 1890s, when she was Charlotte Perkins Stetson. Gilman advocated "gradualist" or "reform" socialism (as opposed to "revolutionary" socialism) at least through the 1890s; she was involved with Nationalism, Populism, and Fabianism, and promoted centralized, commercial services to replace housework.

20. Laura Shapiro, *Perfection Salad: Women and Cooking at the Turn of the Century* (New York: Farrar, Straus and Giroux, 1986), 210.

21. Michael McGerr, *A Fierce Discontent: The Rise and Fall of the Progressive Movement in America, 1870–1920* (New York: Free Press, 2003), 79.

22. Ibid., 79.

23. Suellen Hoy, *Chasing Dirt: The American Pursuit of Cleanliness* (New York: Oxford University Press, 1995), 102.

24. Linda Gordon identifies a similar situation, in which inadequate knowledge of context promoted moralistic judgments in the case of welfare for single mothers in *Pitied but Not Entitled: Single Mothers and the History of Welfare* (Cambridge, MA: Harvard University Press, 1994).

25. Frederick Douglass Opie, *Hog and Hominy: Soul Food from Africa to America* (New York: Columbia University Press, 2008), 58.

26. Robert J. Casey, *Chicago Medium Rare* (Indianapolis: Bobbs-Merrill, 1949), 107; cited in William D. Panschar, *Baking in America: Economic Development. Volume I* (Evanston, IL: Northwestern University Press, 1956), 96.

27. "The Full Dinner Pail," *Daily People* (New York), July 21 1900.

28. Mary Hinman Abel, *Practical Sanitary and Economic Cooking Adapted to Persons of Moderate and Small Means* (Rochester, NY: American Public Health Association, 1890), 177.

29. This campaign promise was roundly rejected by the Socialist newspaper the *Daily People*: "The dinner pail is obsolete. It is an anachronism, a memory of the halcyon days when you could get three dollars for ten hours work, and for three dollars you could get three square meals, one of which was carried in the pail. The average laborer to-day carries his dinner in a paper bag in his pocket, or else in a small box. He does not have enough to make a pail necessary." Furthermore, the author protested the idealization of the dinner pail: "At the very best, the fact that a man must eat a cold, tasteless meal, and one that becomes clammy from its confinement in a tin pail, should arouse the working class." "The Full Dinner Pail."

30. Margaret F. Byington, *Homestead: The Households of a Mill Town* (reprint, Pittsburgh: University Center for International Studies, University of Pittsburgh, 1974), 64.

31. "News for Somebody's Wife," *Daily People* (New York), August 13, 1911.

32. Lucille Baldwin van Slyke, "The Dinner Pail: A Story," *Craftsman* 18, no. 3 (June 1910): 335–46.

33. "Philadelphia Free Soup," *Charities Review* 10, no. 2 (April 1900): 52.

34. Mary Hinman Abel and Ellen Richards, *The Story of the New England Kitchen: Part II: A Study in Social Economics* (Boston: Press of Rockwell and Churchill, 1893), 162.

35. One of the early focuses of the pure food reform movement, frequently discussed in the popular press, was the synthetic dyes used to color cheap candy and ice cream. Journalists liked to portray ragged slum children spending their pennies on unnaturally colored, unhealthy, and probably poisonous confections. See "The Nation's Annual Candy Bill," *New York Times,* January 2, 1910; "Stuff One Gets in Candy. Sulphurous Acid, Glue, and Shellac Some of It," *Daily People* (New York), February 21, 1910.

36. Annual Report, the Starr Centre, 1909, p. 19; Annual Reports collection, box 84, folder "Starr Centre," Urban Archives, Paley Library, Temple University. The graham wafers, pretzels, coffee cakes, stewed prunes, rice pudding, hominy, and bean soup were noted as "very popular."

37. Ibid.

38. Ibid., 20.

39. Ibid. McGerr finds a few other Progressives grappling with the worry that well-meaning public institutions could supplant, rather than support, the home. *Fierce Discontent,* 115.

40. Ellen H. Richards, "Housekeeping in the Twentieth Century," *American Kitchen Magazine* 12, no. 6 (March 1900): 204.

41. Ellen H. Richards, ed., *The Cost of Living as Modified by Sanitary Science* (New York: J. Wiley, 1913), 85; Richards, "Housekeeping in the Twentieth Century," 204.

42. Richards, *The Cost of Living,* 83.

43. Ibid., 25–26.

44. Katherine C. Grier's *Culture and Comfort: Parlor Making and Middle-Class Identity, 1850–1930* (Washington, DC: Smithsonian Institution Press, 1988) remains the best discussion of the manifold cultural implications of middle-class homes and furnishings, especially in the parlor. See especially the introduction on the symbolism of home furnishing.

45. Harvey Green, *The Light of the Home: An Intimate View of the Lives of Women in Victorian America* (New York: Pantheon Books, 1983), 59.

46. Walter Keith, "A Model $2000 House," *Ladies' Home Journal,* March 1897, 25.

47. Clifford E. Clark Jr., "The Vision of the Dining Room: Plan Book Dreams and Middle-Class Realities," in *Dining in America, 1850–1900,* ed. Kathryn Grover (Amherst: University of Massachusetts Press; Rochester: Margaret Woodbury Strong Museum, 1987), 162–63.

48. Priscilla J. Brewer, *From Fireplace to Cookstove: Technology and the Domestic Ideal in America* (Syracuse, NY: Syracuse University Press, 2000), 194–95.

49. Plante, Ellen M. *The American Kitchen 1700 to the Present* (New York: Facts on File, 1995), 117.

50. W. O. Atwater and Charles D. Woods, "Dietary Studies in New York City in 1895 and 1896," USDA Office of Experiment Stations, Bulletin No. 46 (Washington, DC: Government Printing Office, 1898), 26.

51. Ibid.

52. Ibid., 28.

53. The improvement in the family's standard of living suggests that the new rooms were larger, but this information is not directly stated in the report.

54. Atwater and Woods, "Dietary Studies," 28.

55. Christine Frederick, *Selling Mrs. Consumer* (New York: Business Bourse, 1929).

56. Shapiro, *Perfection Salad,* chapter 8.

6. WHAT'S FOR DINNER TONIGHT?

1. Donna R. Gabaccia, *We Are What We Eat: Ethnic Food and the Making of Americans* (Cambridge, MA: Harvard University Press, 1998).

2. Michael Pollan, "Unhappy Meals," *New York Times,* January 28, 2007.

3. Ann Vileisis, *Kitchen Literacy: How We Lost Knowledge of Where Food Comes From and Why We Need to Get It Back* (Washington: Island Press, 2008).

4. Laura Shapiro, *Something from the Oven: Reinventing Dinner in 1950s America* (New York: Penguin, 2004), 47.

5. Susanne Freidberg, *Fresh: A Perishable History* (Cambridge, MA: Belknap Press of Harvard University Press, 2009), 184–90.

6. Harvey Levenstein, *Paradox of Plenty: A Social History of Eating in Modern America* (New York: Oxford University Press, 1993), 108–10.

7. Katherine J. Parkin, *Food Is Love: Advertising and Gender Roles in Modern America* (Philadelphia: University of Pennsylvania Press, 2006).

8. Shapiro, *Something from the Oven,* vxii.

9. Andrew P. Haley, *Turning the Tables: Restaurants and the Rise of the American Middle Class, 1880–1920* (Chapel Hill: University of North Carolina Press, 2011).

10. Levenstein, *Paradox of Plenty,* chapter 3, p. 15.

11. Candy Sagon, "Cooking 101: Add 1 Cup of Simplicity; As Kitchen Skills Dwindle, Recipes Become Easy as Pie," *Washington Post,* March 18, 2006.

12. Although the Food Network does broadcast several shows devoted to "everyday cooking," many of them—like Sandra Lee's *Semi-Homemade Cooking*—rely heavily on premade components. The network's most popular programs are competition shows that are hardly related to home cooking.

13. Shapiro, *Something from the Oven,* x–xix.

14. Here I am borrowing Roland Marchand's concept of advertising fables from *Advertising the American Dream: Making Way for Modernity, 1920–1940* (Berkeley: University of California Press, 1985).

15. Julie Guthman uses the term "alternative food" to describe the various people, groups, and institutions organized around "fresh, local, seasonal, organic, and craft-produced food." Julie Guthman, *Weighing In: Obesity, Food Justice, and the Limits of Capitalism* (Berkeley: University of California Press, 2011), 3.

16. Ibid., 151–53.

17. Freidberg, *Fresh,* 281.

BIBLIOGRAPHY

ARCHIVAL COLLECTIONS

Bureau of Labor Statistics Records, National Archives II, College Park, Maryland.

Business directories, Chicago Historical Society.

Business directories, New York Public Library.

Chicago Foreign Language Press Survey. University of Chicago Special Collections.

Department of Labor, Bureau of Labor Statistics. "Cost of Living Schedules for Urban Families, 1918–1919." Record Group 257, Bureau of Labor Statistics, Entry #36. Stack area 530, row 55, compartment 1, shelf 6, ff, Boxes 1–91. National Archives II, College Park, Maryland

Federal Writer's Project, Library of Congress.

Immigrant in America microfilm collection, Historical Society of Pennsylvania.

Leonard Covello Papers, Historical Society of Pennsylvania.

Margaret Mead records, Historical Society of Pennsylvania.

National Child Labor Committee Collection, Library of Congress, Prints and Photographs Collection, Library of Congress.

National Council of Jewish Women, Oral History Project. Archives of Industrial Society, University of Pittsburgh Library.

Southern Oral History Program Collection, Southern Historical Collection, Wilson Library, University of North Carolina at Chapel Hill.

Urban Archives, Paley Library, Temple University.

"Women, Ethnicity, and Mental Health: A Comparative Oral History Project, 1975–1977." Archives of Industrial Society, Hillman Library, University of Pittsburgh.

Women's Educational and Industrial Union. Schlesinger Library, Harvard University

Abel, Mary Hinman. *Practical Sanitary and Economic Cooking Adapted to Persons of Moderate and Small Means.* Rochester, NY: American Public Health Association, 1890.

Abel, Mary Hinman, and Ellen Richards. *The Story of the New England Kitchen: Part II: A Study in Social Economics.* Boston: Press of Rockwell and Churchill, 1893.

Abbot, Edith. *The Tenements of Chicago, 1908–1935.* Chicago: University of Chicago Press, 1936.

Addams, Jane. *Twenty Years at Hull-House.* Urbana: University of Illinois Press, 1990.

Albrecht, Arthur E. *About Food and Markets: A Teacher's Handbook and Consumer's Guide.* New York: Teachers' College, Columbia University, 1932.

Allen, Leslie H. *Industrial Housing Problems.* Boston: Aberthaw Construction, 1917.

Antin, Mary. *The Promised Land.* Boston: Houghton Mifflin, 1912.

———. *They Who Knock at Our Gates: A Complete Gospel of Immigration.* Boston: Houghton Mifflin, 1914.

Atwater, W. O. "Meat vs. Vegetables." *Harper's Weekly,* October 14, 1889, 1051.

Atwater, W. O., and A. P. Bryant. "Dietary Studies in New York City in 1896 and 1897." USDA Office of Experiment Stations, Bulletin No. 116. Washington, DC: Government Printing Office, 1902.

Atwater, W. O., and Charles. D. Woods. "Dietary Studies in New York City in 1895 and 1896." USDA Office of Experiment Stations, Bulletin No. 46. Washington, DC: Government Printing Office, 1898.

"Bakery Bosses Demand Right and Justice through Arbitration." *Daily Jewish Courier,* April 29, 1918.

"Bakery Owners Declare Guerilla War Against their Workers." *Forward,* December 19, 1920.

Banks, Reverend Louis Albert. *White Slaves, or, The Oppression of the Worthy Poor.* Boston: Lee and Shepard Publishers, 1893.

Beecher, Catharine. *Miss Beecher's Domestic Receipt Book Designed as a Supplement to Her Treatise on Domestic Economy.* New York : Harper & Brothers, 1852.

Bell, Thomas. *Out of This Furnace.* 1941. Reprint, Pittsburgh: University of Pittsburgh Press, 1976.

Bellamy, Edward. *Looking Backward, 2000–1887.* Boston: Houghton Mifflin, 1889.

Benton, Caroline French. *Living on a Little.* Boston: Page, 1908.

Bercovici, Konrad. *Around the World in New York.* New York: The Century Co., 1924.

Bernstein, Nina. "Groceries on the Computer, and Immigrants in the Cold," *New York Times,* December 22, 2007.

Bevier, Isabel. "Nutrition Investigations in Pittsburg *[sic]*, Pennsylvania, 1894–1896." USDA Office of Experiment Stations, Bulletin No. 52. Washington, DC: Government Printing Office, 1898.

Bigelow, W. D., and Burton J. Howard. *Some Forms of Food Adulteration and Simple Methods for Their Detection*. USDA Bureau of Chemistry, Bulletin No. 100. Washington, DC: Government Printing Office, 1906.

Bosworth, Louise Marion. *The Living Wage of Women Workers: A Study of Incomes and Expenditures of Four Hundred and Fifty Women Workers in the City of Boston*. Philadelphia: American Academy of Political and Social Science, 1911.

Brandenburg, Broughton. *Imported Americans: The Story of the Experiences of a Disguised American and His Wife Studying the Immigrant Question*. New York: Frederick A. Stokes, 1904.

"Bread Sold by Weight." *Daily People* (New York), September 12, 1913.

Breckinridge, Sophonisba P. *New Homes for Old*. Reprint, Montclair, NJ: Patterson Smith, 1971.

Brewer, Daniel Chauncey. *The Conquest of New England by the Immigrant*. New York: G. P. Putnam's Sons, 1926.

"Burned by Gas Explosion." *Daily People* (New York), November 6, 1905.

Byington, Margaret F. *Homestead: The Households of a Mill Town*. 1910. Reprint, Pittsburgh: University Center for International Studies, University of Pittsburgh, 1974.

Calkins, Raymond. *Substitutes for the Saloon*. Boston: Houghton Mifflin, 1901.

Campbell, Helen. *Prisoners of Poverty: Women Wage-Workers, Their Trades and Their Lives*. 1887. Reprint, Westport, CT: Greenwood Press, 1970.

Campbell, Helen, Colonel Thomas W. Knox, and Thomas Byrnes. *Darkness and Daylight; or, Lights and Shadows of New York Life*. 1895. Reprint, Detroit: Singing Tree Press, Book Tower, 1969.

Carr, John Foster. *Guide to the United States for the Jewish Immigrant: A Nearly Literal Translation of the Second Yiddish Edition*. New York: Connecticut Daughters of the American Revolution, 1913.

Chapin, Robert Coit. *The Standard of Living among Workingmen's Families in New York City*. New York: Charities Publication Committee, 1909.

Chicago Municipal Markets Commission, "Preliminary Report to the Mayor and Aldermen of the City of Chicago by the Chicago Municipal Markets Commission." Chicago, April 27, 1914.

Clark, Sue Ainslie, and Edith Wyatt. *Making Both Ends Meet: The Income and Outlay of New York Working Girls*. New York: Macmillan, 1911.

"Cost of Living in the United States." U.S. Department of Labor and the Bureau of Labor Statistics, Bulletin No. 357, May 1924. Washington, DC: Government Printing Office, 1924.

"Cost of Production: Iron, Steel, Coal, etc." Sixth Annual Report of the Commissioner of Labor, 1890. Washington, DC: Government Printing Office, 1891.

Covello, Leonard, and Guido D'Agostino. *The Heart Is the Teacher*. New York: McGraw-Hill, 1958.

"A Crusade for Health." *New York Times,* April 1, 1902.

Daley, Agnes. "Life in a New Tenement House." *Charities: The Official Organ of the Charity Organization Society of the City of New York* 5, no. 28 (December 8, 1900): 3.

Davis, Jerome. *The Russian Immigrant.* New York: MacMillan, 1922.

Di Domenico, Angelo. *Graded Lessons in English for Italians: An Aid in Americanization.* Boston: Christopher Publishing House, 1922.

Donovan, Frances R. *The Saleslady.* Reprint, New York: Arno Press, 1974.

Economical Hints, Prepared for the Industrial Aid Society. Boston: Franklin Press and Rand, Avery, 1879.

Farmer, Fannie Merritt. *Boston Cooking School Cook Book.* Boston: Little, Brown, 1896.

———. *What to Have for Dinner.* New York: Dodge, 1905.

Faxon, Florence R. "Shall Bread Be Made in the Home?" *American Kitchen Magazine* 12, no. 3 (December 1899).

Fishberg, Maurice. *Health and Sanitation of the Immigrant Jewish Population of New York.* New York: Press of Philip Cowen, ca. 1902.

"Food Expenditures by Families and Individuals as a Share of Disposable Personal Income." Economic Research Service, United States Department of Agriculture. www.ers.usda.gov/Briefing/CPIFoodAndExpenditures/Data/Expenditures_tables/table7.htm. Accessed September 23, 2011.

"Food Preservation in New York." *Harper's Weekly,* July 4, 1891.

Frederick, Christine. *Selling Mrs. Consumer.* New York: Business Bourse, 1929.

"The Free Lunch Microbe." *New York Times,* July 31, 1904.

"The Full Dinner Pail." *Daily People* (New York), July 21, 1900.

Gephardt, F. C. *Analysis and Cost of Ready-to-Serve Foods: A Study in Food Economics.* Chicago: Press of the American Medical Association, 1915.

Gibson, Campbell. "Population of the 100 Largest Cities and Other Urban Places in the United States: 1790 to 1990." U.S. Census Bureau. www.census.gov/population/www/documentation/twps0027.html. Accessed January 15, 2008.

Gilbert, L. H. "Factors Influencing Nutrition Work among Italians." *Journal of Home Economics* 14 (January 1922): 14–19.

Gilman, Charlotte Perkins. *Charlotte Perkins Gilman: A Nonfiction Reader.* New York: Columbia University Press, 1991.

Greenough, Marietta McPherson. *Better Meals for Less Money.* New York: H. Holt, 1917.

Harbison, Edith Gwendolyn. *Low Cost Recipes.* Philadelphia: George W. Jacobs, 1914.

Howerth, I. W. "Are the Italians a Dangerous Class?" *The Charities Review: A Journal of Practical Sociology* 4, no. 1: 17-40.

"How Much Is That?" *EH.Net: Economic History Services,* ed. Samuel H. Williamson. www.measuringworth.com/ppowerus/. Accessed September 13, 2013.

Hughes, Dora Morrell. *Thrift in the Household.* Boston: Lothrop, Lee, and Shepard, 1918.

"Italian Housewives' Dishes." *New York Times,* June 7, 1903.

J. A. Bell's advertisement. *Chicago Defender,* June 10, 1916.

"Jewish Bakers Win a Raise by the Bosses." *Forward,* May 29, 1923.

"Jewish Women." *Daily Jewish Courier,* July 8, 1912.

Kander, Lizzie Black. *The Settlement Cook Book: Containing Many Recipes Used in Settlement Cooking Classes, The Milwaukee Public School Cooking Centers and Gathered from Various Other Reliable Sources.* Milwaukee, 1901.

Keith, Walter. "A Model $2000 House." *Ladies' Home Journal,* March 1897.

Kirkpatrick, V. G. "War-Time Work of the Visiting Housekeeper." In *Yearbook of the United Charities of Chicago.* Chicago: United Charities of Chicago, 1917.

Kittredge, Mabel Hyde. *Housekeeping Notes: How to Furnish and Keep House in a Tenement Flat.* Boston: Whitcomb and Barrows, 1911.

Lagerquist, Walter E. "Social Geography of the Lower East Side." *New York Times,* April 3, 1910.

Lea, Elizabeth Ellicott. *Domestic Cookery, Useful Receipts, and Hints to Young Housekeepers.* Baltimore, MD: Cushings and Bailey, 1869.

Leeds, John B. *The Household Budget: With a Special Inquiry into the Amount and Value of Household Work.* Philadelphia: J. B Leeds, 1917.

Lincolns, Mary J. *Mrs. Lincoln's Boston Cook Book: What to Do and What Not to Do in Cooking.* Boston: Roberts Brothers, 1884.

"Making Housekeepers in the City Schools." *New York Times,* June 14, 1908.

Marlow, Alvan. "Cheap Restaurants. Mysteries of the Caravanserais of the Wretched." *Daily People* (New York), August 6, 1900.

Martin, Elizabeth Ann. "Detroit and the Great Migration, 1916–1929." Bentley Historical Library, University of Michigan. http://bentley.umich.edu/research/publications/migration/ch1.php. Accessed February 17, 2012.

McCabe, James D. *New York by Sunlight and Gaslight: A Work Descriptive of the Great American Metropolis.* Philadelphia: Douglass Brothers, 1882.

McKibin, Jean, ed. *The Frugal Colonial Housewife.* Reprint, Garden City, NY: Dolphin Books, Doubleday, 1976.

McPherson, Marietta. *Better Meals for Less Money.* Greenough, NY: H. Holt, 1917.

McTaggart, Jenny. "Online Retailing: E-Grocery's Reality Check." *Progressive Grocer,* August 1, 2006.

Melendy, Royal L. "The Saloon in Chicago, Part II." *American Journal of Sociology* 6, no. 4 (January 1901): 433–64

More, Louise Bolard. *Wage-Earners' Budgets: A Study of Standards and Cost of Living in New York City.* 1907. Reprint, New York: Arno Press and the New York Times, 1971.

"The Nation's Annual Candy Bill." *New York Times,* January 2, 1910.

National Industrial Conference Board. *The Cost of Living among Wage-Earners.* Research Report No. 24. Boston, 1919.

Nearing, Scott. *Financing the Wage-Earner's Family: A Survey of the Facts Bearing on Income and Expenditures in the Families of American Wage-Earners.* New York: B. W. Huebsch, 1914.

Nesbitt, Florence. *Low Cost Cooking*. Chicago: American School of Home Economics, 1924.

The New England Cook Book. Boston: Chas. E. Brown, 1905.

"New York's Food—The Same Old Adulteration Going On, Says Health Department." *Daily People* (New York), March 15, 1908.

"News for Somebody's Wife." *Daily People* (New York), August 13, 1911.

Parloa, Maria. *Miss Parloa's New Cook Book and Marketing Guide*. Boston: Estes & Lauriat, 1880.

Pehotsky, Bessie Olga. *The Slavic Immigrant Woman*. Cincinnati: Powell & White, 1925.

"People Unmarried." *Daily People* (New York), September 21, 1913.

"Philadelphia Free Soup." *Charities Review* 10, no. 2 (April 1900): 52.

Reid, Margaret G. *Food for People*. New York: John Wiley & Sons, 1943.

Residents of Hull-House, *Hull-House Maps and Papers*. New York: Thomas Y. Crowell, 1895.

Reynolds, Marcus T. *The Housing of the Poor in American Cities*. 1893. Reprint, College Park, MD: McGrath, 1969.

Richards, Ellen H., ed. *The Cost of Living as Modified by Sanitary Science*. New York: J. Wiley, 1913.

———. "Housekeeping in the Twentieth Century." *American Kitchen Magazine* 12, no. 6 (March 1900).

———. *Plain Words about Food: The Rumford Kitchen Leaflets*. Boston: Home Science Publishing, 1899.

Richards, Paul. *The Lunch Room*. Chicago: Hotel Monthly, 1916.

Richardson, Dorothy. *The Long Day: The Story of a New York Working Girl*. 1905. Reprint, Charlottesville: University of Virginia Press, 1990.

Rischin, Moses. *The Promised City: New York's Jews, 1870–1914*. Cambridge, MA: Harvard University Press, 1962.

———, ed. *Grandma Never Lived in America: The New Journalism of Abraham Cahan*. Bloomington: Indiana University Press, 1985.

Roberts, Peter. *Anthracite Coal Communities: A Study of the Demography, the Social, Educational, and Moral Life of the Anthracite Regions*. New York: Macmillan, 1904.

"Roosevelt Quizzes Girl Dress Strikers." *New York Times,* January 22, 1913.

Rorer, Sarah Tyson. "Indian Corn Kitchen." *Household News,* October 1893, 121–22.

"Rosenthal and Stern the First to Sign Agreement with Jewish Waiters' Union." *Forward,* June 26, 1923.

Roth, Terry. "Street Cries and Criers of New York." November 3, 1938. Library of Congress, Manuscript Division, WPA Federal Writers' Project Collection. "American Life Histories: Manuscripts from the Federal Writers' Project, 1936–1940." http://memory.loc.gov/ammem/wpaintro/wpahome.html. Accessed March 14, 2011.

Russo, Pasquale. *Twelve O'Clock Lunch (The astonishing truth regarding the filthy and unsanitary conditions existing in the Hotels, Restaurants and Lunch Rooms)*. Chicago: Pasquale Russo, 1923.

Sagon, Candy. "Cooking 101: Add 1 Cup of Simplicity; As Kitchen Skills Dwindle, Recipes Become Easy as Pie." *Washington Post,* March 18, 2006.

Sanborn, Alvan Francis. *Moody's Lodging House and Other Tenement Sketches.* Boston: Copeland and Day, 1895.

Schiavo, Giovanni E. *The Italians in Chicago: A Study in Americanization.* Chicago: Italian American Publishing, 1928.

Sears, Roebuck Catalogue, 1897. Reprint, Philadelphia: Chelsea House, 1968.

Simkhovitch, Mary Kingsbury. *The City Workers' World in America.* New York: Macmillan, 1917.

Sinclair, Upton. *The Jungle.* 1906. Reprint, New York: Barnes & Noble, 1995.

Smith, Bertha. "The Gospel of Simplicity as Applied to Tenement Homes." *Craftsman,* October 1905, 81–91.

Smith, Betty. *A Tree Grows in Brooklyn.* Everybody's Vacation Publishing, 1943.

Smith, Jacqueline Harrison. *Famous Old Recipes Used One Hundred Years and More in Kitchens of the North and South.* Philadelphia: J. C. Winston, 1908.

Smith, Mary Stuart. *Virginia Cookery Book.* New York: Harper and Brothers, 1883.

"Socialism and the Family." *Daily People* (New York), Sunday, August 13, 1911.

Streightoff, Frank Hatch. *The Standard of Living among the Industrial People of America.* Boston: Houghton Mifflin, 1911.

"Stuff One Gets in Candy. Sulphurous Acid, Glue, and Shellac Some of It." *Daily People* (New York), February 21, 1910.

Sullivan, J. W. *Markets for the People: The Consumer's Part.* New York: Macmillan, 1913.

Tabb's Quick Lunch advertisement. *Chicago Defender,* February 22, 1919.

"Tenement Number Six." *Daily People* (New York), August 11, 1911.

Thompson, Holland. "Life in a Southern Mill Town." *Political Science Quarterly* 15, no. 1 (March 1900): 1–13.

Townsend, Edward W. *A Daughter of the Tenements.* New York: Lovell, Coryell, 1895.

"The United Hebrew Trades." *The World,* January 8, 1916.

United States Census Bureau. *Report on Transportation Business in the United States at the Eleventh Census 1890.*

United States Senate. *Report on the Condition of Woman and Child Wage-Earners in the United States. Vol. 16, Family Budgets of Typical Cotton-Mill Workers.* Senate Document No. 645, 61st Cong., 2d. sess. Washington, DC: Government Printing Office, 1911.

"Unsanitary Factories." *L'Italia,* June 23, 1906.

Utah Dairy and Food Commission. *Simple Household Tests for the Detection of Adulteration in Food.* Salt Lake City, 1906.

Van Slyke, Lucille Baldwin. "The Dinner Pail: A Story." *Craftsman* 18, no. 3 (June 1910): 335–46.

Veiller, Lawrence. *Housing Conditions and Tenement Laws in Leading American Cities* (prepared for the Tenement House Commission). New York: Evening Post Job Printing House, 1900.

Ward, Elizabeth M. "With Planning and Staples, Dinner Need Not Be a Chore." *Boston Globe,* October 9, 2003.

"Why Was the Price of Bread Raised?" *Daily Jewish Courier,* March 9, 1922.

Wilder, Laura Ingalls. *Farmer Boy.* New York: Harper, 1953.

Wing, Frank E. "Thirty-Five Years of Typhoid: The Fever's Economic Cost to Pittsburgh and the Long Fight for Pure Water." *Charities and the Commons,* February 6, 1909.

Women's Centennial Executive Committee. *The National Cookery Book. Compiled from Original Receipts, for the Women's Centennial Committees of the International Exhibition of 1876.* Philadelphia: Women's Centennial Executive Committee, 1876.

Woods, Bertha M. *Foods of the Foreign-Born in Relation to Health.* Boston: Whitcomb and Barrows, 1922.

Woods, Robert A., et al. *The Poor in Great Cities: Their Problems and What Is Doing to Solve Them.* New York: Charles Scribner's sons, 1895.

Woods, Robert A., and Albert J. Kennedy. *The Settlement Horizon: A National Estimate.* New York: Russell Sage Foundation, 1922.

SECONDARY SOURCES

Ade, George. *The Old-Time Saloon: Not Wet—Not Dry, Just History.* New York: R. Long & R. R. Smith, 1931.

Albala, Ken. *Food in Early Modern Europe.* Westport, CT: Greenwood Press, 2003.

Albrecht, Arthur E. *About Food and Markets: A Teacher's Handbook and Consumer's Guide.* New York: Teachers' College, Columbia University, 1932.

American Reformers. The H. W. Wilson Company, 1985. WilsonWeb. Accessed November 25, 2007.

Apple, Rima D. "Liberal Arts or Vocational Training? Home Economics Education for Girls." In *Rethinking Home Economics: Women and the History of a Profession,* ed. Sarah Stage and Virginia B. Vincenti. Ithaca, NY: Cornell University Press, 1997.

———. *Vitamania: Vitamins in American Culture.* New Brunswick, NJ: Rutgers University Press, 1996.

Aronson, Naomi. "Social Definitions of Entitlement: Food Needs, 1885–1920." *Media Culture and Society* 4 (January 1982): 51–61.

Aurand, Harold W. *Coalcracker Culture: Work and Values in Pennsylvania Anthracite, 1835–1935.* Selinsgrove, PA: Susquehanna University Press, 2003.

Bane, Lita. *The Story of Isabel Bevier.* Peoria, IL: Chas. A. Bennett, 1955.

Barrett, James R. "Unity and Fragmentation: Class, Race, and Ethnicity on Chicago's South Side, 1900–1922." *Journal of Social History* 18, no. 1 (Autumn 1984).

———. *Work and Community in the Jungle: Chicago's Packinghouse Workers, 1894–1922.* Urbana: University of Illinois Press, 1987.

Beecher, Catharine E., and Harriet Beecher Stowe. *The American Woman's Home.* ed. Nicole Tonkovich. Hartford, CT: Harriet Beecher Stowe Center; Rutgers University Press, 2002.

Belasco, Warren. *Appetite for Change: How the Counterculture Took on the Food Industry.* New York: Pantheon Books, 1989.

———. *Meals to Come: A History of the Future of Food.* Berkeley: University of California Press, 2006.

Benson, Susan Porter. *Household Accounts: Working-Class Family Economies in the Interwar United States.* Ithaca, NY: Cornell University Press, 2007.

———. "Living on the Margin: Working-Class Marriages and Family Survival Strategies in the United States, 1919–1941." In *The Sex of Things: Gender and Consumption in Historical Perspective,* ed. Victoria de Grazia and Ellen Furlough, 212–43. Berkeley: University of California Press, 1996.

Bentley, Amy. *Eating for Victory: Food Rationing and the Politics of Domesticity.* Urbana: University of Illinois Press, 1998.

Bittman, Mark. "Is Junk Food Really Cheaper?" *New York Times,* September 24, 2011.

Blackmar, Elizabeth. *Manhattan for Rent, 1785–1850.* Ithaca, NY: Cornell University Press, 1989.

Bluestone, Daniel. "The Pushcart Evil." In *The Landscape of Modernity: Essays on New York City, 1900–1940,* ed. David Ward and Olivier Zunz. New York: Russell Sage Foundation, 1992.

Bodnar, John. *The Transplanted: A History of Immigrants in Urban America.* Bloomington: Indiana University Press, 1985.

Bodnar, John, Roger Simon, and Michael P. Weber. *Lives of Their Own: Blacks, Italians, and Poles in Pittsburgh, 1900–1960.* Urbana: University of Illinois Press, 1982.

Boydston, Jeanne. *Home and Work: Housework, Wages, and the Ideology of Labor in the Early Republic.* New York: Oxford University Press, 1990.

———. "To Earn Her Daily Bread: Housework and Antebellum Working-Class Subsistence." *Radical History Review* 35 (1986): 7–25.

Brestensky, Dennis F., Evelyn A. Hovanec, and Albert N. Skomra, eds. *Patch/Work Voices: The Culture and Lore of a Mining People.* Pittsburgh: University of Pittsburgh Press, 1978.

Brewer, Priscilla J. *From Fireplace to Cookstove: Technology and the Domestic Ideal in America.* Syracuse, NY: Syracuse University Press, 2000.

Brownlee, W. Elliot. *Dynamics of Ascent: A History of the American Economy.* New York: Alfred A. Knopf, 1974.

Burgess, Thomas. *Greeks in America: An Account of Their Coming, Progress, Customs, Living, and Aspirations.* Boston: Sherman, French, 1913.

Burks, J. D. "Clean Milk and Public Health." *Annals of the American Academy of Political and Social Science* 37 (1911).

Carlton, David L. *Mill and Town in South Carolina, 1880–1920.* Baton Rouge: Louisiana State University Press, 1982.

Chudacoff, Howard P. *The Age of the Bachelor: Creating an American Subculture.* Princeton, NY: Princeton University Press, 1999.

Clark, Anna. "The Foodie Indictment of Feminism." Salon.com, May 26, 2010. www.salon.com/2010/05/26/foodies_and_feminism/. Accessed May 31, 2010.

Clark Jr., Clifford E. "The Vision of the Dining Room: Plan Book Dreams and Middle-Class Realities." In *Dining in America, 1850–1900*, ed. Kathryn Grover. Amherst: University of Massachusetts Press; Rochester: Margaret Woodbury Strong Museum, 1987.

Coan, Peter Morton. *Ellis Island Interviews: In Their Own Words.* New York: Facts on File, 1997.

Cochrane, Willard W. *The Development of American Agriculture: A Historical Analysis.* Minneapolis: University of Minnesota Press, 1979.

Cohen, Lizabeth A. "Embellishing a Life of Labor: An Interpretation of the Material Culture of American Working-Class Homes, 1885–1915." *Journal of American Culture* 3, no. 4 (Winter 1980): 752–75.

———. *Making a New Deal: Industrial Workers in Chicago, 1919–1939.* Cambridge: Cambridge University Press, 1990.

Coleman-Jensen, Alisha, Mark Nord, Margaret Andrews, and Steven Carlson. *Household Food Security in the United States in 2010.* ERR-125, U.S. Department of Agriculture, Econ. Res. Serv. September 2011.

Collins, James H. *The Story of Canned Foods.* New York: E. P. Dutton, 1924.

Conlin, Joseph R. *Bacon, Beans, and Galantines.* Reno: University of Nevada Press, 1986.

Counihan, Carole and Penny van Esterik, *Food and Culture: A Reader.* New York: Routledge, 1997.

Cowan, Ruth Schwartz. *More Work for Mother: The Ironies of Household Technology from the Open Hearth to the Microwave.* New York: Basic Books, 1983.

Craig, Lee A., Barry Goodwin, and Thomas Grennes. "The Effect of Mechanical Refrigeration on Nutrition in the United States." *Social Science History* 28, no. 2 (Summer 2004): 325–36.

Crawford, Margaret. *Building the Workingman's Paradise: The Design of American Company Towns.* London: Verso, 1995.

Crocker, Ruth Hutchinson. *Social Work and Social Order: The Settlement Movement in Two Industrial Cities, 1889–1930.* Urbana: University of Illinois Press, 1992.

Cronon, William. *Nature's Metropolis: Chicago and the Great West.* New York: W. W. Norton, 1991.

Cummings, Richard Osborn. *The American and His Food: A History of Food Habits in the United States.* Chicago: University of Chicago Press, 1940.

Davis, Allen F. *Spearheads for Reform: The Social Settlements and the Progressive Movement, 1890–1914.* New York: Oxford University Press, 1967.

Davis, Marni. *Jews and Booze: Becoming American in the Age of Prohibition.* New York: New York University Press, 2012.

Dawley, Alan. *Struggles for Justice: Social Responsibility and the Liberal State.* Cambridge, MA: Belknap Press of Harvard University Press, 1991.

Deutsch, Tracy. *Building a Housewife's Paradise: Gender, Politics, and American Grocery Stores in the Twentieth Century.* Chapel Hill: University of North Carolina Press, 2010.

Diner, Hasia. *Hungering for America: Italian, Irish, and Jewish Foodways in the Age of Migration.* Cambridge, MA: Harvard University Press, 2001.

Diner, Steven J. *A Very Different Age: Americans of the Progressive Era.* New York: Hill and Wang, 1998.

Douglas, Paul H. *Real Wages in the United States, 1890–1926.* Boston: Houghton Mifflin, 1930.

Duis, Perry R. *Challenging Chicago: Coping with Everyday Life, 1837–1920.* Urbana: University of Illinois Press, 1998.

———. *The Saloon: Public Drinking in Chicago and Boston, 1880–1920.* Urbana: University of Illinois Press, 1983.

Eighmey, Rae Katherine. *Food Will Win the War: Minnesota Crops, Cooks, and Conservation during World War I.* St. Paul: Minnesota Historical Society Press, 2010.

Engelhardt, Elizabeth S. D. "Beating the Biscuits in Appalachia: Race, Class, and Gender Politics of Women Baking Bread." In *Cooking Lessons: The Politics of Gender and Food,* ed. Sherrie A. Innes. Lanham, MD: Rowman and Littlefield, 2001.

———. *A Mess of Greens: Southern Gender and Southern Food.* Athens: University of Georgia Press, 2011.

English, Beth. "'I Have a Lot of Work to Do': Cotton Mill Work and Women's Culture in Matoaca, Virginia, 1888–95." *Virginia Magazine of History and Biography* 114, no. 3: 365–66.

Etheridge, Elizabeth W. *The Butterfly Caste: A Social History of Pellagra in the South.* Westport, CT: Greenwood, 1972.

Ewen, Elizabeth. *Immigrant Women in the Land of Dollars: Life and Culture on the Lower East Side, 1890–1925.* New York: Monthly Review Press, 1985.

Filene, Peter G. "An Obituary for the 'Progressive Movement.'" *American Quarterly* 22 (1970): 20–34.

Foner, Eric. "Why Is There No Socialism in the United States?" *History Workshop Journal* 17, no. 1 (1984).

Fox, Bonnie, ed. *Hidden in the Household: Women's Domestic Labour under Capitalism.* Toronto: Women's Press, 1980.

Fox, Daniel M. *The Discovery of Abundance: Simon N. Patten and the Transformation of Social Theory.* Ithaca, NY: Cornell University Press, 1967.

Franklin, Linda Campbell. *America in the Kitchen: From Hearth to Cookstove. An American Domestic History of Gadgets and Utensils Made or Used in America from 1700 to 1930.* Florence, AL: House of Collectibles, 1976.

Freidberg, Susanne. *Fresh: A Perishable History.* Cambridge, MA: Belknap Press of Harvard University Press, 2009.

Gabaccia, Donna. *We Are What We Eat: Ethnic Food and the Making of Americans.* Cambridge, MA: Harvard University Press, 1998.

Gamber, Wendy. *The Boardinghouse in Nineteenth-Century America.* Baltimore, MD: Johns Hopkins University Press, 2007.

———. *The Female Economy: The Millinery and Dressmaking Trades, 1860–1930.* Urbana: University of Illinois Press, 1997.

Gazeley, Ian. "The Cost of Living for Urban Workers in Late Victorian and Edwardian Britain." *Economic History Review,* new series, 42, no. 2 (May 1989), 207–21.

Glickman, Lawrence B. *A Living Wage: American Workers and the Making of Consumer Society.* Ithaca, NY: Cornell University Press, 1997.

Goodwin, Lorine Swainston. *The Pure Food, Drink, and Drug Crusaders, 1879–1914.* Jefferson, NC: McFarland, 1999.

Gordon, Linda. *Pitied but Not Entitled: Single Mothers and the History of Welfare.* Cambridge, MA: Harvard University Press, 1994.

Green, Harvey. *The Light of the Home: An Intimate View of the Lives of Women in Victorian America.* New York: Pantheon Books, 1983.

Greenwald, Maurine W., and Margo Anderson, eds. *Pittsburgh Surveyed: Social Science and Social Reform in the Early Twentieth Century.* Pittsburgh: University of Pittsburgh Press, 1996.

Grier, Katherine C. *Culture and Comfort: Parlor Making and Middle-Class Identity, 1850–1930.* Washington, DC: Smithsonian Institution Press, 1988.

Grover, Kathryn, ed. *Dining in America, 1850–1900.* Amherst: University of Massachusetts Press, 1987.

Guthman, Julie. *Weighing In: Obesity, Food Justice, and the Limits of Capitalism.* Berkeley: University of California Press, 2011.

Gutman, Herbert G. *Work, Culture, and Society in Industrializing America: Essays in American Working-Class and Social History.* New York: Alfred A. Knopf, 1976.

Hales, Peter B. *Silver Cities: The Photography of American Urbanization, 1839–1915.* Philadelphia: Temple University Press, 1984.

Haley, Andrew P. "Turning the Tables: American Restaurant Culture and the Rise of the Middle Class, 1880–1920." PhD diss., University of Pittsburgh, 2005.

———. *Turning the Tables: Restaurants and the Rise of the American Middle Class, 1880–1920.* Chapel Hill: University of North Carolina Press, 2011.

Hall, Jacquelyn Dowd, James Leloudis, Robert Korstad, Mary Murphy, Lu Ann Jones, and Christopher B. Daly. *Like a Family: The Making of a Southern Cotton Mill World.* Chapel Hill: University of North Carolina Press, 1987.

Hareven, Tamara K. *Family Time and Industrial Time.* Cambridge: Cambridge University Press, 1982.

Harvey, Katherine A. *The Best-Dressed Miners: Life and Labor in the Maryland Coal Region, 1835–1910.* Ithaca, NY: Cornell University Press, 1969.

Hayden, Dolores. *The Grand Domestic Revolution: A History of Feminist Design for American Homes, Neighborhoods, and Cities.* Cambridge, MA: MIT Press, 1981.

Hays, Samuel P. *The Response to Industrialism, 1885–1914*. Chicago: University of Chicago Press, 1957.

Heinze, Andrew R. *Adapting to Abundance: Jewish Immigrants, Mass Consumption, and the Search for American Identity*. New York: Columbia University Press, 1990.

Helmbold, Lois Rita. "Beyond the Family Economy: Black and White Working-Class Women during the Great Depression." *Feminist Studies* 13, no. 3 (Fall 1987).

Hess, John L., and Karen Hess. *The Taste of America*. New York: Grossman, 1977.

Hofstadter, Richard. *The Age of Reform*. New York: Knopf, 1955.

Hooker, Richard J. *Food and Drink in America: A History*. Indianapolis: Bobbs-Merrill, 1981.

Horowitz, Daniel. *The Morality of Spending: Attitudes toward the Consumer Society in America, 1875–1940*. Baltimore, MD: Johns Hopkins University Press, 1985.

Horowitz, Roger. *Putting Meat on the American Table: Taste, Technology, Transformation*. Baltimore, MD: Johns Hopkins University Press, 2006.

Hoy, Suellen. *Chasing Dirt: The American Pursuit of Cleanliness*. New York: Oxford University Press, 1995.

Hunt, Caroline L. *The Life of Ellen H. Richards, 1842–1911*. 1912. Reprint, Washington, DC: American Home Economics Association, 1958.

Hunt, Edward Eyre, F. G. Tryon, and Joseph H. Willits, eds. *What the Coal Commission Found: An Authoritative Summary by the Staff* (Baltimore, MD: Williams and Wilkins, 1925).

Hurt, R. Douglas. *American Agriculture: A Brief History*. Ames: Iowa State University Press, 1994.

James, Edward T., et al., eds. *Notable American Women, 1607–1950*. 3 vols. Cambridge, MA: Belknap Press of Harvard University Press, 1971.

James, Randy. "Brief History: Food Stamps." Time.com, September 14, 2009. www.time.com/time/nation/article/0,8599,1921992,00.html#ixzz1diIpyqdp. Accessed November 18, 2011.

Jones, Evan. *American Food: The Gastronomic Story*. New York: E. P. Dutton, 1975.

Jones, Lu Ann. *Mama Learned Us to Work: Farm Women in the New South*. Chapel Hill: University of North Carolina Press, 2002.

Katz, Michael B. *In the Shadow of the Poorhouse: A Social History of Welfare in America*. New York: Basic Books, 1986.

Kennedy, Phillip D. *Hoosier Cabinets*. Indianapolis, IN: Phillip D. Kennedy, 1989.

Kleinberg, S. J. *The Shadow of the Mills: Working-Class Families in Pittsburgh, 1870–1907*. Pittsburgh: University of Pittsburgh Press, 1989.

———. "Technology and Women's Work: The Lives of Working-Class Women in Pittsburgh, 1870–1900." *Labor History* 17, no. 1 (Winter 1976): 58–72.

Kline, Ronald R. "Ideology and Social Surveys: Reinterpreting the Effects of 'Labor-saving' Technology on American Farm Women." *Technology and Culture*, April 1997.

Kurlansky, Mark. *The Big Oyster: History on the Half Shell*. New York: Ballantine Books, 2006.

Kyrk, Hazel, and Joseph Stancliffe Davis. *The American Baking Industry, 1849–1923, As Shown in the Census Reports.* Stanford, CA: Stanford University Press, 1925.

Leavitt, Sarah Abigail. *From Catharine Beecher to Martha Stewart: A Cultural History of Domestic Advice.* Chapel Hill: University of North Carolina Press, 2002.

Lemisch, L. Jesse, ed., *Benjamin Franklin: The Autobiography and Other Writings.* New York: Signet Classic, 1961.

Leonard, Katherine. "Housewives Rejoiced: Canned Food in the American Household, 1900–1930." B.A. thesis, Reed College, 1998.

Levenstein, Harvey. *Fear of Food: A History of Why We Worry about What We Eat.* Chicago: University of Chicago Press, 2012.

———. *Paradox of Plenty: A Social History of Eating in Modern America.* New York: Oxford University Press, 1993.

———. *Revolution at the Table: The Transformation of the American Diet.* New York: Oxford University Press, 1988.

Libecap, Gary D., and Zeynep Kocabiyik Hansen. "'Rain Follows the Plow' and Dryfarming Doctrine: The Climate Information Problem and Homestead Failure in the Upper Great Plains, 1890–1925." *Journal of Economic History* 62, no. 1 (March 2002): 86–120.

Lichtenstein, Nelson, Susan Strasser, and Roy Rosenzweig. *Who Built America? Working People and the Nation's Economy, Politics, Culture, and Society. Volume II: Since 1877.* Boston: Bedford / St. Martins, 2000.

Lubove, Roy, ed. *Pittsburgh.* New York: New Viewpoints, 1976.

Lumpkin, Grace. *To Make My Bread.* Urbana: University of Illinois Press, 1995.

Lynd, Robert S., and Helen Merrell Lynd. *Middletown: A Study in Modern American Culture.* San Diego: Harcourt Brace, 1957.

Marchand, Roland. *Advertising the American Dream: Making Way for Modernity, 1920–1940.* Berkeley: University of California Press, 1985.

Marks, Harry M. "Epidemiologists Explain Pellagra: Gender, Race, and Political Economy in the Work of Edgar Sydenstricker." *Journal of the History of Medicine and Allied Sciences* 58, no. 1 (January 2003): 34–55.

May, Earl Chapin. *The Canning Clan: A Pageant of Pioneering Americans.* New York: Macmillan, 1937.

May, Martha. "The 'Good Managers': Married Working-Class Women and Family Budget Studies, 1895–1915." *Labor History* 25, no. 3 (Summer 1984): 351–72.

McGerr, Michael. *A Fierce Discontent: The Rise and Fall of the Progressive Movement in America, 1870–1920.* New York: Free Press, 2003.

Meine, Franklin J., ed. *Stories of the Streets and of the Town: From the Chicago Record, 1893–1900.* Chicago: Caxton Club, 1941.

Metheny, Karen Bescherer. *From the Miner's Doublehouse: Archaeology and Landscape in a Pennsylvania Coal Company Town.* Knoxville: University of Tennessee Press, 2007.

Miller, Daniel. *A Theory of Shopping.* Ithaca, NY: Cornell University Press, 1998.

Miller, Sally M. "Social Democratic Millennium: Visions of Gender." In *Expectations for the Millennium: American Socialist Visions of the Future,* ed. Peter H. Buckingham. Westport, CT: Greenwood Press, 2002.

Mintz, Sidney. *Sweetness and Power: The Place of Sugar in Modern History.* New York: Viking, 1985.

Morawska, Ewa. *For Bread with Butter: The Life-Worlds of East Central Europeans in Johnstown, Pennsylvania, 1890–1940.* Cambridge: Cambridge University Press, 1985.

Moss, Michael. "Safety of Beef Processing Method Is Questioned." *New York Times,* December 31, 2009.

Mulrooney, Margaret. *A Legacy of Coal: The Coal Company Towns of Southwestern Pennsylvania.* Historic American Buildings Survey / Historic American Engineering Record. Washington, DC: National Parks Service, 1989.

Muncy, Robyn. *Creating a Female Dominion in American Reform, 1890–1935.* New York: Oxford University Press, 1991.

Nestle, Marion. *Food Politics: How the Food Industry Influences Nutrition and Health.* Berkeley: University of California Press, 2002.

Neuhaus, Jessamyn. *Manly Meals and Mom's Home Cooking: Cookbooks and Gender in Modern America.* Baltimore, MD: Johns Hopkins University Press, 2003.

Newby, I. A. *Plain Folk in the New South: Social Change and Cultural Persistence, 1880–1915.* Baton Rouge: Louisiana State University Press, 1989.

Opie, Frederick Douglass. *Hog and Hominy: Soul Food from Africa to America.* New York: Columbia University Press, 2008.

Pacyga, Dominic A. *Polish Immigrants and Industrial Chicago: Workers on the South Side, 1880–1922.* Columbus: Ohio State University Press, 1991.

Panschar, William G. *Baking in America: Economic Development. Volume I.* Evanston, IL: Northwestern University Press, 1956.

Parkin, Katherine J. *Food Is Love: Advertising and Gender Roles in Modern America.* Philadelphia: University of Pennsylvania Press, 2006.

Peiss, Kathy. *Cheap Amusements: Leisure in Turn-of-the-Century New York.* Philadelphia: Temple University Press, 1986.

Plante, Ellen M. *The American Kitchen 1700 to the Present.* New York: Facts on File, 1995.

Plunz, Richard. *A History of Housing in New York City: Dwelling Type and Social Change in the American Metropolis.* New York: Columbia University Press, 1990.

Poe, Tracy. "Food, Culture, and Entrepreneurship among African-Americans, Italians, and Swedes in Chicago." PhD diss., Harvard University, 1999.

———. "The Labour and Leisure of Food Production as a Mode of Ethnic Identity Building among Italians in Chicago, 1890–1940." *Rethinking History* 51, no. 1 (2001): 131–48.

Pollan, Michael. "Unhappy Meals." *New York Times,* January 28, 2007.

Porter, Glenn. *The Workers' World at Hagley.* Greenville, DE: Eleutherian Mills–Hagley Foundation, 1981.

Powers, Madelon. *Faces along the Bar: Lore and Order in the Workingman's Saloon, 1870–1920*. Chicago: University of Chicago Press, 1998.

Roberts, Elizabeth. "Working-Class Standards of Living in Barrow and Lancaster, 1890–1914." *Economic History Review,* new series, 30, no. 2 (May 1977): 306–21.

Rodgers, Daniel T. *Atlantic Crossings: Social Politics in a Progressive Age.* Cambridge, MA: Belknap Press of Harvard University Press, 1998.

———. "In Search of Progressivism." *Reviews in American History* 10, no. 4 (December 1982): 113–32.

Root, Waverly, and Richard de Rochemont. *Eating in America: A History.* New York: Morrow, 1976.

Roscoe, Edwin Scott, and George Lewis Thuering. *The Textile Industry in Pennsylvania.* Engineering Research Bulletin B-74. Pennsylvania State University, College of Engineering and Architecture, University Park, May 1958.

Rosenzweig, Roy. *Eight Hours for What We Will: Workers and Leisure in an Industrial City, 1870–1920.* Cambridge: Cambridge University Press, 1983.

Roth, Leland M. "Company Towns in the Western United States." In *The Company Town: Architecture and Society in the Early Industrial Age,* ed. John S. Garner. New York: Oxford University Press, 1992.

Rutherford, Janice Williams. *Selling Mrs. Consumer: Christine Frederick and the Rise of Household Efficiency.* Athens: University of Georgia Press, 2003.

Schor, Francis Robert. *Utopianism and Radicalism in a Reforming America.* Westport, CT: Greenwood Press, 1997.

Scott, Elizabeth M. "A Little Gravy in the Dish and Onions in a Tea Cup: What Cookbooks Reveal about Material Culture." *International Journal of Historical Archaeology* 1, no. 2 (1997).

Shapiro, Laura. *Perfection Salad: Women and Cooking at the Turn of the Century.* New York: Farrar, Straus and Giroux, 1986.

———. *Something from the Oven: Reinventing Dinner in 1950s America.* New York: Penguin, 2004.

Shergold, Peter R. *Working-Class Life: The "American Standard" in Comparative Perspective, 1899–1913.* Pittsburgh: University of Pittsburgh Press, 1982.

Shiloh, Ailon, ed. *By Myself I'm a Book! An Oral History of the Immigrant Jewish Experience in Pittsburgh.* Waltham, MA: American Jewish Historical Society, 1972.

Shpak-Lissak, Rivka. *Pluralism and Progressives: Hull-House and the New Immigrants, 1890–1919.* Chicago: University of Chicago Press, 1989.

Smith, Peter. "Watch Your Mouth: What Should Food Stamps Subsidize?" *Good,* September 12, 2011. www.good.is/post/should-food-stamps-pay-for-junk-food/. Accessed 18, 2011.

Solomon, Barbara Miller. *Ancestors and Immigrants: A Changing New England Tradition.* Boston: Northeastern University Press, 1956.

Spain, Daphne. *How Women Saved the City.* Minneapolis: University of Minnesota Press, 2001.

Stage, Sarah, and Virginia B. Vincenti, eds. *Rethinking Home Economics: Women and the History of a Profession.* Ithaca, NY: Cornell University Press, 1997.

Stavely, Keith, and Kathleen Fitzgerald. *America's Founding Food: The Story of New England Cooking.* Chapel Hill: University of North Carolina Press, 2004.

Strasser, Susan. *Never Done: A History of American Housework.* New York: Pantheon Books, 1982.

———. *Satisfaction Guaranteed: The Making of the American Mass Market.* Washington, DC: Smithsonian Institution Press, 1989.

Tannahill, Reay. *Food in History.* New York: Stein and Day, 1973.

Tangires, Helen. *Public Markets and Civic Culture in Nineteenth-Century America.* Baltimore, MD: Johns Hopkins University Press, 2003.

Tate, Christine. "Viscose Village: Model Industrial Workers' Housing in Marcus Hook, Delaware County, Pennsylvania." PhD diss., University of Pennsylvania, 2002.

Tedlow, Richard S. *New and Improved: The Story of Mass Marketing in America.* New York: Basic Books, 1990.

Thompson, E. P. *The Making of the English Working Class.* New York: Vintage Books, 1963.

Tignor, Robert, et al. *Worlds Together, Worlds Apart.* New York: W. W. Norton, 2002.

Tomes, Nancy. *The Gospel of Germs: Men, Women, and the Microbe in American Life.* Cambridge, MA: Harvard University Press, 1998.

Troesken, Werner. *Water, Race, and Disease.* Boston: MIT Press, 2004.

Ulrich, Laurel Thatcher. *The Age of Homespun: Objects and Stories in the Creation of an Urban Myth.* New York: Alfred A. Knopf, 2001.

United States Bureau of the Census. *Historical Statistics of the United States: Colonial Times to 1970.* Washington, DC: U.S. Government Printing Office, 1975.

United States Department of Agriculture Food and Nutrition Service website. www.fns.usda.gov/fns/. Accessed September 13, 2013.

Van Wienen, Mark W. "A Rose by Any Other Name: Charlotte Perkins Stetson (Gilman) and the Case for American Reform Socialism." *American Quarterly* 55, no. 4 (December 2003): 603–34.

Vileisis, Ann. *Kitchen Literacy: How We Lost Knowledge of Where Food Comes From and Why We Need to Get It Back.* Washington, DC: Island Press, 2008.

Weigand, Kate. *Red Feminism: American Communism and the Making of Women's Liberation.* Baltimore, MD: Johns Hopkins University Press, 2001.

Wilde, Mark W. "Industrialization of Food Processing in the United States, 1860–1960." PhD diss., University of Delaware, 1988.

Williams, Phyllis. *South Italian Folkways in Europe and America.* New Haven, CT: Yale University Press, 1938.

Williams, Susan. *Food in the United States, 1820s-1890.* Westport, CT: Greenwood Press, 2006.

———. *Savory Suppers and Fashionable Feasts: Dining in Victorian America.* New York: Pantheon Books, 1985.

Wilson, Richard Guy, Shaun Eyring, and Kenny Marotta, eds. *Re-creating the American Past: Essays on the Colonial Revival.* Charlottesville: University of Virginia Press, 2006.

Wright, Gwendolyn. *Building the Dream: A Social History of Housing in America.* New York: Pantheon Books, 1981.

Ziegelman, Jane. *97 Orchard: An Edible History of Five Immigrant Families in One New York Tenement.* New York: Smithsonian Books, 2010.

INDEX

progressives 7, 18–23, 26–27, 41, 69, 93–95, 112, 115, 127, 129–32, 142–43, 148–49

public markets, 54–56

pushcarts, 5, 56–57, 60, 71–72, 81, 83–86, 90

railroads, 7, 10, 12, 30–33, 48, 54, 92

ready-to-eat food, 6, 52, 60, 64, 66, 70, 78, 83–85, 90, 111, 143–44

refrigeration, 5, 29–33, 59

restaurants, 52, 60, 70–85, 137, 145

Reynolds, Marcus T., 58–59, 66, 68

Richards, Ellen, 21, 25, 127, 134–39, 147

running water. *See* plumbing

Russian immigrants, 6, 43, 75, 83, 88–89, 114

saloons, 3, 52, 60, 71–74, 78–85, 129, 131, 142, 144

sauerkraut 5, 79, 83, 86, 105, 117

school lunches, 3, 19, 84, 130–34

scrip, 97–98, 119

seasonality, 28–34, 49

settlement houses (social settlements), 2, 19–24, 41–42, 132–33, 138

Simkhovitch, Mary, 69

single men and women, 13, 16, 24, 46, 51–52, 64, 66, 72, 74–79, 83, 102–3, 106–7, 148

sinks. *See* plumbing

socialism, 18, 78, 83–84, 124, 127–29

South Carolina, 32, 95, 99, 107

standard of living, 17, 106, 115

storage, 32, 37–38, 49, 52–59, 85, 115, 145

stoves, 2, 37–47, 65–66, 85, 100–101, 111, 115, 118, 128–29, 137, 142

textile mills, 8–9, 16, 24, 89, 92–103, 107–8, 112–19

toilets. *See* plumbing

tubs. *See* plumbing

United States Coal Commission, 94, 116, 119

utilities, 2, 20, 36, 39–43, 130, 141, 148

wages, 2, 8–11, 13–20, 25–26, 44, 63, 66–67, 89, 92, 98–99, 103–5, 119–25

women's wage work, 15–16, 37, 51, 61, 64, 66, 69, 76–77, 81, 102–3, 118, 125, 137–38, 147

wood. *See* fuel